Horse power

Horse power
The politics of the turf

CHRISTOPHER R. HILL

with a Foreword by the Rt. Hon.
VISCOUNT WHITELAW, C.H., M.C.

Christopher R. Hill

MANCHESTER
UNIVERSITY PRESS

Published by Manchester University Press
Oxford Road, Manchester M13 9PL, UK
Distributed exclusively in the USA and Canada
by St. Martin's Press, Inc.
Room 400, 175 Fifth Avenue, New York, NY 10010, USA

British Library cataloguing in publication data
Hill, Christopher R.
    Horse power: the politics of the turf.
    1. Horse racing—Political aspects—Great Britain— History—20th Century
    I. Title
    306'.483   SF335.G7

Library of Congress cataloging in publication data applied for

ISBN 0 7190 2501 X *hardback*

Typeset in Palatino with Bramley display
by Koinonia Ltd, Manchester

Printed in Great Britain
at the University Printing House, Oxford

Contents

Foreword

I have always taken a personal interest in racing and I have many friends who have been closely concerned in its administration over the years. And so it was only natural when I became Home Secretary in 1979 that I should take a close interest in the affairs of racing with which the Home Office was concerned. I was therefore interested to learn that Christopher Hill was writing a history of horse racing in recent times and delighted to have been asked to write this short foreword to his book. He has had the benefit of the full co-operation of all those bodies and individuals concerned in the developing relations between Jockey Club, the Tote, the Betting Levy Board and the bookmaking organisations. As a result he has produced *Horse Power – the Politics of the Turf,* which gives a comprehensive and fascinating account of a period of years when I believe much has been done for the lasting benefit of racing in Britain. The book should also help the various components of racing to understand each other better.

WHITELAW

Acknowledgements

I am greatly indebted to a number of bodies in all sections of the racing industry who contributed to my research fund. They included the Jockey Club, the Horserace Betting Levy Board and the Horserace Totalisator Board. The 'big four' bookmakers contributed, on the suggestion of the late Lord Wigg, who was then Life President of the Betting Office Licensees' Association (BOLA). They are Coral Racing, Ladbroke's, Mecca Bookmakers and the William Hill Organisation.

In addition the Lord Leverhulme Charitable Trust and the Macdonald–Buchanan Charitable Trusts generously provided invaluable financial assistance.

The Nuffield Foundation made it possible for me to gather comparative material in France, Germany and Hong Kong.

I am grateful to the Racecourse Association which gave my research assistant and myself entrance badges to racecourses.

Note on sources

Numerous individuals and organisations provided valuable research material. My principal archival debt is to the late Lord Wigg, who allowed me unrestricted access to all his racing papers, including the Levy Board papers generated during his period as chairman.

I am also grateful to the following who provided me with access to their archives: the National Association of Bookmakers, *The Sporting Life*, and the Thoroughbred Breeders' Association. John Winter and Hugh McCalmont kindly provided me with documents on the formation and activities of the Bloodstock and Racehorse Industries' Confederation (BRIC) and the Newmarket strike of 1975 and Tom Kelly generously lent me notebooks containing articles which he had written weekly in the *Sporting Chronicle* over a number of years.

Virtually everyone whom I approached in the racing world took a constructive interest in the project, and I am indebtd to a multitude of people and organisations for their generous assistance, and very often hospitality as well. Interviews were given on the understanding that the information imparted and opinions expressed were not to be attributed in the text. Some of the individuals who allowed me to interview them or who corresponded with me are listed below, with apologies to any whom I may have inadvertently overlooked:

The Hon. Robert Acton; Hamish Anderson; Richard Baerlein; Eric Barber; the Hon. Edward Beckett; John Biggs; Alex Bird; Michael Bramwell; Phil Bull; Captain Tim Bulwer-Long; Col. J. Cameron-Hayes; the Rt. Hon. Mark Carlisle, QC, MP; Michael Clayton; the late John Crabb; Martin Crawshay; Geoffrey de Deney; Noel Digweed; Jeffrey Dilling; Jonathan Dimsdale; John Dunlop; Rod Fabricius; Anthony Fairburn; Frank Fleming; Ossie Fletcher; Louis Freedman; Edward Gillespie; Sir William Goring, Bt.; Captain E. Graham; Francis Habbershaw; Jocelyn Hambro; Geoffrey Hamlyn; Field Marshal Lord Harding of Petherton; David Harris; Lt.-Col. Robin Hastings; the late Col. Sir Denys Hicks; John Henderson; Lord Howard de Walden; Stanley Jackson; Tom Kelly; Brigadier Sidney Kent; Dr Paull Khan; the late Lord Kilmany; Peter King; Sir Timothy Kitson; Charles Layfield; Sir David Llewellyn; Miss Mary Lund; Hugh McCalmont; Robert McCreery; Captain John Macdonald-Buchanan; Lord Mancroft; the Earl of March and Kinrara; the late John Marriage, QC; Martin Mitchell; Roger Mortimer; Tim Neligan; Lt.-Col, T. W. Nickalls; Lavinia, Duchess of Norfolk; Mark O'Connor; Major-General Bernard Penfold; Major Christopher Philipson; Sir Stanley Raymond; Nick Robinson; Pat Rohan; Robert Sangster; Sam Sheppard; Hugh Sidebottom; the late Major-General Jeremy Spencer-Smith; Peter Spencer-Smith; Geoffrey Summers; Major David Swannell; Lord Vestey; Brigadier H. J. de W. Waller; Michael Wallis; Mrs Bridget Walters; Lord Weinstock; Viscount Whitelaw; the late Lord Wigg; the late Lord Willoughby de Broke; Kenneth Witney; John Worrall; Marcus Wickham-Boyton.

The following, as well as giving interviews, were kind enough to read and make comments on parts of the text. I am especially indebted to Viscount Whitelaw for writing the Foreword and to Sir Ian Trethowan and Sir Woodrow Wyatt for bravely grappling with the whole text. Naturally any errors or omissions remain my responsibility.

Major the Hon. Sir John Astor; F. Christopher; Len Cowburn; Martin Crawshay; Robert Fellowes; Michael Filby; Christopher Foster; Harold Hodgson; Kenneth Kemp-Turner; Viscount Leverhulme; Brian McDonnell; Lord Manton; Miss Margaret Meades; Lord Plummer; Lord Porchester; Lord Renton, QC; Tristram Ricketts; John Sanderson; Lt.-Col. P. Victory; Gordon Wasserman; Peter Willett; John Winter; Michael Wrigley.

Acknowledgements

Mrs Hardy has again done all the typing with great patience and skill, and without once complaining about my handwriting. I am most grateful to her.

My greatest debt is to Hugo Watson Brown, who was the ideal research assistant. I very much doubt whether the research would have been completed if I had not had the benefit of his many and various abilities.

I
Setting the scene

This book has two purposes. First, it analyses the politics of a fairly small group of people (about twenty thousand) whose lives are devoted to the interlocking activities of breeding and racing thoroughbred horses. To a lesser extent it is about the larger group (perhaps sixty thousand) who live off betting, mainly on horses, but also on greyhounds, Miss World, and whether it will snow on Christmas Day. Secondly, it explains some of the links between racing and the wider world of politics in Westminster and Whitehall.

The book is not about party politics in the sense of Conservative and Labour. But politics exists in all aspects of social life, including sport, and racing is no exception. With the growth of leisure, much of it involuntary, and of the number of pastimes available to occupy it, has come a livelier interest in how our sports have grown up, how they are organised, and why. There is also a growing literature on the connection between sport and politics, to which I see this book as a contribution. I do not, however, subscribe to the school of thought which sees sport as a means employed by capitalists to suppress the working class.[1]

Racing provides a spectacle; millions of English men and women dabble in it, if only by having a bet on the Grand National or the Derby. It is both a colourful part of the English heritage and a tax-raising machine for the State. Few of its devotees have a close knowledge of its extraordinarily complex organisation, though most know a great deal about their own particular corner of the total picture. Fortunately, most of them are happy to share their thoughts, often forcefully, and, as may be seen in the list of acknowledgements, I have had the good luck to talk to a great variety of racing's 'insiders'.

The tightly-knit world of racing – one author has called it a 'sub-culture' within society at large[2] – is riddled with politics, as the insiders readily admit. Pressure groups proliferate, representing all the major interests, like owners, trainers, breeders, the racecourses themselves and the bookmakers, as well as the minor, but no less essential contributors to the total scene, like the farriers.

Politics abounds, both within and between the groups. The Racecourse Association has the almost impossible task of representing all grades of racecourse from Ascot to Ludlow. The trainers are split between the rich south and the relatively impoverished north. Members of the owners' association range from those with one leg of an animal which may give his owners a lot of fun but will never set the turf on fire, to those who spend millions. The breeders are, perhaps, the most homogeneous of the major groups, since there are many interests, like the control of disease, which hold the members together.

Two bodies preside over the racing world: one is the venerable Jockey Club, a private club, first mentioned in print in 1752 (the precise date of its foundation is unknown) and incorporated by Royal Charter in 1968 (until 1968 jumping had been controlled by a separate though closely related body, the National Hunt Committee. I shall, however, unless the context requires otherwise, refer simply to the Jockey Club as racing's ruling body). The Club is served by Weatherby's, an hereditary civil service, which in 1769 obtained control, by somewhat buccaneering tactics, of what was then called *The Sporting Calendar* (since 1773 *The Racing Calendar*), and has retained it ever since.[3] The other body is the Horserace Betting Levy Board, which was set up in 1961 to raise a levy from bookmakers and distribute it for the good of racing. The new resources brought into racing by the Board naturally encouraged the growth of interest groups and so of political activity. Relations between the Board and the Jockey Club, which until 1961 had been the only source of power in racing, have sometimes been very bad, and often uneasy.

I have been able to go in detail into the questions at issue between the Jockey Club and the Levy Board during the least happy period of their relationship, the years when the late Lord Wigg was Chairman of the Board, because Lord Wigg himself was good enough to give me unrestricted access to his racing papers shortly before he died.

I had thought that the best way to explain the complexities of racing's politics would be to start in 1960, with the passage of the Act which legalised betting shops, and made possible the raising of

a levy from bookmakers under a second Act, passed in 1961. However, I found that to explain why betting shops were legalised instead
of a monopoly of off-course cash betting being given to the totalisator,
I had to go back to the beginning of the 1950s. The preparation and
passage through Parliament of the 1960 and 1961 Acts were accompanied by intricate negotiations between the Jockey Club, the bookmakers and the Home Office, the Department of State responsible
for racing. I have attempted to link the intense behind-the-scenes
activity with what went on on the public stage, and have been greatly
assisted by access to documents kept at the National Association of
Bookmakers.

Since most of the book is about the government, administration
and politics of racing, it has not been necessary to separate jumping
from the Flat. However, in discussing such subjects as the ways in
which racing and breeding have become international big business
in recent years, I have concentrated on flat racing.

When I began to study racing I was told 'the higher you go in
racing, the less you will find it has to do with horses, the more with
politics and administration'. Another senior figure told me 'Always
ask the people you interview what racing is for.' I am glad he said
it: otherwise I might have become absorbed in politics and finance
to the exclusion of the horses. As it was, I found a great variety of
answers: racing is a sport, an entertainment, a necessary but (for
some breeders) rather tiresome test, a money spinner (for many
bookmakers and a few punters), a career ladder for the professionals,
a means to social advancement and business success for some owners, a ruling passion, a way of life, and, in Phil Bull's words, 'the
great triviality'.[4]

It is often said that racing is in crisis. But one cannot talk about
'racing' as a whole. It is far too complex a series of overlapping circles,
between and within which there is conflict and co-operation. Nor
can one evaluate the problems of racing, breeding and betting, without putting them into their historical context. To do this we need to
take a mental snapshop of the racing world as it was in the early
1950s.

Surviving two wars

Racing has survived two world wars. As George Lambton, the noted trainer, recounts, it was stopped by the Government early in the 1914-18 war on the ground that public opinion was against it. However, the racing lobby organised a campaign, with the help of the financier Horatio Bottomley (who was later imprisoned for fraud) to show that the continuance of racing in war time was, in fact, not disapproved of by the public, and that to stop it would be a disaster for the breeding industry. The result was that Lloyd George telephoned Bottomley 'You can have your racing if you can arrange matters with the railway companies' and the day was saved. It is interesting that, writing as long ago as 1924, Lambton saw that racing and breeding were industries, as well as sports.[5] The tension between those two aspects of the activity, and the ways in which it shows itself in its politics, is one of this book's major themes.

In the war of 1939-45 much the same thing happened, except that the decision to cease racing was taken by the Jockey Club, and not the Government. Racing's major modern historian, Roger Mortimer, is unlike Lambton in seeing racing until 1939 as having been 'essentially a sport, rather than a business or industry'. Wartime racing continued until the 1940 Derby, which was held at Newmarket, instead of Epsom, 'when the special trains and a long stream of cars and coaches aroused a suspicion in some minds that the nation as a whole was not treating the war with the seriousness it unfortunately deserved'. Questions were asked in the House of Commons, and the Stewards of the Jockey Club decided that racing must stop.

However, it started again three months later, and continued throughout the war, though on a much reduced scale. Mortimer records that there was a good deal of opposition to it 'so that the Jockey Club was faced with the tricky task of keeping the pulse of the sport beating without incurring criticism for impeding the war effort'. He adds that 'An element of class resentment began to creep in. People who saw nothing wrong in big crowds at football matches and dog racing, had the strongest objection to anyone going to a race meeting, racing in their eyes being the pastime of the rich.' To some extent they were right: as Mortimer himself says 'Class distinction gave the lie to the old saying that "on the turf and under it all men are equal"',[6] but vast crowds used to go racing, and the proportion who were rich or upper-class cannot have been high.

The post-war years

Racing and gambling booming after the war and 'the volume of money in circulation was augmented by the huge profits from black market operations'.[7] But very soon English owners and breeders began to get worried by the French 'invasion' during which many English Classics and other major races fell to them from 1947 onwards. Names like those of Marcel Boussac and Madame Suzy Volterra began to top the lists of winning owners and breeders, and the French invasion was accompanied by another mounted from Ireland. (Cottage Rake, trained by Vincent O'Brien, won the Cheltenham Gold Cup in 1948, 1949 and 1950.) The Americans, too, played their part, once the so-called 'Jersey Act' had been repealed in 1949. (This was not an Act of Parliament, but a decision made by the Jockey Club in 1913, on a proposal by Lord Jersey, effectively to close the Stud Book to American-bred horses.)[8] In 1954 an American-bred colt, Never Say Die, won the Derby, the first to do so since Iroquois in 1881. Iroquis was ridden by the great Fred Archer, who shot himself in 1886.

Even after the second world war, the government of racing was conducted by the Jockey Club and National Hunt Committee in a relaxed and traditional manner, although a good many of its members, as Mortimer puts it, 'thought they heard the distant rumbling of tumbrils if there was the slightest suggestion of change'.[9] This is not to say that all members were resistant to change – we shall see in chapter VII that a group of them produced a far-sighted report during the depths of the war[10] – but many were still contentedly in the grip of pre-war attitudes. The adjustment of the social classes to the necessity of behaving differently to one another after the war was a slow process, and it would be unfair to reproach members of the Jockey Club for having failed to move more rapidly than anyone else.

It was not only members of the Jockey Club who would nowadays be considered old-fashioned. The great trainer H. S. Persse, writing on training in a collection published in 1940, was a firm disciplinarian. He had no use for Trade Unionism (we shall see, in Chapter IX, that some of the Newmarket trainers thought not very differently in 1975) and believed that a union would be as likely to turn into 'a clearing house for stable information' as to benefit the lads themselves. 'Nowadays,' he wrote, 'boys are very thin-skinned. If found fault with, they go to other trainers, who oft-times will take them without any reference. . . Boys are the very devil, the bugbear of a trainer, needing to be watched almost all the time.' But he liked apprentices, and used to make a point of meeting their parents. This was not, however, from any concern for their welfare, but because he wanted to guess from the parents' size whether their son was likely to remain small enough to make a jockey.[11]

Some courses disappeared during the Second World War, but there were still more than have survived until now. The difficulty of getting to the races, usually by train, and the discomfort of racecourses were often great, but the crowds seem not to have complained, and to have been content with a very poor view of the racing. Broadcast commentaries were not introduced until 1953, and even information about runners, riders and so on was not relayed over the loudspeakers until 1946. Prize money, was, by modern standards, incredibly low though it was boosted by the introduction of commercial sponsorship in 1957. Sponsorship itself was encouraged by the growth of television and the consequent publicity achieved.

By 1950 the boom was beginning to break. Attendances at racecourses dropped by fifteen per cent. It was still the age of going-out for the day or to the cinema, rather than staying at home and watching television, but there was beginning to be more choice of amusement and of how to spend one's money. But a couple of years later racing's leaders were beginning to see that its financial base was precarious. The Hon. (later Sir John) J. J. Astor, an MP from 1951 to 1959, did much to publicise racing's plight.

A Tote monopoly?

At first Astor believed that the Tote (the universally used abbreviation for the Totalisator) should be given a monopoly of betting. This would entail the abolition of bookmakers so that the Tote would make greatly increased profits, which it would be able to disburse for the benefit of racing.

I shall go later into the reasons for the failure of the Tote monopoly movement, and at present only explain the logic of Astor's position. The Tote is a method of betting whereby the money bet is placed in a 'pool'; a percentage is deducted for the benefit of the Tote (I shall not discuss the various methods of doing so) and the remainder paid out to the backers of the winning and placed horses. Thus the odds are unpredictable, or were so until recent years, when modern technology made it possible for the changing odds to be instantly calculated, and displayed on screens at the betting kiosks.

By contrast, a 'punter' (as a person who places a bet is familiarly known) who bets with a bookmaker has two possibilities. He may place a bet at agreed odds, which vary during the period before a race according to the amount of money the bookmaker has taken on the various horses, so that a punter a few minutes earlier or later may be offered different odds, which will be more or less favourable. Alternatively, he may bet at Starting Price (SP), that is, the price which the majority of bookmakers are offering when the race begins. In the days when cash betting off course was illegal, most bookmakers could bet only at SP, as they were not in touch with the course, and so not aware of the changing odds.

Astor's reasoning was that the Racecourse Betting Control Board (RBCB), which governed the Tote, had been founded, largely on the initiative of the Jockey Club, in order to benefit racing, as well as to provide punters with an alternative method of betting. The RBCB had been set up by Act of Parliament in 1928 (the moving spirit behind the Act had been Lord Hamilton of Dalzell, Senior Steward of the Jockey Club in 1927), and the Tote commenced its operations on the flat at Newmarket and Carlisle in July 1929. Since the Tote's purpose was to finance racing, and since racing's finances were rocky, it seemed reasonable to create conditions in which it could maximise its contribution to racing, by giving it a monopoly of off-course betting. (However, it should be noted that Lord Hamilton himself had not favoured the abolition of on-course bookmakers.)[12] A contributory reason for seeking a monopoly was that the Tote's profits had never been very large, partly because the minimum stake was so low – 2s at first, raised to 4s in 1957.

The idea of a Tote monopoly gradually gave way to that of a levy on bookmakers, to be applied to the benefit of racing. In December 1955, the Duke of Norfolk, the retiring Senior Steward of the Jockey Club, was, according to *The Times*, to brief the Chancellor of the Exchequer on the Industry's plight.[13] He intended to ask the Chancellor to lighten the Tote's tax burden (then forty-seven per cent); to reconsider the burden of entertainment tax (which was removed from all live entertainment in April 1957) and to implement the recommendation of the 1951 Royal Commission on Betting, Lotteries and Gaming that off-course betting should be legalised.[14] The Duke thought the bookmakers might thereafter be subjected to a levy, but still perhaps be abolished altogether eventually.

Viscount Astor (brother of J. J.) developed the case in the House of Lords six months later. The best races were being won by the French and the best stallions being exported; the racing industry had a capital of about £20 million, which annually earned £1½ million or more in dollar exports, but which cost the people participating £2 million to £3 million a year. (His brother had put the figure at over £3 million.) Owners put up forty per cent of the stake money themselves, with the result that most of them could not make ends meet without betting. This in turn meant that they tended to breed horses of the sprinter type, and the faster two-year-olds which were good gambling vehicles, instead of classic type horses bred to stay a mile and a half as three-year-olds. Furthermore, the British public were getting poor facilities at British racecourses at much higher cost than in Ireland or France.[15]

Ten years later Roger Mortimer produced another argument for a Tote monopoly. He was complaining of the younger stable staff, who might bring English racing to a grinding halt. They were inveterate clock-watchers, devoid of any sense of dedication to their work and plainly resentful of the order and discipline without which no stable can be run efficiently. A Tote monopoly, however, would bring greatly increased prize money; trainers would be able to charge their owners realistic fees, and so to pay considerably higher wages, which in turn would attract a better type of man to the job.[16]

Faced with consistent pressure from the early 1950s onwards, the bookmakers were naturally dismayed, but not trodden down. They realised that paying a levy would be better than being abolished, though at first they seem not to have seen the difference between a levy and a conventional tax on betting.

They were also opposed to the proposal to take betting off the streets and into betting shops. Under the Betting Houses Act of 1853 and the Street Betting Act of 1906, all off-course betting, except on credit, was illegal. Naturally no notice was taken of the prohibition, and a great variety of illegal forms of betting flourished throughout the country. In some places betting shops were ignored by the police, in others the police were bribed to turn a blind eye, in others bookmakers had offices to which customers were not admitted, but from which they despatched agents (known as 'runners') to collect bets in streets, factories, hospitals, and so on.

The bookmakers' opposition to betting shops solidified as the decade went on. They feared that legal betting would lead inevitably to a tax on betting, as it did. They objected to the petty restrictions which they felt sure would be imposed on the conduct of betting shops, as indeed they were. They feared that if betting shops turned out not to be a success, their failure could be used as an excuse for the introduction of a Tote monopoly. Some small bookmakers did not relish the extra expense of running shops; others feared that they would fall into the jaws of the big fish, and, contrariwise, at least one large credit bookmaker (William Hill) was afraid that preference in the allocation of licences would be given to the small men. Nevertheless, when it became clear that legislation, and a levy, were inevitable, the bookmakers strenuously developed their organisation, and eventually reached more or less acceptable compromises with the Government. A social revolution was brought in, not kicking and screaming, but with relative decorum.

The 1950s, and, to an even greater extent, the 1960s, were an era of great events and of changes in society at large, as well as in the narrow world of racing. It was also a period of commanding figures, of whom the most obviously dominant in racing was Colonel George (later Lord) Wigg, who was Chairman of the Horserace Betting Levy Board from 1967 to 1972. He had come from a humble background to be a long-serving Labour Member of Parliament and close confidant of Harold (later Lord) Wilson when the latter was Prime Minister. He had served in the Army, and come to love it, and he had a passionate interest in racing. On paper there could hardly have been a better Chairman of the Board.

In fact, as later chapters will show, his character and class-consciousness made him exactly the wrong man to deal at all amiably with the Jockey Club. He certainly got results, but many of them might have been achieved by an emollient man with half the expenditure of energy, and none of the distrust and general aggravation which Wigg generated.

It must also be said that, by encouraging the growth of betting, and so of the levy, he encouraged racing's dependence on the levy, and stimulated the industrial, rather than the sporting, aspects of the activity. It is ironic that a man so devoted to racing should have produced such results.

Since Wigg there have been no dominant characters. Instead there seems to have been a general movement in the racing world away

[9]

from flamboyance towards administrative competence and what is now called a 'low profile'. Racing is indubitably well run, but it must seem rather dull to those who remember the excitement of the earlier days. Most of the remainder of this book is devoted to an account of those invigorating times.

Notes

1 This view is very cogently put in J. Hargreaves, *Sport, Power and Culture*, London, 1986. See also e.g. P. Fuller, 'Introduction', J. Halliday and P. Fuller (eds.), *The Psychology of Gambling*, pp. 1-114. He believes that 'Gambling divides the working class against itself', p. 37.

2 P. Khan, *The Sport of Kings: a study of traditional social structure under change*, unpublished Ph.D. thesis, University of Swansea.

3 R. Mortimer, *The Jockey Club*, London, 1958, pp. 32-4.

4 Phil Bull is an owner–breeder and the publisher of *Timeform*, who has for many years been a persistent, and often constructive, critic of the racing establishment.

5 The Hon. George Lambton, *Men and Horses I Have Known*, London, 1963 (first published 1924), pp. 308-10.

6 R. Mortimer, *The Flat: flat racing in Britain since 1939*, London, 1979, pp. 7, 19, 21, 13.

7 *Ibid.*, p. 47.

8 Mortimer, *The Jockey Club*, pp. 140-3.

9 *Ibid.*, p. 106.

10 Jockey Club, *Report of the Racing Reorganisation Committee to the Stewards of the Jockey Club*, London, February 1943.

11 H. S. Persse, 'Training', Lord Harewood and Many Authorities, *Flat Racing*, n.d. but 1940, p. 321.

12 Lord Hamilton has left an interesting account of the Tote's origins in his paper 'The Tote' in Lord Harewood & Others, *Flat Racing*, pp. 378-94. For his views on bookmakers see p. 394.

13 *The Times*, 9 December 1955.

14 Royal Commission on Betting Lotteries and Gaming, *Report* (Cmd. 8190), 1951.

15 198 *H.L.* Deb., col. 99, 27 June 1956.

16 R. Mortimer, *The Tote Racing Annual 1966*, London, n.d. but 1966, pp. 11-12.

II

The 1950s: the prelude to legislation

The Betting and Gaming Act, 1960, could not have been introduced without co-operation between Home Office, Jockey Club and bookmakers. This is not to say that the bookmakers welcomed it, but they realised that they could gain more by negotiation than from obstruction.

The Act, which legalised cash betting off course, was based largely on the recommendations of the Royal Commission on Betting, Lotteries and Gaming, chaired by Henry Willink, which reported in 1951.[1] The gap, by governmental standards, was not especially long, but without sustained pressure in the 1950s in both Houses of Parliament, it might well have been longer.

The legislation was of the greatest importance to racing, because it legalised betting shops and opened the way to the levy on bookmakers' profits. The levy was introduced under the Betting Levy Act, 1961, which established the Horserace Betting Levy Board as a statutory body to raise and spend the levy. Nor, without the 1960 Act, could there have been Betting Duty, which was eventually introduced in October 1966.

The Jockey Club had for many years shown itself aware that racing needed more money; having failed to obtain a share of the betting tax introduced in 1926, it had played a leading part in promoting the Racecourse Betting Act of 1928, which permitted the setting up of the Racecourse Betting Control Board, or 'Tote Board'. The wide-ranging and far-sighted Ilchester Committee (the Racing Reorganisation Committee), which the Jockey Club appointed in the darkest days of the war and which reported in February 1943,[2] looked to the Tote as an important source of increased finance, and as late as the mid 1950s the Jockey Club seems still to have thought that the higher income which racing needed should be got from increased contributions by the Tote, rather than by trying to promote a Tote monopoly.

There were, however, some individuals working for a Tote monopoly. As long ago as Derby Day 1953, Lord Porchester (who since 1969 has been the Queen's racing manager, and a member of the Jockey Club since 1964), elated by Pinza's victory in the Derby, found himself next to Winston Churchill at dinner at Blenheim and ventured to tell him that the best thing he could do for racing would be to abolish bookmakers. Churchill's response was stern: why, he asked, should bookmakers not be allowed to earn their living like anyone else? In any case, the word abolish should never be used: it should be struck from one's vocabulary. But Churchill forgave Porchester his temerity, because he, too, had backed Pinza.

During the 1950s some MPs, notably the Hon. John Astor, had been active in promoting the case for a Tote monopoly. Astor had taken great pains in 1953 to work out estimates of the difference between the cost of racing to owners and breeders and their income from it, a deficit which he put at over £3 million annually (excluding stakes they subscribed themselves). He presented the figures on 25 November 1953 to a parliamentary committee on racing, the Bloodstock Breeding and Racing Committee, which he had formed to promote turf interests, with a view to getting back into racing, via the Tote, some of the money bet off course, once off-course betting was legal. However, Astor, who, when he entered the House of Commons in 1951, had been convinced that a Tote monopoly was the answer to racing's problems, had by 1956 concluded that it was no longer feasible. It had become clear to him that it was a non-runner because there was no support from the Jockey Club, which represented the racing industry. Nor was there any obvious support from punters, or public, and the bookmakers had a well-organised anti-Tote lobby in the House.

By 1956 his objectives were to promote debates to discuss the merits of legalised betting, and to promote thought about how money from both bookmakers and Tote might be returned to racing, preferably with their co-operation. If co-operation failed, debates might at least reveal the large volume of off-course betting, and the substantial profits from it, both of which the bookmakers habitually minimised.

The bookmakers' lobby: I – origins

Astor's task was not easy. The bookmakers had been organised for many years, and their history of lobbying and successful collective action goes back at least to Churchill's short-lived tax on betting turnover, which was introduced in 1926 and removed in 1929.

The bookmakers organised for self-protection in what Richard Kaye calls 'the bad old days after 1918 when a state amounting to gang warfare existed on racecourses'.[3] The first body, the Bookmakers and Backers Racecourse Protection Association, was founded in August 1921, and the unpublished record of the speeches at its first annual banquet, held on 6 December 1921, shows that the London-based bookmakers were determined (as Walter Beresford, their first president, put it) '. . . to remove the stigmas from our name. I know we have got a very bad name. . .'. Much of the trouble had been with Birmingham: 'Up to now, the good class Birmingham people have interviewed certain other men in that city, and they have assured us that if Birmingham men do start these feuds again, they will be responsible, and they will deal with these people who have caused trouble amongst us.' These, and further remarks in Beresford's speech, strongly suggest that the London bookmakers feared bookmakers based in other parts of the country, who presumably wanted to keep rivals off their local racecourses, though not as much as they feared the 'terrorists'. The latter, Beresford said, were as harmful to SP bookmakers as to those on course '. . . because if there is no bookmaking on the racecourse there will be no business for SP men. And if this terrorism and blackmailing is allowed to go on unchecked, it will put a stop to bookmaking altogether.'

Another speaker ('Tom' Harris, proposing the health of the visitors) urged bookmakers in the provinces to form similar associations, which would eventually be federated in a single national body. He saw no difficulties over raising a large income for the association, but the first consideration was to ensure members' safety, whatever part of the country they might be in.

The Association's president, Edmund Davies, thanked the Jockey Club and the Racecourse Association for their support, and said that, thanks to the bookmakers, south country racecourses were perfectly safe. He had been to one of them recently: 'The sun was shining, the air was delightfully pure, and the surroundings were altogether very exhilarating. I said to a bookmaker there: "I remember this racecourse twenty-five years ago, and in those days a man like your-self would not have been able to carry on." In fact, he would have been knocked about. It is now like coming into an al fresco drawing room.'

The federally organised national association, to which Harris had looked forward at the inaugural dinner, came into being in 1932, as the National Bookmakers' Protection Association, and changed its name to National Association of Bookmakers in 1964. The NAB continues to this day, though it now has a rival in the Betting Office Licensees' Association, which broke away in 1973. The NAB is a body rooted in a tradition of protecting the interests of the small man and of the wish to become respectable. Its founders were on-course bookmakers, who saw, and still do see, the real professional as the man who stands on his 'joint' (the box on which he stands at the races) and calls the odds. But, because the NAB is a federation of regional bodies, whose local pride must always be borne in mind, it is in constant danger of fission and of independent action by member associations, which sometimes have not had total confidence in the central body's ability to protect their interests.

The bookmakers' lobby: II
– Parliament and the Tote monopoly, 1951-9

By the period with which we are concerned the bookmakers were well practised in guarding their own interests. On 23 April 1951 the National Bookmakers' Protection Association (Excutive Committee, 31st meeting) took note of the then very recent Royal Commission on Gambling's conclusion that it would be desirable to introduce betting shops. Although it was known that not all the NBPA's grass-roots membership was opposed to betting shops, the committee thought it wise, even at that early stage, to prepare a memorandum setting out the case against them.

There was sustained pressure on the Government, in both Lords and Commons, to introduce legislation based on the Royal Commission. The process started in the Lords, where, on 8 February 1956, Lord Silkin drew attention to the Willink Commission and to the fact that no action had been taken on its recommendations.

Some peers were totally opposed to gambling, other favoured it in moderation, but all the ten who took part (including Lord Mancroft, who, as Joint Parliamentary Under-Secretary of State at the Home Office, wound up for the Government) thought that something must be done. Mancroft (who was to be Chairman of the Tote from 1972 to 1976) assured the House that the Report was not gathering dust. There had so far been no legislation, because the Government's timetable had not allowed it, and because any legislation was bound to be controversial and take a great deal of time. He recalled that the Betting and Lotteries Act of 1934 had occupied over twenty Parliamentary days 'and many of those days were actually nights'.

But the Government recognised that at present the law was 'an ungodly jumble', and was particularly concerned about its unenforceability. The Government believed that any satisfactory law would control all major forms of commercial gambling and would register those who provided the facilities; it would apply fairly to all sections of the community, and as much information about gambling as possible would be made available to the public. Legal off-course cash betting and the registration of bookmakers sprang to mind, and in this connection Mancroft said that he had seen betting shops in southern Ireland: 'They are neither attractive nor unattractive; they are as negative places as one can imagine, but apparently they work well.'[4]

There followed debates in both Houses. The first of these took place on 9 March 1956[5] on Arthur Lewis's motion urging the House to take note of the labours of the Royal Commission of 1951, and the Government to repeal all the existing gambling legislation and replace it with one comprehensive Act. Lewis himself wanted only to deal with gambling on horses and dogs, and was particularly interested in dogs because he had a dog track in his constituency, but he had no objections to other members discussing different sports.

Astor seconded the motion and quoted figures from the Royal Commission's Report to show that forty to forty-five per cent of the adult population bet regularly. It was often, he said, asked whether this was socially beneficial or a liability, but there was evidence that most people bet moderately and the Commission had concluded that moderate gambling had no bad social effects. Ernest Bevin had considered racing beneficial during the war. There were, however, dangers of police corruption in the present state of the law, which also enshrined class discrimination, and he urged the Government to find time for legislation. Astor continued: 'I am sure everyone will

[15]

agree that as the sports. . . provide the medium for gambling, they should be allowed enough money back into their sport to keep it healthy.' He concluded: 'I would rather win the Derby than an election.'[6]

George Wigg, who as Lord Wigg was to be Chairman of the Horserace Betting Levy Board from 1967 to 1972, did not think that any government would do anything about betting, though he thought it ought to tackle the problem of street betting. Meanwhile, the governing bodies of sports should put their own houses in order. The Jockey Club was 'a terrible organisation', which ought to tackle such problems as the superfluity of racecourses in the country.[7]

The debate stimulated W. F. (later Lord) Deedes, Joint Under-Secretary of State at the Home Office, to make an announcement which, although similar to Mancroft's, was somewhat more specfic and was momentous because it marked the beginning of serious consultation between the Home Office and interested bodies. He said that the Home Office agreed with the conclusion of the report that the present legal situation was unsatisfactory. He went on that the Government accepted the Commission's conclusion in favour of off-course betting shops, but added that although the Commission's conclusions were clear, it would be difficult to draft and find time for a Bill.

Although Deedes' statement had not committed the Government to introduce legislation by any particular date, it was clearly to be taken seriously, and that short debate contained the seeds of much that was to follow. At its 37th Meeting on 6 April 1956 the book-makers' Executive Committee commented that the position was now very grave for them.[8] They were still divided on the issue, and it was imperative for the Committee to find out what the majority really wanted. It appeared that both sides of Parliament were, broadly speaking, in favour of betting shops, and the Chairman had already been approached by the Home Office, which wished to receive a small deputation to discuss with the Under-Secretary of State matters regarding the proposed legislation.

It was not long before a further move was made in the Lords. On 27 June 1956 Viscount Astor (John Astor's brother) initiated a debate, welcoming the Government's intention to introduce a comprehensive Bill dealing with betting. This opportunity enabled him to present his case in some detail, in a speech which was obviously the result of much thought and preparation. In it he deployed the arguments for aid to racing, which were gradually becoming familiar to Parliament and the public at large. He then developed the case for a Tote monopoly, as in France, and in the twenty-four States of the USA where racing was legal. He linked the positive benefits to racing of a monopoly with an attack on some bookmakers, whose lower fringe corrupted the police, and who, because of the large amounts of money passing through their hands, could afford to finance other crimes as well. There were many 'fine respectable honest book-makers': 'But the present system makes a border-line between betting and crime which I am sure the police, and all interested in law and order, would be delighted to see finished once and for all by the establishment of the same totalisator monopoly in this country as has proved successful in our main competitors.'[9]

However, Lord Astor, like his brother, seems by then to have given up any serious expectation that the Government would, in fact, introduce a Tote monopoly, and therefore went on to urge that, as a second-best solution, the Government should license and control bookmakers.

He made the case, in greater detail than had been done publicly hitherto, for a levy on bookmakers' turnover, both on and off course. This, he said, was successful in Ireland, and there was no reason why it should not succeed in Britain, despite the failure of Winston Churchill's earlier tax. He also foreshadowed several other major aspects of the eventual legislation: the Tote, he thought, should be allowed branch offices and a monopoly of the use of its own odds; runners and cash betting by post should be legalised.

There was, he went on, 'a sinister alliance between the Churches Committee on Betting and bookmakers to oppose betting shops. . . The Church Committee think that to have betting shops would encourage betting and make it too respectable. The bookmakers seem to prefer the present system, where they act without control, without licence and without taxation. . .'[10]

This powerful speech, and the whole debate which it introduced, drew a flood of publicity. In the short term it provoked a statement by the Home Secretary in Parliament on 2 July that there was no foundation for statements that there were highly-organised gangs frequenting racecourses in different parts of the country and en-gaging in violence. In the longer term the speech was extremely influential; it gave the public notice of what racing and breeding interests expected from any betting legislation, and most of what it asked for was achieved only a few years later.

Replying to the debate, Lord Mancroft stated that the Government was satisfied that betting shops and off-course cash betting by post should be legalised, that other methods of betting should incur harsher penalties than was at present the case, and that bookmakers should be subject to a comprehensive system of control. However, since he had last spoken on the subject he had realised that the whole question was more complicated than he had thought, and he still could not say when legislation would be introduced. Astor's suggestion of a levy (though Mancroft did not use the word) was a novel one. It had not been discussed by the Royal Commission, but that did not rule it out for consideration. Meanwhile the Home Office was in touch with no fewer than twenty different bodies.

Parliamentary concern was reflected in the press. For example the Aga Khan wrote to *The Times* on 27 December 1956 (one of a series of letters from various contributors under the heading 'Saving British Racing') calling for a Tote monopoly, on the grounds that it had done so much for French racing. The best British horses, he added, were all being exported to the USA, which drew the spirited riposte from Lord Rosebery, in a letter published on 31 December, that in this respect the Aga Khan was the worst offender, having sold all his four Derby winners to the USA.

Lords Windlesham and Astor returned to the attack in the Lords on the 6 May 1958 and again asked when legislation could be expected. Astor made another speech, setting out again the case he had made in June 1956 for a Tote monopoly or, failing that, a levy (this time he used the word). Lord Chesham, for the Government, again had to reply that no date could be set for legislation. The Lord Chancellor (Viscount Kilmuir) gave a somewhat similar reply in response to further pressure from Windlesham on 16 December 1958. This time he admitted that Astor's proposals for a levy had greatly complicated matters, and, by implication, that they had delayed the Bill.

In the Commons the next step had been taken on 20 November 1957, when George Wigg presented his Betting Reform Bill to extend the powers of the Racecourse Betting Control Board. This Bill was discussed four days later at the 43rd Meeting of the Bookmakers' Executive Committee, whose members thought that it was likely, but not certain, to be talked out. They agreed that the position must be watched carefully and that members should be in touch with their

MPs. On 16 January 1958 the 9th meeting of the bookmakers' Inner Cabinet (which had been set up in June 1956) worked out the details of the campaign against the Bill. They attacked it in a leaflet, with a cartoon on the front page headed 'Do You Want A Wigging?' which was distributed by post to clients of member associations. In March the Inner Cabinet was informed that Wigg had been much upset by the leaflet. They thereupon expressed willingness to send a delegation to meet Wigg and John Astor at the House of Commons to hear their explanation of the provisions of the Bill, although they were clear in their own minds that no amendment could be made to it which could make it acceptable to them.

The leaflet shows that the provision of the Bill which most worried the bookmakers was that they would no longer be permitted to take bets at Tote odds. The RBCB would also be able to accept cash bets by post and to allow callers at Tote offices to bet on credit. Bookmakers could do neither of these things, and protested that the Bill was 'the thin end of the wedge to a complete tote monopoly'. They urged their readers to write at once to their MPs objecting to any form of monopoly and pointing out that the 1951 Royal Commission had been strongly against dealing with betting legislation piecemeal. In the event the Bill was counted out at Second Reading on 16 May 1958, a result which was naturally the cause of great satisfaction to the bookmakers.

The next attempt at legislation was Sir Eric Errington's Betting Reform Bill, which the Inner Cabinet considered similar to Wigg's Bill, but better drafted, so that their objections to it were virtually the same. They had no objection to the RBCB putting its own house in order, but they saw the Bill as more than an administrative measure to deal with the Tote's internal affairs, because it also attacked the interests of bookmakers. Since, according to the bookmakers' Parliamentary Agent, this Bill had Home Office support, it was unlikely to fail at Second Reading, and would therefore have to be amended in Committee. The three main provisions which the Inner Cabinet thought required amendment were, first, the Tote's proposed monopoly of postal cash betting; secondly, the monopoly by the Tote Board and its agents of pool betting at Tote odds; thirdly, the penalties for those ignoring the monopoly. It was important, therefore, that 'friendly MPs' should volunteer to serve when the Bill reached the Committee stage. If it did not prove possible to defeat the Tote's proposed monopoly of cash betting by post, the alternative strategy would be to try and get the same provision extended to bookmakers. However, this alternative had disadvantages, since some bookmakers were opposed to the legalisation of cash postal betting, and the extension would also require the alteration of the Long Title of the Bill, which would be a major operation.

Errinton's Betting Reform Bill reached Second Reading on 13 March 1959, and enjoyed rather longer debate than had its two predecessors.[11] Errington explained that the Bill dealt only with the Tote and that other betting should be left to government legislation. He argued that the Bill would bring the functions of the RBCB up to date; they had been amended only once, in the 1934 Betting and Lotteries Act. It would also bring into effect the less controversial recommendations of the Royal Commission, and its overall aim was to raise the Tote's turnover, and so to increase the amount of money which could be ploughed back into breeding and racing. Although some bookmakers might be opposed to the Bill, the increased prosperity of the Tote would be to their ultimate advantage.

The Bill did not seek a Tote monopoly, only a copyright in Tote prices. 'I may be a bit of a muggins, but one would not be such a muggins as to introduce a Bill of that character' (that is, one providing for a Tote monopoly). Nor did the Bill allow the Board to open betting shops. 'Finally, the Bill is not the thin edge of the wedge of any deep, dark, secret development that anybody has in mind by which to get at other people engaged in the betting industry.'[12]

Ernest Davies, who seconded the motion, echoed Lord Astor's remark of June 1956 in saying that opposition to the Bill came from 'almost a sinister or unholy alliance between the Churches on the one hand and bookies on the other. . . They are strange bedfellows indeed'.[13]

John Astor made a point with which one can sympathise: 'Debates on gambling seem to have a recurring pattern. Hon. members make the same speeches on it year in and year out, and nothing very much seems to happen.'[14] His feeling was that if the Conservatives were to win the forthcoming election they would bring in gambling legislation. He went on that neither the public nor the House wanted a Tote monopoly, nor was the way to help racing to oblige off-course bookmakers to contribute to it, because the money would be too difficult to raise. The best way to help racing would be to expand the scope of the Tote. If the Tote were offering cash and credit facilities on and off course, perhaps quadrupling its turnover from

£27 million to £100 million, that would help enormously.

In opposing the Bill, Stephen (later Sir Stephen) McAdden (who from now on regularly appears as a stalwart defender of bookmaking interests, particularly those of the smaller bookmaker) said that Errington had remarked that ninety per cent of the people in this country who wanted to bet could do so already. Tote Investors had offices all over the country. The object of this Bill, therefore, seemed to be to provide betting facilities for the other ten per cent who were not credit-worthy. It seemed a rather fantastic proposition to ask people to support a Bill so that those who were not creditworthy could make themselves even less creditworthy by gambling. He was, as one would expect, against the Tote having copyright in its own prices.

David Renton, Joint Under-Secretary of State at the Home Office, said that there was no government time left for this Private Member's Bill, and that, as in 1928, the Government believed that there should be a free vote on the measure – in marked contrast to its attitude when it eventually introduced its own legislation. Provided certain amendments were made in Committee the Government was broadly neutral to the Bill, and content to leave its future to the judgement of the House. In fact, it was talked out on 24 April 1959.

Why the Tote monopoly movement failed

By this time, it seems, most of the impetus behind a Tote monopoly had died away. A sign of the times was that a new body, called the Racing and Breeding Liaison Committee, with representatives from the Racecourse Association, the Racehorse Owners' Association and the Thoroughbred Breeders' Association, had been founded early in 1958[15] to improve the industry's finances by tapping the enormous sums wagered off course. But the committee did not think the public wanted a Tote monopoly.

That the impetus for a monopoly had died so easily seems extraordinary now, when we are accustomed to hear that a great opportunity to establish a Tote monopoly was missed in 1960. After all, the Tote existed largely thanks to the Jockey Club's initiative, and its purpose, apart from providing an alternative betting medium, had, ever since its setting up in 1928, been to put money into racing: the natural thing when legalising off-course cash betting might well have been to hand it over to the Tote – or so it seems with the clear vision of hindsight.

But just as most of us realise now that a Tote monopoly is politically off the cards, so the idea seems to have been politically dead by 1960 – indeed, John Astor had formed this opinion as early as 1956, although, as we shall see in a later chapter, he was still arguing the case for it ten years later. In fact, it appears that even in 1960 the leaders of racing either believed that the time for a Tote monopoly was already past, or were not convinced that they really wanted it. Of course, it would not have been easy to achieve, and perhaps could not have been achieved at all, even if the Jockey Club had fought wholeheartedly for it since 1951. Be that as it may, it would surely have been much easier then than in 1976, when the Tote, under so experienced a politician as Woodrow Wyatt, still thought it worthwhile to make strenuous representations for a monopoly to Lord Rothschild's Royal Commission on Gambling.[16] By contrast, Astor's earlier committee having died for lack of support, there seem to have been virtually no representations at all in 1959-60.

Thus there was never an effective lobby for a monopoly, partly because the bookmakers themselves were an effective force, but also because many of the rulers of racing did not believe in it enough to carry conviction even with themselves. Though they desired the benefits to racing they could not accept the personal inconvenience that might come with it. In retrospect this may seem to have been foolish, since a Tote monopoly off course would not have interfered with the pleasure of striking a bet with a favourite bookmaker on course. (Again, this point was not lost on Astor, but unfortunately he was not elected to the Jockey Club until 1959.) The principal pleasure lies in getting the bookmaker to improve the odds – 'six to five seeing it's you' instead of eleven to ten. It is also reassuring to know in advance what you stand to win, and of course the Tote seemed dull and was not sophisticated enough to handle complicated bets, while bookmakers are – or were – colourful characters with Rolls Royces.

The bookmakers' lobby: III
– betting offices and the levy

Meanwhile, a year before Lewis's Bill of 1956, the bookmakers had been under pressure from the Racecourse Association (RCA). It was reported at their 35th Executive Committee Meeting, on 2 March

1955, that the RCA had written to the National Bookmakers' Protection Association intimating that it would like to discuss the possibility of obtaining contributions from SP bookmakers towards the upkeep of racecourses. Faced with this pressure, and worried by a recent press campaign against bookmakers, the NBPA decided to set up a publicity department and to keep on the Parliamentary lobbyist whom they already employed. In April 1956 they also resolved to employ a firm of solicitors to act as Parliamentary Agents, who would keep a close watch on any Bill to legalise betting shops which might result from W. F. Deedes's announcement in March that the Government had such legislation in mind. It was agreed that the Committee (its full name was by now the National Bookmakers' Protection Association and Associated Bodies' Joint Committee) should ask each constituent association to levy at least £5 a head from its members to finance the bookmakers' campaign, which, at that stage, was not expected to last long, since it was thought that the Bill would be introduced in November 1956 and come into force in January 1958. The bookmakers' fears were somewhat reinforced by a paper which had just been published in Northern Ireland, which showed that the advent of betting shops had imposed considerable restrictions on bookmakers' activities there, and had led to the introduction of betting tax.

The RCA withdrew its request for a formal meeting with the bookmakers in the light of the new situation created by the proposed introduction of legislation. Nevertheless, a meeting was held, at which the bookmakers informed the RCA that, in view of pending legislation and the possibility of the introduction of betting tax, it was not possible at present for the bookmakers to consider making any grants to racecourses. From now on the bookmakers, as they became increasingly essential to the orderly preparation of legislation, became heavily involved in other meetings, though they did continue to see the RCA from time to time.

On 17 April the bookmakers went to see the Stewards of the Jockey Club. The Senior Steward, Lord Willoughby de Broke, started with the misconception that the bookmakers themselves had requested the meeting with the Home Office which was to be held two days later; once that had been cleared up, he continued that he was anxious to persuade the Government to allow the Jockey Club and the National Hunt Committee to form a joint negotiating committee representing all racing interests, to advise the Government at various stages of the legislation, and asked the bookmakers whether they wished to be represented on this body. The bookmakers, who might have been expected to jump at the chance, were not able to give an immediate reply, but said that the proposal would be placed before their General Council. (This caution and concern to ensure that delegates do not act out of line with the main body's wishes, are typical of the bookmakers' dealings, necessarily so in view of their federal structure, and perhaps one of the secrets of their success.)

Two days later they duly met Sir Austin Strutt, an Assistant Under-Secretary at the Home Office. In reply to a request for a full statement of the Government's intentions, he drew attention to Deedes's statement, which had said that the Government wished to implement the main recommendations of the Royal Commission, including the legalisation of cash betting by post, the requirement for all bookmakers to be registered, and the establishment of licensed betting offices. It seems that by now the bookmakers must have canvassed their members' view on betting shops, since the leader of their delegation stated in reply that the Joint Committee represented ninety-nine per cent of all bookmakers and that they were no more in favour of betting shops than they had been when they gave evidence to the Royal Commission. Their associations would prefer some other method of depositing cash bets, such as postal boxes (a proposal which was taken up by a number of Members of Parliament in the debates on the Betting and Gaming Bill), and asked whether it was too late to make renewed representations to this effect.

Strutt replied that the Home Office would consider very carefully the views of bookmakers on such issues of principle, but that the decision lay with Ministers, and the Government's declared intention was to follow the recommendation of the Royal Commission, which had already stated that the bookmakers' proposals to it had been impracticable. Any alternative proposals presented now must, therefore, be directed to practical alternatives.

The bookmakers then turned to the great transitional difficulties which would occur if betting shops were brought in; there was a difficulty about deciding between rival claims to set up betting shops in a given area and there might well be hardship on bookmakers if discretion were given to local licensing bodies rather than a judicial body. To this, Strutt replied that this was exactly the sort of point on which the Home Office had foreseen practical questions arising, though many of them were, in fact, covered in the Royal Commission's Report. He thought that in the first place the Associations should confine themselves to major issues of principle, and subsequent points of detail which might emerge during the preparation of the legislation could be the subject of informal discussions between the Home Office and one or two representatives of the Associations. The bookmakers concluded the meeting with an assurance that, although they would have to report back to their Associations, they would wish to assist the Home Office as far as possible.

In May 1956 the Jockey Club put into effect its intention (announced in the *Racing Calendar* of 6 May) to bring together all the interested parties, and held a meeting of the Joint Betting Bill Committee, which was chaired by the senior steward and attended by the bookmakers, representatives of the Jockey Club itself, the National Hunt Committee, the RBCB, Tote Investors, the Thoroughbred Breeders' Association, the RCA, Tattersalls' Committee, the Racehorse Owners' Association and the press. The Committee's intention, as Roger Mortimer recounts, was to agree the principles on which the proposed legislation should be based.[17]

The bookmakers by now felt the need for the 'Inner Cabinet', to which reference has already been made, to carry on day-to-day business, and this body was appointed at their 39th Executive Committee meeting on 14 June 1956. The Committee approved a four-point statement, which was to form the basis of its position at future meetings:

(1) It agreed that any monies taken out of racing by way of licence fee or registration fee should be returned to racing for the benefit of the racing public, e.g. the provision of additional amenities and reduced admission fees.

(2) They were opposed to the suggestion that the registration of bookmakers be placed in the hands of the RBCB. Instead, the bookmakers should be represented on whatever body was responsible for licensing, because they possessed the necessary experience. However, if this was not practicable then licensing should be done by a petty sessional court.

(3) They remained opposed to betting shops and preferred that the Street Betting Act of 1906 should be repealed.

(4) They thought adequate provision must be made for the control of undesirables seeking to obtain licences.

When the Jockey Club's Betting Bill Committee met on 18 June, substantial agreement had been achieved on three of these points and an appropriate letter had been agreed with the bookmakers and despatched from the Jockey Club Register Office to the Home Secretary. (It seems probable that point 3 above was the one upon which agreement could not be reached.) The next step in the drawing together of these disparate parties, bookmakers, Jockey Club and Home Office, was an invitation from the Home Office to the Stewards of the Jockey Club to present the facts of the economic plight of racing and to put the case in principle for betting on horse-racing to contribute to the sport. This was a milestone, as the case had never previously been put to any Government, although Lord Astor had made it in the debate of June 1956.

In September 1956 the Senior Steward, Lord Willoughby de Broke, brought the public up to date on these events at the St Leger dinner, when he revealed that, as soon as the Government had announced its intention to legalise betting offices, the Jockey Club had set up a committee of principal racing interests (referred to above), and made contact with the Home Office. He went on that the Stewards' aim was to make as much money as possible available to racing and breeding:[18] the result was that the idea of a levy now became firmly linked, in public, with that of legalising cash betting off course.

In drafting their scheme for the Home Secretary, Major G. Lloyd-George, the Stewards 'were careful to emphasise that their scheme was based on an assumption that the government had accepted the principle that betting on horse racing ought to contribute to horse racing; and that if that assumption was incorrect, they were not prepared to proceed further in the matter.'[19]

In November, the Stewards again saw the Home Secretary, but the negotiations failed, because Major Lloyd-George could not produce a scheme which the Stewards could support. Despite this failure, the Stewards seem to have been obsessively jealous that no other bodies, except the bookmakers, should have a hand in dealings with the Government, other than through the Joint Betting Bill Committee, and remained convinced that there was no need for a turf lobby in the Commons, because they were themselves in close touch with Ministers.

They may indeed have been in touch, but it seems to have been a perennial problem for the Jockey Club, and perhaps still is, to judge the level at which to exert pressure within the Government and civil service, and too often to go straight to the top. In that respect, George Wigg could have taught them much. Furthermore, to anticipate a little, when it came to the Betting and Gaming Act of 1960, the only memorandum which impressed the Home Secretary, R. A. Butler, was the one sent to him by the Tote: the others, in his view, did not make it at all clear what racing really wanted.

Meanwhile, to return to 1956, the bookmakers were naturally alarmed by continuing references to a Tote monopoly, and at their next meeting at the Home Office (6 December 1956), where they were received by Sir Frank Newsam, the Permanent Under-Secretary, they pointed out that neither the Tote monopoly nor the possibility of a bookmakers' financial contribution to racing had been included in the report of the Royal Commission. It now appeared that the Government's Bill was likely to include matters not covered by the Royal Commission, and the bookmakers asked to be informed exactly what these were, so that they could comment.

Newsam replied that the Government had not yet decided what would be in the Bill, but would welcome the bookmakers' views on any new proposals, particularly the suggestion that they should contribute to racing. It was agreed that the bookmakers should submit a second memorandum to the Home Office, covering the following new points:

(1) The idea that cash bets might be put into boxes as an alternative to betting shops.

(2) The possibility of a Tote monopoly of betting shops.

(3) Financial contributions by off-course bookmakers to racing.

(4) The possible bases for assessing the contributions which might be (*a*) a flat rate, (*b*) the number of a bookmaker's employees, (*c*) turnover, or (*d*) profits.

(5) The practicability of separating accounts and profits on horse-racing from dog-racing and other sports.

The bookmakers continued to be extremely nervous, partly because of a statement by Lord Willoughby de Broke (published in the press and the *Racing Calendar* on 13 December 1956), indicating that a suggestion of a partial Tote monopoly off course had been made at the Home Office by the Stewards of the Jockey Club. The statement confused the bookmakers, because it contradicted a letter sent by the Jockey Club to all members of its Joint Betting Bill Committee on 22 November, in which it was made clear that the suggestion of a partial Tote monopoly had emanated from the Home Office and been rejected by the Jockey Club. The points which the Stewards had discussed with the Home Office were: (1) that licensed betting offices (the correct name for what were, and are, often colloquially called betting shops) should be operated by the RBCB and would receive cash bets only; they would also be allowed to employ runners and agents; (2) off-course bookmakers would be licensed only for credit betting and cash postal betting; (3) there would be no provision in the Bill for any of the proceeds of off-course betting with bookmakers to make any contribution to racing. In other words, it appears that at this stage the Jockey Club was being offered a bargain, whereby it would give up the idea of a levy in return for the partial Tote monopoly which would be entailed by the limitation of off-course bookmakers to credit and postal betting. The Steward's letter went on that they had replied that such a partial monopoly in favour of the Tote would prove unworkable, and that they could not support any Bill which would not provide for *all* betting on racing to contribute to racing. The bookmakers' confusion was subsequently dispelled, but it is not surprising that some Inner Cabinet members had doubts about remaining in the Jockey Club's committee.

From now on the bookmakers' deliberations, and their negotiations with other bodies, were concerned at least as much with the levy as with the legalisation of cash betting off course. Although the legislation was delayed (the bookmakers thought this was because of the Suez Canal crisis) they remained convinced that it would come, and perhaps be included in the Queen's Speech in November 1957. They were also convinced that there would be some form of tax or levy, and the real question was: who would receive the proceeds thereof? Some progress was made on this point when, at a meeting of the Jockey Club's Joint Committee, the bookmakers got agreement to the principle that any monies taken out of racing by way of registration or licence fee should go back to benefit racing as a whole.

The bookmakers were subjected to further pressure in the shape of a demand by Mrs Mirabel Topham, the owner of Aintree, that the rentals of Exchange Telegraph's telephones on course should rise in 1957 from £240 per annum to £5,000 per annum, the equivalent of £500 a day. Since the bookmakers were the customers for the Extel commentary, this demand was seen as a means of raising an indirect levy on behalf of a single racecourse which, if successful, could spread all over the country. Extel had already rejected a demand from the Racecourse Association that the company should collect a levy from the bookmakers amounting to about £2 million, and Extel and the bookmakers now agreed that they would refuse to make the additional payments demanded by Mrs Topham. If necessary, press telephone lines could be used instead of those rented by Extel, and subsequently Extel successfuly defied attempts by the course executives at Aintree and Manchester to prevent them from supplying their subscribers with any service. Mrs Topham, however, did not give up, and on 4 March 1957 she proposed that on-course bookmakers should pay the promoters of each race a sum related to the betting turnover on that race, and that a committee of bookmakers should discuss the ways and means with the Racecourse Association. She also contended that the copyright of sporting events was vested in the promoters of races by the 1956 Copyright Act.

Yet another proposal for extracting money from the bookmakers had been made by three southern racecourses to the Southern Bookmaker's Protection Association, to the effect that starting price bookmakers should subsidise the televising of mid-week racing by ITV. The Thoroughbred Breeders' Association had also joined in the campaign, with a resolution at its Annual General Meeting in December 1956 that the bookmakers should be forced to bet to Tote odds, either by a Tote monopoly being created on course, or by the on-course bookmakers being prevented from rendering a Starting Price return.

Faced with all these pressures, it is not surprising that the rails bookmakers at this point decided to form an association of their own. (The rails bookmakers are the big bookmakers who bet on the rails between the Members' Stand – in which they are not allowed to operate – and the Grand Stand. Non-racegoers may wish to note that the Grand Stand is sometimes referred to as Tattersalls, which is not to be confused with Tattersalls the Auctioneers, nor with Tattersalls' Committee, which settles disputes between punters and bookmakers!) Kaye states that they were driven to do so by the absurdity of the Pitch Rules, which 'might have been written by Kafka, or the author of the Athanasian Creed'.[20] (The Pitch Rules, made by the bookmakers themselves, govern the positions they occupy on racecourses.) The new Association was urged by the NBPA not to make separate representations to the Jockey Club, but instead to apply for representation on the Joint Betting Bill Committee. Archie Scott, the popular and influential Old Etonian bookmaker, who played such a considerable part in bookmakers' politics over the next few years, appears in the NBPA papers for the first time on 20 February 1957 as Chairman of the Rails Bookmakers' Association. He and William Hill joined the bookmakers' Executive in May 1957, when Scott also became a member of the Inner Cabinet.

The 40th meeting of the Executive Committee, on 5 April 1957, was told that Mrs Topham's continuing efforts to extract money from the bookmakers, coupled with the RCA's apparent knowledge of what was going on, had led the Stewards of the Jockey Club to express active disapproval of some of the methods being used by the various bodies. The bookmakers were taking legal advice on the copyright question, and agreed that it was important to keep on good terms with the RBCB and the Jockey Club itself. They were unanimous that the Jockey Club was the body with which they should negotiate. It appears, therefore, that after the doubts about the Jockey Club, which had been caused by Willoughby's press statement, the bookmakers were now again prepared to be on good terms with the Club. At the May meeting of the Inner Cabinet the members noted that the Home Office had been receiving a great deal of information from bookmakers' sources and that the bookmakers' failure to speak with a single voice was a great danger to their profession. This had been shown in 1926, when Churchill had introduced betting tax. Now it appeared that associations of bookmakers in Scotland and in Leeds had made separate representations to the Home Office.

On 9 July 1957 the Inner Cabinet's 7th meeting discussed a memorandum prepared by its Parliamentary Agent which set out the pros and cons of what now seems a rather surprising new suggestion, namely that the bookmakers should seek to obtain a Royal Charter. Their purpose was to create an organisation which would have sufficient authority to raise a levy itself, instead of being subject to a governmental agency. However, Sir Dingwall Bateson, Chairman of the Racecourse Betting Control Board, advised that a Royal Charter would be a roundabout way of achieving that objective, and the Inner Cabinet agreed that, although it should continue to look into the possibility of obtaining a Charter, time was short. In the interim a sub-committee should be set up, to include representatives of the bookmakers, the stewards and the RBCB, to consider alternatives. Whatever conclusion might be reached, the Inner Cabinet considered that it would be impossible to evolve any workable scheme for raising any substantial contribution to racing from bookmakers unless they could obtain adequate control of their own affairs.

The bookmakers met the Jockey Club and the RBCB on 25 September 1957, and recorded at their Executive Committee in November (at which Archie Scott was elected Chairman) that the meeting had ended 'on a rather happy note'. Both the stewards and the RBCB had insisted that racing needed more money, to which the bookmakers had replied that if such funds were to come out of betting, then they should go back to racing, and not be used for the general purposes of the Exchequer. It does, indeed, appear that a substantial measure of agreement had, at this point, been reached. The request by the Racecourse Association for talks with the off-course bookmakers had been turned down, as they were still negotiating with the Jockey Club and RBCB and had promised not to negotiate with any other body. However, the Jockey Club disagreed, and thought that it would be advisable for the bookmakers to meet the RCA to explain to them the difficulties involved.

At their November meeting the bookmakers also returned to their need for a constitution, which was being prepared by Mr Hancock, their Parliamentary Agent. Hancock said he did not think the Privy Council would agree to the grant of a Royal Charter and that a Private Member's Bill was a stronger possibility. However, it was extremely difficult to draft a constitution, as it would have to be agreed by all the constituent members. There were also legal difficulties, since a constitution could not allow the parent body to accept as members people who were operating outside the law, and many existing bookmakers would remain in that position if cash betting off course were not included in the Bill. There was some argument about whether a Private Member's Bill would be desirable, since one member thought that it might be used as the outline of machinery for setting up a tax system when a tax was introduced (it does not appear at this point that a distinction was being made between what is now called levy and the Betting Duty which was introduced much later). On the other hand, until some form of constitution was arrived at, it would not be possible to make any progress in supplying contributions to racing, and in that case the Jockey Club would have to be so informed, and the good relations which had been built up with the Club would vanish; the uneasy calm which had existed for about a year would end, and the bookmakers' opponents would spring up again.

Two important new developments occurred at the 10th meeting of the Inner Cabinet on 23 February 1958.

First, the idea was floated of a fund to protect punters against defaulting bookmakers. It was thought that such a fund would improve bookmakers' status with the Government and public, since at present it was possible for people to say that one advantage the

Tote had over the bookmakers was that the former did not default.

Secondly, although it was not possible to meet the RCA's demands for money while the bookmakers had no legal backing, it did seem possible that voluntary contributions on a more limited scale (say, £100,000) might be obtained from bookmakers if the idea were sponsored by the Stewards. The Executive Committee's 45th meeting, held on the same day, was told that the only hope of achieving a response from bookmakers to an appeal for annual payments lay in persuading the Stewards of the Jockey Club to put their names to the scheme, which might, perhaps, be called the 'Stewards' Fund', but the only inducement that could be offered to bookmakers was an advertisement in the sporting press, which would indicate the public relations advantages which might be expected, and suggest that contributions might be allowable against income tax. Such a scheme might produce as much as £100,000, but research was necessary to find out how many people could be expected to pay. Shortly afterwards, on 14 April, the bookmakers met the RCA; they explained that they were making approaches to the Stewards of the Jockey Club with respect to a voluntary fund, and asked the Chairman of the RCA to restrain his members from making life difficult for the bookmakers meanwhile.

The 12th meeting of the Inner Cabinet, on 16 July 1958, returned to further consideration of its own Bill, which was now being drafted. It was agreed that further thought should be given to the Northern Ireland example to see how the legalisation of off-course betting had worked out in practice there. In further discussion of the bookmakers' Bill, the Parliamentary Agent agreed that its chances of passing into law were slight, but that it was worth drafting because it would help the bookmakers to formulate their views and could later be used as a source of amendments to the Government's Bill during its committee stage. The effort expended would therefore not be wasted.

The principal purposes of the bookmakers' Bill were to establish a board of bookmakers who would register members and be empowereed to raise a levy from them. It would be an offence for any unregistered person to operate as a bookmaker. The Betting Houses Act of 1853 would be repealed and perhaps also the Street Betting Act of 1906. The clause relating to the levy would apply to all types of bookmaking, including greyhounds, but provision was made for the contributions to go only to horse racing. (This, however, was a point which required further thought.) The need for secrecy was emphasised, as otherwise the impression might be created that the bookmakers were actually committed to the introduction of the Bill.

Meanwhile the Stewards had in June agreed in principle to the bookmakers' proposals for a fund and agreed that it should be called 'The Racecourse Improvement Fund supervised by the Jockey Club and the National Hunt Committee'. However, the Stewards did not wish to participate in the distribution of the money collected, but approved of the RCA's suggestion that a committee, on which the bookmakers would be represented, would plan the distribution and that such plans would be submitted for approval to the Stewards. They also agreed with the point upon which the bookmakers had always insisted, that the bulk of the money should go to public amenities.

On 9 December 1958 William Hill, the bookmaker, made the Gimcrack speech at York, as owner of the Gimcrack Stakes winner, Be Careful, and took the opportunity to discuss bookmakers' interests. The number of bookmakers on course was decreasing, and their average gross profit could not be much above two per cent. He could see no reason why off-course bookmakers, who no doubt made a better living than those on course, should not make a contribution to racing. If bookmakers were granted legal status, and were all registered with the NBPA, they would be able to raise considerable sums and clean the undesirables out of the profession.

He personally loathed the idea of betting shops, but if betting were to be legal at all, it should be legal by all methods, including in shops. However, the shops would need strict regulation.[21]

In March 1959 the NBPA's Executive Committee was dissolved, and replaced with the National Bookmakers' and Associated Bodies Joint Protection Association. (The Association was dissolved on 31 December 1964.) The new body's committee resolved at an emergency meeting on 31 May 1959 that it did not want to see betting shops legalised, but if cash betting had to be legalised then it was in favour of legislation based on its own Bill, which would assure registration of bookmakers by their own associations and give those associations power to levy money for the benefit of racing. Betting shops under this arrangement would be organised on the Northern Ireland model, and if the bookmakers' associations were not the controlling bodies, then the bookmakers must be equally represented on whatever body was eventually in control.

The Racecourse Amenities Fund was discussed again at the 20th meeting of the Inner Cabinet on 8 June 1959, when a letter from William Hill dated 29 May was read, pointing out that 'it is a little galling to me personally to think part of this company's contributions. of £5,000 is going to such courses as Ascot, Epsom and Goodwood, where not only is membership refused. . . but where I am also refused admittance even on a member's introduction voucher, solely because I am a bookmaker.' It was agreed to say at the next meeting of the Fund that bookmakers were not prepared to give money to courses where bookmakers were treated in such a way. Nevertheless, it was agreed that someone should be hired to make a personal approach to all bookmakers to encourage contributions to the fund. (By the late 1960s the voucher system was virtually dead, though it lingered on at the main meetings at York and Goodwood. Of course in those days the membership of racecourses was far more exclusive than it is now.)

On 3 July 1959 a bookmakers' deputation called on the Stewards, and gave them their resolution of 31 May. They also informed the Stewards that they had prepared a draft scheme dealing with betting legislation, which might be submitted to the Home Office at a future date. It transpired that the Stewards had already visited the Home Office and submitted their own scheme, a copy of which they now gave to the bookmakers. They also told the bookmakers that the Home Office wished to close all enquiries into the betting legislation before the House went into recess on 30 July, and it was therefore desirable to put any remaining views to the Home Office immediately.

The bookmakers found it necessary to accept this invitation because the Stewards' latest scheme would still have put registration of bookmakers and collection of levy under the control of the RBCB, and there were other unacceptable points. They therefore applied for an interview at the Home Office, which agreed to receive a deputation on 22 July. Meanwhile, on 16 July the bookmakers met the Stewards at Newmarket, again at the Stewards' request, and E. W. Weatherby (of Weatherby's, the firm which runs racing on behalf of the Jockey Club) said that, since the last meeting with the bookmakers, he had seen Home Office officials, who had suggested modifications to the Stewards' scheme. These removed *in toto* the bookmakers' objections to that scheme, since it was now proposed that

[34]

the bookmakers would be licensed by the Government, but under the overall control of a central government body of only three persons, which would control two boards. The first would be a modified form of the present RBCB, answerable for control and running of the Tote, while the other would be a board of bookmakers responsible for the organisation and control of bookmakers.

It was considered advisable by the Home Office that the bookmakers should continue the Racecourse Amenities Fund for a further year. The government was prepared to incorporate into the Bill statutory powers enabling the Board to levy money for the benefit of racing, although that power would only be used if the requisite sum of money were not forthcoming as a result of voluntary contributions to the Amenities Fund. The bookmakers regarded these proposals as the best they had seen so far.

The Home Office was uncertain on four points regarding the levy, and had asked the Stewards to assist in solving them, and the Stewards in turn had asked the bookmakers for help. First, how much money did racing need? Second, what was the requisite sum, which, if it were not raised by the Amenities Fund, would require the application of statutory powers? Under what scheme was it suggested that statutory powers should be granted? And fourth, how, and by whom, would money be distributed to racing? The sum suggested by the Home Office to cover the first two points was £3 million, presumably a figure put to the Home Office by the Jockey Club, since this was the sum it also put to the Peppiatt Committee. (This Committee is discussed briefly below, and in more detail in Chapter IV.)

On 22 July there followed the meeting at the Home Office, which was attended by Sir Charles Cunningham, a senior official, and four of his colleagues. The meeting, which was described as very friendly, lasted one and a quarter hours, during which great interest was shown in the bookmakers' draft scheme, which Cunningham had read thoroughly. The bookmakers stated that they considered £3 million an excessive figure and that it would be wise to start lower and work up. They thought the money raised should be distributed in the same way as the Amenities Fund, and according to the same criterion, namely, that it should be spent on improving amenities for the comfort of the public.

Finally, Cunningham asked what would occur if the Minister were to come down more in favour of the findings of the Royal Commission. Scott replied that although bookmakers could not agree to that being the best possible legislation, they would do their best to make sure that it would work.

The Bill was formally announced in the Queen's Speech on 27 October 1959:[22] 'A Bill will be introduced to amend and modernise the law on betting and gaming.' Harold Macmillan (later Earl of Stockton), the Prime Minister, amplified the announcement:[23] 'There will be time for a number of measures, some of them long overdue, of various social reforms. Among these is the modernisation of the law on betting and gambling, the former of which has been left undisturbed for fifty and the latter, I am told, for more than a hundred years.' R. A. (later Lord) Butler, the Home Secretary, duly presented the Betting and Gaming Bill on 30 October, when it was given its First Reading.

On 2 November he said, in a reply to a written question from Sir Hendrie Oakshott, which echoed the Lord Chancellor's remarks in the previous December about Lord Astor's 'reorientation':

> The Stewards of the Jockey Club, and other bodies concerned with the sport of horse racing and the breeding of race horses, have made representations to me that any Bill relating to betting should include provision for a compulsory levy on off-the-course betting on horse races, the proceeds to be devoted, like the surplus from the totalisator, to the support of horse racing and breeding. This proposal was not considered by the Royal Commission on Betting, Lotteries and Gaming, 1949-52; it raises important issues of principle and presents serious practical difficulties.[24]

Butler and the Secretary of State for Scotland had therefore decided to appoint an Inter-departmental Committee under Sir Leslie Peppiatt to consider the desirability and practicability of bookmakers contributing to racing and breeding and, if they favoured it, to advise on its amount and how it should be raised.

On 3 November 1959 Hancock reported to the 21st meeting of the Inner Cabinet that the Betting and Gaming Bill's Second Reading would take place soon, and would probably go upstairs to Committee rather than being considered by a Committee of the whole House. That would be the time to put down amendments. In Archie Scott's opinion, there was no possibility of defeating the betting shops, and the best that could be done now was to see that the legislation reflected the bookmakers' views as far as possible. If betting shops were not in the right hands, he believed that they could be a threat to bookmakers generally because they might provide excuses for the authorities which could be used in favour of granting a Tote monopoly in a few years' time.

There followed an emergency meeting of the Committee on 9 November, when Scott asked members for points in the Bill with which they were dissatisfied, so that he could arrange for them to be ventilated in the Second Reading debate. He continued that he viewed the Bill with despondency, as he thought it a means by which the Tote could set itself up to handle off-course betting, in the hope of ousting the bookmakers once its business was established. One of the principal worries expressed at this meeting was that the magistrates would issue permits to people with very little bookmaking experience who, in turn, might lose all their money and then welsh, thus undermining the good reputation of bookmakers in general, which they had established with the public over the last forty years. One member thought the betting shop system would be unworkable without more police supervision, and feared that after the Tote had gained sufficient offices, the Government would bring in another Bill outlawing betting shops on the grounds that they were a social evil.

Conclusion

This account of the bookmakers' lobby in the 1950s shows that, although its members' activities were in large part illegal, it was able to operate effectively and to establish good relations with its negotiating partners in the Home Office and the Jockey Club. The bookmakers seem to have been taken seriously by the Home Office, not only because common adversity produced a greater degree of unity among them than they had ever achieved before, but also because they were well advised and thorough, and had taken the trouble to produce a draft Bill of their own.

For their part, as one veteran recalls, the bookmakers were pleased to be well received at the Home Office, and thought Butler a man of sense for consulting them – the experts. A great many of the points which they made in negotiations before the Bill was presented to the House of Commons had been accepted by the Home Office officials, so that there was a surprisingly large measure of agreement before the Bill began its lengthy passage through Parliament. Numerous points which had been discussed in advance were discussed again, exhaustively, but few completely new points were produced.

The bookmakers themselves showed good sense in their dealings with the Jockey Club. Although they could not fail to realise that the Club's interest was to extract as much money from them as possible, they saw, once they had accepted that a levy was the inevitable sequel to the legalisation of betting offices, that their interest lay in trusting the Jockey Club (though, as we have seen, their faith was sometimes shaken) and approaching the future in a spirit of partnership.

It was not easy for bookmakers to accept that betting offices would be legalised. However, the smaller bookmakers supported it in the end, because, however much they felt that their activity, although illegal, was perfectly respectable, they also felt that it would be comfortable to end the confusion between being regarded as petty criminals, whilst at the same time providing a service desired by a large section of the public. Part of their reward was that, when it came to the allocation of licences under the Act, many formerly illegal proprietors were given preference.

The large bookmakers were in a different position, because the bulk of their business was on credit, and therefore legal. At first they were uninterested in betting shops, and feared that rackets and gangsterism would result. In fact, however, there was little violence, and as early as 1962 Ladbroke's began to take over existing betting shops. The flotation of their shares, when they became a public company in 1967, was a runaway success, and by 1969 they owned four hundred shops.[25]

The Home Office, too, had a hard task to reconcile the conflicting interests. The officials had relied heavily on the report of the Royal Commission of 1951; they knew that Ministers would do the same, and that they would not depart from their determination to legalise betting offices. At the same time the Jockey Club exacerbated the bookmakers' fears of an eventual Tote monopoly by continuing to insist, until the eleventh hour, that they should be registered by the RBCB, which would also collect the levy from them. The bookmakers, on the other hand, were determined to control their own affairs, partly because they feared the Tote, and partly because they wished to confirm the professional status of bookmaking. By persuading both sides to accept a formula which would put bookmakers under the control of a statutory body, the Home Office not only eased the passage of the Betting and Gaming Act 1960, but did much of the groundwork for the Betting Levy Act, 1961.

Notes

1 Royal Commission on Betting, Lotteries and Gaming, 1949-51, *Report* (Cmd. 8190), 1951.
2 Jockey Club, *Report of the Racing Reorganisation Committee to the Stewards of the Jockey Club*, London, 3 February 1943.
3 R. Kaye (with R. Peskett), *The Ladbrokes Story*, London, 1969, p. 198.
4 195 *H.L. Deb.*, col. 839, 8 February 1956.
5 549 *H.C. Deb.*, cols, 2487-2578, 9 March 1956.
6 *Ibid.*, cols. 2507 and 2509.
7 *Ibid.*, col. 2513.
8 References to the bookmakers' internal affairs are taken from papers held at the National Association of Bookmakers, to which body I am most grateful for access to them.
9 198 *H.L. Deb.*, col. 101, 27 June 1956.
10 *Ibid.*, col. 103.
11 601 *H.C. Deb.*, cols. 1618-1702, 13 March 1959.
12 *Ibid.*, col. 1621.
13 *Ibid.*, col. 1634.
14 *Ibid.*, col. 1650.
15 *The Times*, 12 February 1958.
16 Royal Commission on Gambling, *Final Report*, 1978 (Cmnd. 7200), vol. I. The Tote's evidence is discussed in paras. 8.18 to 8.35.
17 R. Mortimer, *The Flat*, London, 1979, p. 127.
18 *The Times*, 12 September 1956.
19 Mortimer, *The Flat*, p. 128.
20 Kaye, *The Ladbrokes Story*, p. 158.
21 *The Times*, 10 December 1958.
22 612 *H.C. Deb.*, col. 51, 27 October 1959.
23 *Ibid.*, col. 75.
24 612 *H.C. Written Answers*, cols. 24-5, 2 November 1959.
25 Kaye, *The Ladbrokes Story*, p. 266.

III
The Betting and Gaming Act, 1960

> Though the present system may be illegal it is understood. It is under-
> stood sufficiently to be evaded, and when the time comes for people to
> pay their fines they do so and then carry on until their turn comes round
> again.
>
> (George Wigg, in the Committee Stage
> of the Betting and Gaming Bill, 11 February 1960)[1]

Though the idea of a levy was by now firmly established, the purpose of the Betting and Gaming Bill was not, unhappily for the industry, to do something for racing, but to honour the campaign commitment to clean up the corruption that resulted from illegal bookmaking. However, the industry knew that it would not have to wait long. We have already seen that it had been insisting for several years that racing must benefit from the money gambled on it. On 8 December 1958 the retiring Senior Steward of the Jockey Club, Lord Sefton, had given a hint of the Stewards' resolution by making it clear at a meeting of the Club that, although it had never asked for betting legislation, if a Bill was unsuitable the Club would oppose it unless it provided for a contribution to be raised from gambling.[2] In fact, the Bill did not contain any such clause, but by then it was clear that a levy would follow shortly, and if the Government's intention to introduce it had not been announced in time, the Bill could still be opposed in the House of Lords.

The immediate purpose was for R. A. Butler, who had been Home Secretary since 1957, and hoped to succeed Harold MacMillan as Prime Minister (for which post he was defeated by Sir Alec Douglas Home in October 1963), to get betting off the streets, just as he had done with prostitution, so removing two of the most obvious causes of police corruption and establishing himself as a great reforming Home Secretary. He also saw racing and breeding as important employers and export earners, but betting as something that had to be tolerated.

Butler's purpose was to legalise betting, not to encourage people to bet (so the shops were not to be comfortable; 'loitering' and continuous betting would not be allowed), nor at that stage to make anything out of it for the Government, though Betting Duty followed some years later. The Betting and Gaming Bill did not have an easy time in Parliament; Butler introduced it himself, but might easily have given up, had his will not been stiffened by his lieutenants – as he had given up over other legislation in the past. As it was, he took no part in the very long committee stage, and was severely criticised for failing to do so, perhaps because the immensely heavy work load laid upon him by MacMillan gave him no choice but to leave the Bill to his joint Under-Secretaries, Dennis Vosper (later Lord Runcorn) and David (later Lord) Renton. (Vosper was in charge of the 1960 Act, assisted by Renton, and Renton of the 1961 Act, assisted by Vosper.) However, the evidence is mixed: the former Conservative Minister, Sir David Llewellyn, has recalled having heard from several sources that Butler had assiduously put it about that his work at the Home Office occupied only half a day a week, and that it was generally thought he said this because he wanted some different, additional, post.[3]

It is interesting that Butler himself did not, at least in retrospect, regard the Betting and Gaming Act as one of his major achievements, nor as completely successful. As he says in his memoirs, published in 1971:

> It drove betting off the streets, where it was illegal and strained the police, but the House of Commons was so intent on making 'betting shops' as sad as possible, in order not to deprave the young, that they ended up more like undertakers' premises.[4]

However, it must be added that this passage may be an example of Butler's self-delusion, since the 'sadness' had been deliberate Government policy, designed to make the Bill more acceptable to the Churches and moralists.

The Government, rather cleverly, did not allow a free vote on the Bill, on the stated ground that it was not primarily a matter of conscience, but an administrative measure to tidy up the law. The Government also, no doubt, had in mind the need to emphasise its own certainty, despite the great disparity of advice that it had been

receiving, of the rightness of its actions, which might have been
called in question by a free vote. The latter was allowed by Labour,
which made predictable, though not excessive, political play with
the Government's failure to allow the same.

When Butler introduced the Bill's Second Reading on 16 November
1959, he explained that it was not the purpose of the criminal law
to deprive men of the right to decide about what was moral and
what immoral, but to prohibit activity injurious to society itself, and
to protect those who needed it. The 1906 Street Betting Act had
prohibited betting in the streets, but telephones had led to credit
betting, largely by the middle classes. The 1951 Royal Commission,
on which the Bill was based, had estimated that three and a half
million people bet an average of 8s a week with cash bookmakers,
against an average £2.10s–£3.10s by those with credit accounts. Butler
now wanted to start betting offices, as had been recommended by
the Commission, because at present the law was unenforceable and
held in contempt, and led to bad relations between police and public.
He would also allow runners in factories, provided the bets they
collected were taken back to the betting offices.

The Tote, which had given Butler an assurance that, since its operations were not liable to Duty, it would not seek to enter the football
pools' market, had battled for the exclusive right to offer Tote odds,
and had obtained Counsel's opinion to the effect that the skill used
in compiling the odds conferred a copyright. The result was that the
Tote's exclusive rights to conduct pool betting and to offer Tote odds,
and a right to authorise others to use its odds, were included in the
Bill, perhaps not surprisingly, if the Tote's memorandum was really
the only one Butler had understood.

British attitudes to gambling were expressed in all their rich
variety, antiquity and often hypocrisy in the debates on the Bill.
There was considerable division of opinion as to whether the objective of legalising betting without encouraging it could best be fulfilled
by legalising the *status quo*, which most members in the early, rather
ill-informed, stages of the Bill's passage through Parliament thought
meant street betting (they learnt only gradually how diverse the
status quo was), or whether betting shops were the answer. *The Times*
thought both should be allowed, leaving licensing justices to decide
the mix.[5] However, Niall MacPherson, the Under-Secretary of State
for Scotland, said that evidence from Scotland indicated that, since
the introduction of betting shops there, street betting had decreased

to the extent that it was no longer considered a problem. Some Members thought the best answer might be to establish special letter boxes into which people could post their bets: the difficulty here, however, was that children might be led astray.

Butler's main intention was to legalise betting shops and prevent street betting, and he presented as a quite separate point the demands by racing and breeding interests that bookmakers should make a financial contribution to racing, which had caused him to set up the Peppiatt Committee to enquire into the question. However, some MPs felt strongly that, although the questions of betting offices and the levy were separable in principle, they were inseparable in practice. If Peppiatt were to find that the levy was undesirable or impracticable, or both, these MPs felt that their decision between betting shops, the continuance of street betting, or a combination of the two, would be affected, and there was therefore considerable annoyance that the committee had been appointed too late for its findings to be available at any stage of the Betting and Gaming Bill's passage through the Commons.

Chuter Ede, the influential former Home Secretary, thought the Street Betting Act of 1906, which forbade street betting, one of the worst pieces of class legislation ever put on the statute book. But, though he favoured betting shops, he did not believe they would prevent street betting. Nor did he approve of a General Bookmakers' Council, which would decide on who was suitable to become, or remain, a bookmaker; he understood that this idea was supported by the Jockey Club, of which he appears to have been no admirer.

Rather few MPs discussed the morality of gambling, but George Thomas (later Viscount Tonypandy) thought it a sin, which became no less sinful if conducted in a shop. He estimated that four thousand shops would be needed in London alone, and thought gambling would undermine the values of our civilisation. Patrick Gordon Walker, on the other hand, who called on the Government to follow the Labour example and allow a free vote, did not think betting a sin but a folly which should be allowed, though in the hope that education would cause it to be replaced by better forms of social activity. He quoted the Royal Commission of 1951, which had said that the spread of gambling was one of the symptoms of an age in which people had more leisure and could not make good use of it – or did not know how to. The remedy lay not in restrictive legislation, but in education and the provision of facilities for more healthy recreation.[6]

In the late 1980s it looks as though they may have been right, and that the growth of education may indeed provide one of the explanations for the changing age profile of betting shop habitués, currently reported by bookmakers. Young punters (it is said – there seems not to have been systematic research) are not being recruited, but prefer to save up their money for cars or gramophone records. A very similar point was made by the prescient Dennis Vosper, when the employment of 'young persons' by bookmakers was being considered in Committee: 'People under 18 with surplus spending power do not devote that money so much to betting as to other things. They expend it on dancing, "pop" records and so on.'[7]

Gordon Walker went on that, in setting up betting shops, the Home Secretary would be like a charwoman sweeping dust under the carpet, as he had been over the Street Offences Act, which got prostitutes off the streets. He also saw the danger of betting being dominated by the big chains and a number of Members feared domination by Vernons and Littlewoods. William Rees-Davies, on the other hand, reported that William Hill's were opposed to betting shops because licensing magistrates might be expected to favour the smaller bookmakers. The latter wanted the Act to contain a limitation on how many shops a single proprietor might own, and the Home Office was sympathetic, but could not see how to put the idea into effect. Stephen McAdden confirmed that the bookmakers' associations were opposed to betting shops. The only people, he said, who wanted shops were the Racecourse Betting Control Board, which was jealous of bookmakers' access to non-racegoers. Nor, though he did not use the word, did he like the idea of a levy – 'I think that sometimes a lot of "chi chi" is talked about the great sport of racing, and one gets the impression that it is only kept in existence as a result of the efforts of a few indigent noblemen at great sacrifice to themselves'[8] – and it was not right that betting offices should be opened to help such people.

There was opposition from a variety of other sources. The Scout (a *Daily Express* journalist) pointed out that the large established bookmaking firms, whose business was legally done over the telephone, were against betting shops, or 'half crown joints'.[9] A few days later, Warren Hill said that no one wanted betting shops except the Tote propagandists, and the fact that the Whips were on in Parliament made the man in the street think the Bill was just a cover for a Tote monopoly. The Jockey Club was tired and out of its depths in politics, though fully capable of administering the rules of racing. What was more, Warren Hill went on, the Jockey Club's own financial position was not clear, and this weakened its demand for a levy on off-course betting. Nor had it revealed how such a levy would be spent, so that the suspicion was going about that it might merely be used to help owners.[10]

In a later article he added that he did not believe the Jockey Club's contention that the bookmakers wanted to pay a statutory levy.[11] In yet another article he pointed to the public's disquiet that betting, on which expenditure was only a tenth of that on alcohol or tobacco, should be regarded as a crime, and bewilderment that there should be thought to be a moral difference between betting in a shop and elsewhere. The public feared that betting shops would only encourage immoderate gambling, and did not believe that street betting could be stamped out by Act of Parliament.[12]

At the Committee stage the arguments which had been touched on at Second Reading were reproduced at immense length: the Official Report occupies 1,282 columns, 986 of which are concerned with betting and only 296 with gaming.

A major amendment of principle was moved by Reginald (later Lord) Paget, that instead of introducing betting offices, the government should legalise the *status quo*, by repealing the Street Betting Act. He would, however, not oppose 'local option', which would allow betting shops to continue where they already existed, and later produced an Amendment to this effect. He feared that once betting offices were introduced, large chains would grow up, as had happened with the football pools, of which he said: 'Indeed, I should say, from watching their performances, that the only thing they have heard about ethics is that it is a county east of London.' The notion that betting offices, if introduced, should be uncomfortable, was absurd: 'It is on a par with an epigram I once found in a Victorian tract to the effect that conjugal bliss was all right so long as both parties wore long combinations.'[13] The point was supported by Eric Fletcher, who, like a number of Members, produced evidence, frequently contradictory, from Ireland. He had seen betting shops in the North, where they had recently been legalised, and had found them dingy and unpleasant and 'Like so much else one finds in Ireland, they are quaint places.'[14]

In Committee it became clear how little MPs knew about the present state of illegal betting, and how very varied was its treatment in different police areas. Perhaps the most striking contribution was from Charles Longbottom, MP for York, who said that there were between forty and fifty betting shops in the City, with the result that there were no street runners, though there were plenty of factory and hospital runners. The shops were conducted in a most orderly way, the police turned a blind eye on them, and they had not been raided since 1938. Yet forty miles away at Scarborough they were regularly raided: and at nearby Filey they were not allowed at all. Longbottom said: 'I know some bookmakers in Scarborough who know almost the day they will be raided. They know how much money they will have to pay and budget accordingly throughout the year. Others are raided almost as if it were an annual festival.'[15]

Stephen McAdden, who throughout the debates showed himself the friend of the small bookmakers, though not of the chains, said that as far as he knew, bookmakers in London were against betting shops, where they would be an innovation, but that they should be legalised in Scotland, where they already existed.

This remark chimed with an important element of Vosper's case for the introduction of betting shops, which was that they had largely suppressed street betting in Scotland (where they were illegal) and Northern Ireland, where they had been legalised in 1957. He agreed that a large proportion of bookmakers had been opposed to betting shops ever since the Royal Commission, but he was none the less determined that they should be introduced. Betting in the streets, the Royal Commission had said, was not 'the natural method of providing facilities for cash betting', but had grown up because betting in offices was forbidden. Later, Butler was to say that the streets were not 'suitable' places for betting, though no real explanation was ever produced of how the Government had decided what was natural or suitable; nor was any convincing answer given to the attitude to street betting expressed by Chuter Ede (who had been Labour's Home Secretary from 1945-1951) that 'people regard it as one of their essential liberties to break the law in this way.'[16] The Government's real case seems to have been that street betting led to police corruption. Even this, in order not to offend the police, had to be put in the form that it led to the *danger* of police corruption, though of course it could be regretfully admitted that there were *a few* cases of actual corruption.

Sir James Duncan, the Member for South Angus, told the Committee that the Scottish Starting Price Bookmakers' Association was opposed to street betting and in favour of shops, as were the East Midlands BPA and the Racecourse Association. He, and other members, did not believe that the introduction of shops would have any effect on the total quantity of betting, an important point, since in those pre-levy days the Government was concerned merely to provide outlets for people's existing propensity to bet, not to encourage them to bet more. James McInnes added that, in his own city of Glasgow, there had been almost a thousand street bookmakers; now there were virtually none, but instead there were 350 betting shops, owned by 260 inividuals.

George Wigg, who had been absent from the Committee's first few sessions because he was recovering from an operation, now began to show his expertise. It was no accident, he said, that betting shops existed in Scotland. Until the First World War, he added, punters who wanted to bet by post (which was illegal in Britain) had sent their bets 'over the water' to Holland or Switzerland. When the war came, Scottish bookmakers had no longer been able to collect their bets from their associates abroad: 'Their livelihood had gone. How were they to get the bets? It was illegal to get bets through the post, so if the chief constable did not accept a bribe, the Glasgow Police, through the kindness of their hearts, from that day onwards shut their eyes to a practice which remains illegal to this day.' He agreed that there were numerous prosecutions in Scotland, (at Second Reading the House had been told that there had been proceedings against 16,812 people for 3,907 betting and gaming offences in 1958), but they were done on a rota arranged between the police and the bookmakers. But though Wigg could be pungent about the relationships between police and bookmakers, he also feared the power of organised bookmaking in Scotland: 'there is a degree of centralisation growing up which puts enormous economic power into fewer and fewer hands'.[17]

The Committee debated runners at length – Wigg thought that in these days of rat-catchers being called 'rodent technicians', they should be renamed 'accredited agents'. Rees-Davies, who spoke with the expertise of a racing journalist, thought that to license them would lead to disputes over pitches and to a renewal of the gang warfare that had existed many years ago. 'It used to cost, I think, 7s 6d if one wanted to have someone razer-slashed in London or Brighton at that time.'[18] He argued that the real reason for bookmakers' opposition to betting shops, instead of a system of runners bringing bets back to offices to which punters were not admitted, was that shops would have higher overheads, and so lead either to lower profits or lower odds offered to the punter. However, this assertion provoked an immediate counter-example from Eric Johnson, who drew attention to a letter in *The Sporting Life* of 28 January, from an individual who operated nine betting shops, and found his outgoings lower than in the days when he had had to pay runners.

Some members displayed considerable knowledge of how factory runners operated. For example, Sir James Duncan said that they were provided with bags, which might be collected by the bookmaker at the factory gate, or delivered by the runner to the bookmaker's office. The bets were timed and locked in a bag, with six partitions for the six races. Only the bookmaker could unlock the bag. Meanwhile, the runner had the cash, but, as he was receiving a regular commission of fifteen per cent, he would be unlikely to 'welsh' with a single afternoon's takings. In the street the system was rather different; according to Reginald Paget, a bag with a clock locking device would call attention to itself,and there the custom was for bets to be written on slips of paper, which would be wrapped round the stake money and handed to the runner.

Vosper reiterated the Government's determination to suppress street betting, and therefore street runners, but to allow runners in factories, and to allow such individuals as the milkman to collect bets and so to function as runners. There were legal difficulties about whether a factory runner could be held to be occupying a 'place', and so contravening the Bill. However, in a case brought under the 1853 Act, which the 1960 Bill closely followed, it had been held that a 'place' must be one effectively occupied by the person. Provided, therefore, that the factory runner moved about the factory, he would be occupying neither the whole factory, nor any particular spot within it, and could not be held to be occupying a 'place'. It was intended that a Government amendment would cover cases where the runner did not move about the factory, but instead collected bets at a defined place.

As for the legal position of the milkman, if he accepted a bet in a house's garden, he would be in a private place, not covered by the Street Betting Act, but if the house door gave directly on to the street, the milkman might be held to be loitering with intent to collect bets.

However, Vosper could not find that any such case had ever been brought, and considered it so unlikely that the courts would be called upon to decide the point in the future that it did not need to be covered by Government amendment. Vosper would not, however, go so far as to allow bets to be taken in, for example, newsagents' shops, which would have been an offence under the Betting Act of 1853, not the Street Betting Act of 1906, and would remain an offence under the new Act.

We have seen that some members feared the growth of chains of bookmakers and that one of them was the Labour stalwart George Wigg, who at that time regarded himself as very much the small bookmakers' friend. Another, a Conservative, was Stephen McAdden, who moved an amendment to the Bill which would have limited any individual to holding three betting licences; Robert Mellish, the Member for Bermondsey, supported him, but would have liked the limit to be only one licence. Already, huge prices were being paid for options on properties which could be used as betting shops in his constituency, so that the small man would have no chance. Vosper, too, liked the small man, but, as so often, he argued the practical impossibility of achieving the desired end through legislation. He thought three shops rather too low a number, but in any case doubted whether it would be a wise precedent to try to impose smallness on a business by legislation.

In addition to all the arguments against betting shops which have been noted so far, there were others based on class and ethics. Chuter Ede said of the prohibition of street bookmaking, in words which could have been used by his friend and admirer George Wigg:

> The trouble is that this is merely an effort to make something which people in high places regard as being too proletarian conform to a pattern which they regard as respectable. Yet one finds some members of the community who object to being compelled to make their private transactions and their social habits conform to the standard set by a class to which they do not belong.[19]

As for ethics, there were *quasi*-moral utterances from both sides of the House about such 'evils' as continuous betting, but only one Member, J. T. Price, rejected betting root and branch on ethical grounds, and even he, having recognised that legislation was needed, was prepared to help make it work, and hoped that the 'great finance houses' could be kept out. However, he was also out-

spoken against the evil of gambling as a whole, and could not understand why Members who, in the debate on the Street Offences Bill,
had rejected the Continental example of State brothels, should now
be prepared to set up similar establishments for betting. Later he
said: 'Here we have legislation admittedly conceived in corruption
and we are going to put on the Statute Book a new Act which has
been born in sin.'[20]

Once the Committee (where, just as at Second Reading, there was
no free vote for the conservatives) had decided that street betting
should continue to be illegal, and that betting shops were to be
legalised, much of its work concerned matters of relative detail. There
remained, however, four major areas of concern. These were: the
needs of the rural areas; the involvement of young people in betting;
the conditions under which bookmakers should operate; and the
position of the Tote.

It had been recognised on both sides of the Committee that people
in the rural areas were as likely to wish to bet as were those who
lived in towns, but that in many areas the population would be so
dispersed as to make it not worth a bookmaker's while to open a
shop. There was much discussion of newsagents or other shopkeep-
ers, or even publicans, being allowed to take bets, a solution which
the Government could not accept. Nor was Vosper persuaded that
Britain should follow the French example of using cafés as agents of
the *pari-mutuel*, but he did produce a major amendment whereby a
betting shop need not be reached directly from the street, but could
have indirect access via a hall or passage, provided that punters did
not have to *pass through* another place of business to reach the betting
shop – which could, however, be *attached* to another place of business. Thus country districts would be assisted. It would even be
possible in theory for a room in a pub to be licensed, though Vosper
thought 'the justices would think long before they granted such an
application',[21] or a betting shop might be established in a club. It
would also be up to the planning authorities to decide whether shops
might be opened near such bodies as youth clubs or churches, to
both of which there had been objections.

Many members of the Committee were worried about the corrupt-
ing effect of gambling on young people, though there were others,
like George Wigg, who were robust enough to think that the young
should be guided rather than restrained, and that moderate experience of betting early in life would act as an inoculation against excess

later. He urged the Committee not to believe that people who did not bet were in some way superior to those who did, and added for good measure 'Any politician who does not have a bet should not be trusted', echoing, perhaps unconsciously, Lord Rosebery, who used to say of trainers that if they did not bet they could not be trusted really to care whether or not their horses won.[22]

Many points of detail were covered in the very lengthy discussions of the conditions under which bookmakers should operate. In response to the question whether an aspiring bookmaker should first obtain a licence from the justices and then seek planning permission for his premises, or *vice versa*, Ministers took the common-sense line that the two applications should proceed at the same time. The matter descended, however, into farce, because Renton had had to seek a ruling from the Minister of Planning and Local Government as to whether a betting shop should count as a shop, in which case the conversion of an existing shop into a betting office would not entail a change of use and therefore not be subject to planning permission. The Minister of Planning and Local Government was slow to make up his mind, and Renton was obliged to report, amid laughter, that: 'His present and provisional view is that he does not think that it will require an amendment of the Use Classes Order in order to establish that a betting office is a shop and not an office.'[23] Later, however, the question was settled with a decision that betting shops would constitute a new class of premises, so that planning permission would be required for all of them.

The hours during which betting shops should be open engaged much attention. One idea was that they should be closed during racing hours. This suggestion was made not in order to encourage people to go to the races but to discourage continuous betting. However, Vosper did not endorse closing during racing hours, partly because it would be difficult to enforce. (He had found in Dublin that the authorities had never tried to enforce restrictions on payment of winnings during racing hours, which had been introduced as long ago as 1931.) It would also destroy the parity which the Bill sought to promote between cash and credit punters, and, as Simon Wingfield Digby pointed out, if the shops were shut, punters would not be able to find out the odds or the draw of the horses they fancied. Nor, although Vosper disapproved of continuous betting, did he see how it could be prevented in practice. Robert Mellish, on the other hand, had talked to some street bookmakers, who by now accepted the inevitability of betting shops but wanted them to close by 2.30 p.m., since virtually all their business was done in the morning, and with the great growth of commuting to work, people no longer particularly wished to collect their winnings on the same day as they had placed their bets.

The possibility was raised of extending betting shops' hours when there was evening racing. Rees-Davies, however, asserted that most bookmakers were content to close at 6.30, and that evening racing was not popular with trainers, the racecourses, or their staff. He thought that if people wanted evening racing they should bet on course. (Evening racing later became something of a bone of contention between the Levy Board and the Jockey Club. The Board was reluctant to spend significant sums on meetings which generated no levy, because the betting shops were closed, while the Jockey Club was concerned to keep racing alive as a sport, and thought the Board should look upon evening racing as a loss-leader, which would attract to the course people who were not free in the day-time.)

Inside the shops, only limited information was to be provided, including 'the blower' (the instrument which delivers the commentary from racecourse to betting shop) and *The Sporting Life*, but not television or radio. Nor were music and dancing to be permitted! George Wigg argued against television, because it tended to prevent active participation, and Vosper again summed up the Government's attitude:

> We are enabling the business of betting to be carried on efficiently, and we are providing a service to potential punters. The provison of radio and television programmes would be going too far, in my opinion. We wish to provide sufficient facilities to attract the punter away from the streets, where some hon. Members still believe that he will wish to operate, and persuade him to conduct his business in the betting office. But we do not want to encourage him to stay in a betting office longer than is necessary. Nor do we wish to attract other people who would not normally frequent a betting office.[24]

There remained the important question of how entry to the bookmaking business was to be regulated. The bookmakers had always set great store by having some say themselves in the licensing procedure, and McAdden, who had already accompanied a delegation of bookmakers to see Vosper on the previous day, 29 February 1960, when they had made exactly that point, now moved that anyone seeking a permit should be required to inform the National Bookmakers' Protection Association and Associated Bodies' Joint Committee. The Association was anxious to keep unreliable characters out of bookmaking, and was a more suitable body to be consulted than Tattersalls' Committee, because the latter dealt generally with the larger disputes between bookmaker and punter, whereas the Association was accustomed to settle disputes over quite small sums.

Mellish supported him. The NBPA had done more than any other organisation to clean up the gangs to which Rees-Davies had referred. It was a respectable body, and Mellish himself was invited to their annual dinner: 'Hon. Members would be surprised to know the kind of people who go to that dinner. The Duke of Norfolk is often there.'[25] Chuter Ede, however, disagreed about the Association's value: 'I was concerned thirty years ago with breaking up the race course gangs. This was done not by this Association but by the sentences imposed on the gangsters who were caught.'[26] The NBPA, he argued, was only a voluntary body. It was an astounding proposal to give it such recognition in law. Vosper agreed: it was open to any member of the public to appear before the licensing justices, and that should give the bookmakers sufficient protection.

The Committee concluded its discussion of Part I of the Bill with a new clause, moved by John M. Temple, to control bookmakers' advertising, both in newspapers and on their shop fronts, which caused George Wigg to make another of his outbursts against holier-than-thou attitudes, hypocrisy, and the upper class in general. The last, he thought, believed that:

> The lower orders, to which I have the honour to belong, do not know [how to spend their time and money], and they must be supervised and watched over at every stage. All that the upper level and more righteous people have to do is to think a little about putting some new Clauses on the Notice Paper in order to change our social habits. The Home Office, of course, drawing its strength from the great school at Oxford, is caught up in the same piece of nonsense.[27]

Sir James Duncan read out an extract from a circular to Members from the Churches: 'We consider that the licensed betting office should appear plainly for what it is. It should have no other external features than the name of the bookmaker and the nature of the business.'[28] McAdden pointed out that credit bookmakers could not survive without advertising, whereas betting shops probably would not need to. Arthur Holt confirmed that illegal bookmakers did not seem to advertise at present: 'I met some of the people who go to these places regularly. They had no difficulty whatever in knowing exactly where these places were, and they had known for a long time. This is not altered by the fact that enquiries of the Chief Constable at the same time led to my being informed that no such betting offices existed in the town.'[29]

In conclusion, Vosper promised to consider the arguments. He made no commitment to introduce a clause on advertising, but could see a real reason to differentiate between cash and credit betting in that the latter was obliged to advertise. (This had been urged upon him by the delegation of bookmakers on 29 February.) Eventually a clause was put into the Bill, which closely followed the Churches so far as betting shops were concerned, whilst permitting credit bookmakers to advertise, though subject to limitations.

The Tote and the Betting and Gaming Bill

The Bill gave the Tote copyright in its prices and the power to license others to use them; the provision was fiercely attacked in Committee, largely by Stephen McAdden, but the debate showed that the Tote was also not without friends.

Gordon Walker, although not a Tote monopolist, read with approval from a report in *The Times* of advice on betting received by the Premier of Western Australia from Sir George Ligertwood. *The Times* had reported him as saying 'that the betting shop is contrary to the interest of the community; that the shops have had an adverse effect on racing as a sport, and are likely in time to bring it to a standstill; that they have encouraged betting and increased its volume; and that the system has allowed off-course bookmakers to make substantial profits and dispose of their licences for big sums in goodwill.'[30]

The Tote would now be able to open its own betting shops. McAdden therefore moved another amendment, by which the justices would be obliged, when considering a bookmaker's application for a licence, to disregard any Tote shop in the area. Vosper was able to reassure him by confirming that if there were local demand for Starting Price betting, the justices would be obliged to consider bookmakers' applications, even if the Tote were already operating in the area. However, he thought the bookmakers had the advantage over the Tote, because they existed in far greater numbers and 'will probably be much quicker off the mark in seeking applications.'[31] Wigg,

[54]

as a member of the RBCB, naturally defended it stoutly. He pointed out that the Board would license bookmakers to use the Tote odds, either as the Board's agents or on commission, on terms to be negotiated later. Wigg himself wanted to retain the racecourse bookmaker: 'He is that little bit of sparkle that makes racing in England different from racing abroad.'[32]

For commercial reasons, he would not disclose in advance the terms on which the Board would license bookmakers to use its odds: 'Bookmakers have a very good lobby and unlimited amounts of money. If they think they are being treated unfairly, they will go to the hon. Member for Southend East (Mr McAdden) and we shall hear all about it.'[33] Wigg's point about the lobby was well timed, since only two days earlier a report to the bookmakers' Joint Committee had summed up a number of recent successes. The deletion of clauses had been achieved which would (1) have prohibited loitering, whether inside or outside betting shops, (2) have prescribed special hours for the payment of winnings (the removal of these two opened the way to continuous betting) and (3) have forbidden betting shops to give their customers any information (such as that contained in a newspaper) other than the results of races and the odds. In addition, the requirements as to layout of premises had been modified, the blower was to be allowed, and preference in the granting of licences was to be given to applicants who had been continuously in business for a year to 2 November 1959.

Renton, answering the many points raised by McAdden, made a speech unequivocally favouring the Tote's copyright. He made it clear that newspapers would be free to publish Tote prices; the point of the Bill was to clarify the Tote's position *vis-à-vis* bookmakers: 'For many years "bookies" have been getting money for nothing by using what should clearly have been stated from the outset of the Board's activities to have been a right of property in the Board.'[34] Since Tote betting offices would operate only at Tote odds, it was only fair that bookmakers should pay for the right to use its prices.

The Bill's last stages

Once the immensely long Committee proceedings were complete, it may be said that all was over bar the shouting, though the remaining stages occupy many columns of Hansard.

At Report (the stage at which a Bill, as amended in Committee, is reported to the House), Chuter Ede made a last-ditch attempt to secure the legalisation of street betting, though he was prepared to retain betting shops where they were already well established. He was supported by Robert Mellish, who believed that the amendment in favour of street betting would have passed if the Committee had been allowed a free vote. He did not insist that the whole country should follow the same practice, but, as so often, was primarily interested in the affairs of his own constituency. Wigg, too, supported Ede's amendment. He was afraid of a monopoly by the major chains, and took the opportunity to state yet again his belief in the social value of the small bookmaker.

Butler was present on this occasion, and reiterated the Government's, by now familiar, case against street betting. He took with equanimity the numerous barbed complaints about his absence from the Committee: he had, he said, 'done the penance' of reading its proceedings, but he would have preferred to be there, 'because, in listening, one sees the different, glistening, forms of human nature. . .'[35]

In response to questions about his proposed timetable for the Bill, Vosper said that the bookmakers, the RBCB and other interests would be consulted as soon as the Bill's likely fate in 'another place' (the quaint circumlocution by which each House is invariably described in the other) was known. The target date, by which bookmakers' permits would have been issued, and betting offices would become legal, was 1 May 1961. It would therefore be necessary for Peppiatt's proposals for a levy on bookmakers, on which Vosper had made a statement a few days earlier, to come into effect on the same date. (These proposals are outlined in the next chapter.)

On 11 May, when the Bill passed its Third Reading in the Commons, Dennis Vosper summed up: eighty-eight hours had been spent on discussing the measure so far, with Members' concern having at all times been to find the balance between individual freedom on the one hand and the prevention of excess on the other. The Bill had remained unchanged in its general form, but runners would now be able to take bets from any work place or place where people resided together (he was referring to e.g. hotels and hospitals), not just in factories, so that there would be five channels available for a person wanting to make a bet: the telephone, the post, a roundsman (like the milkman), a runner, or the betting shop.

Ede observed that in the depression people had found the pools a comfort, because they allowed them to exercise a little choice, and George Wigg supported him: 'During the war, the continuation of racing was essential to the national well being. . . the effect on the man in the factories, working long hours with very difficult conditions, was to make life a little brighter for them. . . .' and added one of the pungent remarks with which he so often enlivened debates on racing: 'When the French win the Derby they are, to some extent, spitting on Nelson.'[36] Towards the end of his life he used to say that he himself had played a part in keeping racing going during the war. He had arranged with the Member for Stoke, Ellis Smith, to introduce him to Ernest Bevin, who had the ear of the austere Sir Stafford Cripps. Wigg, Smith and Bevin got stuck in the lift at the Grand Hotel, Manchester, so Bevin had plenty of time to listen, and in due course talked fruitfully to Cripps.

The Lords' amendments

The debates in the Lords resulted in several amendments to the Bill being passed, which had earlier been ventilated in the Commons, and which the Commons accepted when the Bill was returned to them. Some Peers displayed considerable expertise, others a refreshing innocence. For example, a pleasant picture of learned heads being put together is evoked by Lord Meston's remarks: 'I must confess that until I came here I did not know what a 'blower' meant, but the noble and learned Viscount the Lord Chancellor has explained the instrument to me.'[37]

Support for the levy, with the threat of a Tote Monopoly in the background, showed itself in the Lords. Lord Norrie, who had been Governor-General of New Zealand, made a very well informed speech about the benefits conferred on racing in that country by a Tote monopoly. He did not favour such a monopoly in Britain, but thought it might be gradually introduced if the proposals for a levy did not work out successfully. (The Peppiatt Report was being debated in the Commons on the same day, 23 May.) Lord Mancroft, who was to become Chairman of the Tote twelve years later, went further. He would not object to the bookmakers disappearing altogether, but meanwhile was certainly in favour of their making a contribution to racing. In response to these and similar contributions, Earl Bathurst, for the Government, said: 'Bookmakers are part and parcel of the racing scene and I do not believe that we should be justified in putting them out of business. . .'[38] but Peppiatt's proposals were to be put into effect, though not as part of this Bill: 'I have heard, by tick-tack from another place, that my right honourable friend [the Home Secretary] will give an assurance that, because it will be more satisfactory and tidier, a new Bill will be introduced for this purpose in the next session. . .'[39]

A number of Peers tried, unsuccessfully, to link the question of defaulting bookmakers with a plea that the time had come, now that betting shops were to be legalised, for betting debts to be made recoverable at law. As Lord Boothby said at the Committee stage (this was a Committee of the whole House): 'This Bill, of course, is rooted in the hypocrisy so dear to the hearts of the English people. . . It legalises betting yet takes no steps to enforce that bets properly and legally laid should be paid in one way or another.'[40]

An unsuccessful effort was made to prohibit bookmakers' runners in factories. The Government could not accept it because of the danger to industrial discipline if workers left their factories to go to the betting shop, because of the difficulties of enforcement, and because it wanted to promote various methods of betting, instead of relaying exclusively on betting shops. As Lord Stonham put it: 'This sort of thing is going on in every one of my factories, without difficulty, without fighting, without bloodshed or the prospect of it, and in all the five hospitals of which I am chairman.'[41]

Lord Silkin put forward an amendment, which had already been discussed in the Commons, that companies should not be allowed to apply for bookmakers' permits. The Government could not accept this as it stood, but Lord Bathurst promised to examine the point again, and eventually, thanks to the persistence of the Duke of Devonshire and Silkin, an amendment was passed obliging any bookmaking company whose board changed during the year to inform the police, so that the latter, if they thought a new board member not a fit and proper person, could apply to the justices for the company's permit to be revoked.

Lord Spens, with acknowledgement to Sir James Duncan's effort in the Commons, moved various amendments about advertising, on behalf of the Churches. At this point the Archbishop of Canterbury intervened, to clarify the Church's attitude. After a long apology for the failure of any Bishop to be present at Second Reading, the Archbishop said: 'If the Church gives general support to this Bill, as it does, it is not because – and I have to stress this – the Church in any way whatsoever supports or encourages betting or gambling.'[42] But the Church recognised that gambling could not be abolished, and therefore the Government must control it. He added the subtle point that whereas the Government says 'the more betting and gambling, so much the worse', the Church's view is 'the less betting and gambling the better'. The new system of controlling gamblers must be tried on its own merits, which meant without advertising.

In reply, the Lord Chancellor said that he understood the amendment, which the Government now accepted, to refer to betting offices only. The Churches' arguments, with which he concurred, were that those who wanted betting offices would find them unaided,and that advertising would lead to the danger of chains of betting shops growing up, which the Government did not want.

The Commons approved the Lords' amendments on 27 July. These, in summary, were to raise the minimum age of bookmakers' runners from eighteen to twenty-one, to vary the penalties for street betting, to oblige companies to notify the authorities if new directors joined their boards, to allow permits to be removed during the year, and to prohibit advertising by betting shops. The last of these, which Wigg described as hypocrisy and bunkum, was later cleverly evaded by a bookmaker who, as required by law, announced in 'a newspaper circulating in the area' that he was applying for a betting office licence. However, the paper he chose was *The Sporting Life*, and the Court held on 1 May 1963 that he was within his rights![43]

The Bill received the Royal Assent on 29 July 1960. Thereafter there were regular questions to Ministers about the progress being made in issuing betting office licences and bookmakers' permits. On 22 June 1961, Vosper, replying to Simon Wingfield Digby's suggestion that some permits had been unreasonably refused, said that matters were proceeding smoothly, though there had been some difficulties.[44]

On 21 June the Secretary of State for Scotland had been able to announce that 434 betting licences had been granted in Glasgow, though the number of shops actually operating was rather lower.[45] On 9 November 1961 Renton, again answering Wingfield Digby, said that 8,779 bookmakers' permits and 7,926 betting office licences had been in force in England and Wales on 1 June 1961. His information was that street betting had been sharply reduced, and he announced that the penalties for it, under the Street Betting Act of 1906, were to be increased on 1 December.[46]

On 30 July 1962 William (later Viscount) Whitelaw, Parliamentary Secretary, Ministry of Labour, answering Willie Hamilton, said that 32,000 people had been employed in betting in England in May 1961, and 4,300 in Scotland, compared with 27,500 and 2,600 respectively in May 1951. The percentage increase over ten years had therefore been far higher in Scotland than in England, though the Minister did not make the point.[47]

Various questions were directed to obtaining changes in the regulations governing betting shops. On 9 November 1961 Renton, rather surprisingly in view of the detailed interest taken by the Government in betting offices, had to reply that he had no power to compel them to display clocks.[48]

Later, he told Leo Abse, who had asked whether the compulsory closing time of 6.30 p.m. could be raised in view of the increase in evening racing, that the Secretary of State was considering representations from the bookmakers' organisations that they should be allowed to remain open until later when there was evening racing.[49] However, on 31 May he added that the National Greyhound Racing Society was against later opening (presumably because this would keep people away from the dog tracks and so reduce their totalisators' turnover) and said that the Government did not intend to be rushed into a decision.[50] (Nor has it been: the hours during which betting shops must be closed – 6.30 p.m. to 7.00 a.m. – were still being earnestly discussed in 1987). On 17 May 1962 James Callaghan asked for a review of the Betting and Gaming Act, in view of dissatisfaction expressed by a number of small bookmakers about the granting of an excessive number of licences to large bookmaking firms, but Renton refused, on the ground that a review would be premature.[51]

Conclusion

In planning the Betting and Gaming Act, the Government had no alternative but to consult the bookmakers, who had the grass-roots strength which came from having punters in every town and village, as well as an effective lobby in Parliament. This was long before the days when MPs had to register their interests, but of course those who, in fact, did represent bookmakers were widely suspected in the House, and viewed with some distaste. (It was a very different story when Brian Walden was openly recruited to assist them in the early 1970s and gained universal respect in the House and in

Whitehall for his presentation of the bookmakers' case.) The book-makers had friends on both sides of the House, but their lobby was stronger among Labour MPs, who knew more about betting in factories and on the streets. On the other hand, Wigg, also a Labour Member, was particularly helpful to the Government in getting the Bill through, and may even have threatened some Labour recalcitrants with the spectre of a Tote monopoly. He had certainly believed in this as a solution to racing's problems in the early 1950s and despite his later work for the Levy Board and the Betting Office Licensees' Association, may have gone on hankering for it, however much he realised it was a non-runner politically.

Parts of the debates on the Bill are tedious, and they provide evidence enough that Members of Parliament sometimes take themselves rather too seriously. But taken as a whole, they provide, as Gordon Walker acknowledged, an education in the state of betting in Britain in the 1960s.

They also illustrate an aspect of Parliamentary democracy at work. It is true that a Government can sometimes ride roughshod over opposition, but it could not treat the bookmakers high-handedly. Instead, it consulted them extensively and over several years before the Bill came before Parliament, and continued to receive deputations during its progress. Although they would not sacrifice their main objectives, the legalisation of betting shops and the continued prohibition of betting in the streets, Ministers were aware that so major a piece of social legislation must rest upon consent. In large measure they had obtained this before the debates began, so that, although the bookmakers promoted opposition to the Bill at every stage, they had in a sense accepted defeat before the battle started. The Government seems also to have retained the bookmakers' confidence throughout, largely because it shared their concern that bookmaking should become a legally recognised and socially respectable profession, because it understood and took seriously their point of view, and was prepared to compromise on numerous points, provided that the Bill's essential principles were safeguarded.

The two other main pressure groups were the Jockey Club, with its penumbra of specialised racing interests, and the Churches, both of which had, by comparison with the bookmakers, a built-in respectability which assured them a hearing. The Jockey Club maintained a 'low profile' in the debates on the 1960 Act. It must have been aware that, particularly in the Commons, it had opponents (like

Chuter Ede), but in any case it had no need to argue its case very strongly, since the principle of the levy had been accepted by Ministers, and all that remained was for it to be put into effect.

The Churches directed themselves in the main to the single issue of advertising, and, as we have seen, they were reasonably successful in limiting it. They owed this, not only to their spokesmen in the Commons but to their persistence in the Lords, where the Archbishop of Canterbury's intervention cannot have been taken lightly, and where Peers from both sides of the House supported them.

The Government's readiness to listen to the experts, and to give way in the face of good arguments, were especially apparent in the Lords. The Lord Chancellor showed himself prepared, throughout the proceedings (and said so on several occasions), to consider new points with the utmost open-mindedness, and to reconsider those whose proponents returned to the attack.

The debates in the Lords illustrate the general virtues of that House. Its Members are, on the whole, free from the need to make purely political points. Because the House's functions are primarily deliberative, debates tend to be well-informed, serious and orderly, with the result that all points of view may receive a hearing. Although, as in the debates on the 1960 Bill, amendments are frequently withdrawn, this is usually done (as, indeed, was the case in the Committee stage in the Commons) in response to a promise by the Government to think again. This, in turn, extends the basis of consent for a measure, or at least acquiescence in it, because such a promise assures the mover of an amendment (and, if he has been briefed, the group that has briefed him), that he is being taken seriously, even if he does not win his point in the end.

The bookmakers had expended relatively little effort on the Lords' debates, and their friends were not greatly in evidence, though their Inner Cabinet had discussed possible amendments on 2 May, and the main Committee had noted on 24 May that the last chance to put down amendments was imminent. But by now it was clear that the proposals to legalise betting shops and to continue to ban betting in the streets would not be defeated.

It is ironic that the larger bookmakers, who many MPs feared (rightly, as it has turned out) would grow in power once the Bill was passed, were the most opposed to it, because they had most reason to fear the levy. Although the Bill and the levy were separate issues, they became, as we have seen, inextricably entwined in the minds of the Government, the Jockey Club and the bookmakers themselves. The larger bookmakers believed that the levy, and the Betting Duty which they realised must follow, would drive bookmaking underground. Nevertheless, they feared most of all that if a levy were fixed by the Gaming Board or some similar body, they might not be represented on it. They also probably preferred a compulsory levy to the voluntary Amenities Fund.

Most of the leading bookmakers in those days bet on course, and were in close touch with owners, so they could see the necessity of such a fund. But not all bookmakers subscribed to it, and in 1959 it brought in only £60,000, of which £45,000 was passed on the racecourses. Once Archie Scott, the bookmaker who became a member of the Peppiatt Committee, had convinced them that the levy was inevitable, all bookmakers, large and small, were determined to have as much say as possible in raising and distributing it.

We shall see in the next chapter how the Peppiatt Committee's proposals were translated into law in the Betting Levy Act of 1961.

Notes

1 *H.C.*, Standing Committee D, col. 397, 11 February 1960.
2 *The Times*, 15 December 1958.
3 Sir David Llewellyn was writing as 'Jack Logan' in his weekly column in *The Sporting Life*, 26 October 1984.
4 R. A. Butler, *The Art of the Possible*, London, 1971, p. 203.
5 *The Times*, 9 December 1959.
6 613 *H.C.* Deb., col. 827, 16 November 1959.
7 *H.C.* Deb. Standing Committee D, col. 938, 22 March 1960.
8 613 *H.C.* Deb., col. 1083, 17 November 1959.
9 *Daily Express*, 22 December 1959.
10 *The Sporting Life*, 6 January 1960.
11 *Ibid.*, 14 January 1960.
12 *Ibid.*, 20 January 1960.
13 *H.C.* Deb., Standing Committee D, cols. 46 and 45, 8 December 1959.
14 *Ibid.*, col. 211, 2 February 1960.
15 *Ibid.*, col. 85, 10 December 1959.
16 *Ibid.*, col. 252, 4 February 1960.
17 *Ibid.*, cols. 174, 175 and 177, 28 January 1960.
18 *Ibid.*, col. 183.
19 *Ibid.*, col. 740, 8 March 1960.
20 *Ibid.*, cols. 837-8, 15 March 1960.
21 *Ibid.*, col. 686, 3 March 1960.

22 *Ibid.*, col. 490, 18 February 1960.
23 *Ibid.*, col. 519, 23 February 1960.
24 *Ibid.*, cols. 793-4, 10 March 1960.
25 *Ibid.*, col. 636, 1 March 1960.
26 *Ibid.*, col. 639.
27 *Ibid.*, col. 951, 22 March 1960.
28 *Ibid.*, col. 953.
29 *Ibid.*, col. 968.
30 *Ibid.*, col. 259, 4 February 1960.
31 *Ibid.*, col. 714, 3 March 1960.
32 *Ibid.*, col. 876, 15 March 1960.
33 *Ibid.*, col. 918, 17 March 1960.
34 *Ibid.*, col. 904.
35 622 *H.C.* Deb., col. 1336, 5 May 1960.
36 623 *H.C.* Deb., cols. 485-6, 11 May 1960.
37 223 *H.L.* Deb., col. 1147, 23 May 1960.
38 *Ibid.*, cols. 1181-2, 31 May 1960.
39 *Ibid.*, cols. 1195-6.
40 224 *H.L.* Deb., col. 152, 31 May 1960.
41 *Ibid.*, col. 138.
42 *Ibid.*, col. 311.
43 Churches Council on Gambling, *Gambling – Why?*, London, 1964.
44 642 *H.C.* Deb., col. 1652, 22 June 1961.
45 642 *H.C.* Written Answers, col. 148, 21 June 1961.
46 648 *H.C.* Deb., col. 1137, 9 November 1961.
47 664 *H.C.* Written Answers, col. 6, 30 July 1962.
48 648 *H.C.* Written Answers, col. 71, 9 November 1961.
49 658 *H.C.* Written Answers, col. 108, 19 April 1962.
50 660 *H.C.* Deb., cols. 1563-4, 31 May 1962.
51 659 *H.C.* Written Answers, col. 140, 17 May 1962.

IV
The Levy and the Harding years

The Peppiatt Report

Once the Betting and Gaming Act was out of the way, the Betting Levy Bill came on the scene. The way had been paved by the Peppiatt Report, itself the child of Home Office thinking, though none of the officials concerned knew anything about racing. The Home Office had become convinced that Tory back-benchers would stop the Betting and Gaming Bill if no levy were promised, and the appearance of Peppiatt's Report in April 1960 was in time to reassure backbench opinion. As Rothschild put it:

> The Government were promoting the Bill on social grounds: to rid the streets of illegal betting. The bookmakers wanted to be legalised. The racing industry believed that the establishment of betting offices would reduce attendance at race meetings. It was prepared to support the Bill on condition that racing got a share of the proceeds of off-course betting. There was some horse dealing between the racing interests and the bookmakers. The result was the unanimity of views expressed to the Peppiatt Committee.[1]

Thanks to the horse dealing, some of which has been described in the last chapter, it was generally expected that Peppiatt's Committee would find in favour of a levy. This it did: it was impressed by the

> almost unanimous opinion, on all sides of the racing industry (including the bookmakers), that a levy is required. It is not our view, however, that without a subsidy horse racing will rapidly decline or die. . . Nor do we think that it is necessary to establish that horse racing is declining to justify a levy. . . the infusion of fresh money should be regarded not as serving to bolster a declining industry but as an aid to improving it.[2]

The bookmakers were naturally prominent among those who gave evidence to Peppiatt. In their written memorandum of December 1959 they stated that the National Bookmakers and Associated Bodies Joint Protection Association represented approximately five thousand bookmakers in eighteen organisations. They had been in favour of making a financial contribution to racing ever since the resolution in June 1956 by the Jockey Club's Joint Betting Bill Committee. They stated that they believed, as they had said in their submission to the Home Office of 11 July 1959, that a board of bookmakers, with a chairman appointed by the Secretary of State, should be responsible for registering its members and raising a levy from them for the benefit of racing. The board would be empowered to levy what it thought a suitable amount from each bookmaker, up to £1,000 a year, and would make payments in consultation with the bodies involved in racing.

At the 24th meeting of the Inner Cabinet on 22 December 1959, it was agreed that the bookmakers' oral evidence to Peppiatt on 4 January 1960 should be on the following broad lines: it was desirable to have a levy on off-course bookmakers provided always that it was within their capacity to pay, and that the money it raised was used for the benefit of the racing public by way of improved amenities and the reduction of admission charges. The question that had to be asked was how much racing actually needed, given that the racecourse accounts which the Chairman had collected suggested that their profits had been increasing lately. The Jockey Club's figure of £3 million was excessive.

The meeting agreed that it would be practicable for the bookmakers' organisations to collect the levy, which should amount to about £1 million per annum, if they were given statutory authority. It was important to combat the Jockey Club's view that the Tote was at a disadvantage to off-course bookmakers, and it was vital to make clear to Peppiatt that if a levy on bookmakers were followed by a betting tax, the result would be a Tote monopoly.

The Committee took a great deal of evidence, some of it from the Street Bookmakers' Federation (which must still have been illegal!) and reported in April 1960, just after the Betting and Gaming Bill had completed its long Committee stage in the Commons. The Peppiatt Committee came to the conclusion that racing should help itself, not get a grant from the Exchequer. The scheme would have to be compulsory and established under statute, somewhat, though not exactly, akin to 'the levy on cinema takings for the benefit of British film production; the sugar surcharge mechanism; the levy on the cotton industry; and the levy payments under Agricultural Marketing Schemes'. The levy should be on bookmakers rather than on backers, though the Committee shrewdly added 'we are not at all convinced that in the end means would not be found to pass on at least a part of it directly or indirectly. . .'[3]

The Committee noted that in 1958 racing had received £685,000 from the Racecourse Betting Control Board and a further £450,000 from bookmakers' entry fees to racecourses. The Jockey Club had argued that racing needed a subsidy of £3 million, which would be one and a half per cent of turnover, assuming the 1951 Royal Commission's turnover figure of £200 million was correct, but the committee thought that £3 million was too much. It recommended the creation of two new bodies, the Bookmakers' Levy Board, to raise funds, and the Central Board, to distribute them, and that the former should seek to raise £1 million to £1,250,000 in its first full year. This, as we have just seen, was about the sum the bookmakers themselves reckoned they could provide.

The Committee made fairly detailed recommendations about how the Board should be constituted and operate, and how bookmakers should be graded and their profits assessed. It thought profits from sports other than horse racing should be included, and added 'We are assured that it should not be impracticable for accounts to be separated in this manner'.[4] This is an interesting remark in view of the bookmakers' continuing insistence in 1987 that the separation is not possible; the Levy Board still uses, as a rough guide, the eighty per cent horses, twenty per cent dogs conventional distinction, which it established in the Wigg era, though bookmakers are required to substantiate any non-horse-racing deduction over fifteen per cent.

On 3 May 1960 Vosper made a statement in the Commons on the Peppiatt Report. He announced that the Government accepted the Report in principle, and this acceptance (he added in reply to a question) included 'some reference' to the figure of £1,250,000 which Peppiatt had identified as racing's annual need.

The Betting and Gaming Bill, Vosper continued, was due to be debated on Report in the same week, and it would not be possible for the Government to prepare amendments, which would reflect its views on Peppiatt, in time for that debate. A great deal of work would be required to draft the necessary legislation, but it would be done in time to fit in with the timetable proposed by Peppiatt: in other words, an Act to introduce the levy would be passed by the early months of 1961.

A debate on the Report was introduced by Eric Johnson on 23 May, the same day as the Betting and Gaming Bill reached Second Reading in the Lords. He defended the levy at length, and was not convinced by the Committee's arguments against the levy being based on bookmakers' turnover, as opposed to profit.

He also disagreed with the Committee over the amount of money needed, and thought that the £3 million suggested by the Jockey Club was an absolute minimum. Nor did he believe the Committee's figure, which it had obtained from the NBPA, that eighty-seven per cent of all bookmakers made less than £3,000 a year. In discussing the bookmakers' capacity to pay he drew attention to figures from Ireland, where in 1958 bookmakers had paid £1,024,000 to the State and to the Racing Board on a turnover of only £14,684,000.

Butler declared his own attitude to the levy. 'I had always thought that the Betting and Gaming Bill should be accompanied by proposals for a levy. . .' 'If the sport is to go on, further prize money and further encouragement to the raising of bloodstock is vital for this old-fashioned and popular industry in this country.' He emphasised that the levy was not intended in any sense as a subsidy to any individual owner: 'I should not like anybody to think that we are adopting any proposal to transfer public money from one section of the public to another.[5]

Butler intended to prepare his Bill on the basis that bookmakers would pay levy on profit rather than turnover, unless he was converted in the course of debate. He was inclined to agree that £1,250,000, as suggested in Peppiatt, was sufficient, rather than £3 million. However, the exact sum would be a matter for the Central Board and the Bookmakers' Levy Board to decide; nor did he see how it would be possible to put into the Bill a maximum figure to be raised by the Board.

Chuter Ede spoke against the idea, which had always been dear to the bookmakers' hearts, that the scheme should be operated by the bookmakers themselves, a body of men for whom he had no great admiration. Nor was he certain that the National Bookmakers' Protection Association was as representative as it claimed to be, for he had received a letter from a small bookmaker, who complained that the Peppiatt Committee's composition had cut it off from the interests of the small men, who had no desire to join the NBPA, but from whom the Committee expected to obtain eighty-seven per cent of the levy.

Eric Fletcher struck another note of discord from the Opposition benches. He complained, as many Members had done in earlier debates, that the Peppiatt Committee's report had been received too late to be considered during the passage through the Commons of the Betting and Gaming Act. He then went on to uncover the interests behind that Act in terms so forthright that they are worth quoting at length:

> the most potent argument in persuading the House of Commons to legalise betting shops was in order to set up a system for the registration of bookmakers so that a levy could be raised on their takings for the benefit of racecourse owners and race horse owners.
>
> It is no secret that the Home Secretary has been under considerable pressure on this subject from the Jockey Club and other vested interests. It is no secret because Lord Sefton, the Senior Steward of the Jockey Club, made it plain in a speech at the end of 1958 – a year before the Betting and Gaming Bill was introduced – that the support of the Stewards of the Jockey Club for the Betting and Gaming Bill would be forthcoming only if there was provision for a levy, because, he said, it was essential that money bet on horse racing should contribute to horse racing. We must remember that the price paid for the support of the Jockey Club for the proposal to license and legalise betting shops was the promise to introduce the levy.
>
> I am not saying that the proposed levy is wrong merely because it was instigated by the Jockey Club, but it is essential that the House should consider whether the proposal for a levy corresponds with the public interest as well as with vested interests.[6]

It would have been difficult to answer so frank and, indeed, devastating an analysis of the forces behind the 1960 Act and the proposals for a levy, and no one tried to do so. Numerous points were touched upon which were later developed in the debates on the Betting Levy Bill, but the remaining speech of most significance was by Enoch Powell, then a Conservative. He could see no logical reason to subsidise racing, but his real purpose was to attack the general principle of what is often called 'hypothecated taxation', which he called 'assigned revenue', that is, 'revenue designed in advance for a specific purpose or application. . .'. It was also revenue which was raised and spent outside the House's direct control, and so was 'a departure from. . . the principle that all revenue which is raised by the authority of this House shall be paid into the Consolidated Fund and that all payments which are made by the authority of this House shall be made out of the Consolidated Fund.'[7] Powell's intervention made little difference at the time, but, like some of his other utterances, that one has been remembered over the years, while much else that was said has been long forgotten.

The Betting Levy Bill

After the debate on the Peppiatt Report there remained a great deal of work to be done on finalising the Betting Levy Bill, though the Home Office officials must have been helped by the fact that they had been thinking about it since 1956. So, too, had the bookmakers, and once the Peppiatt Report had been published, the impending Bill moved to the centre of their attention. They had welcomed the Report, though, of course, with some reservations, and by their 31st Inner Cabinet meeting, on 11 October 1960, they were drafting a scheme of the kind envisaged in the Report. The Bill was prepared at high speed and final proposals had to be presented to the Home Office by 25 October. The bookmakers at this stage were still hoping that assessment of bookmakers would be left entirely in the hands of a Central Bookmakers' Committee, assisted by regional sub-committees.

At the Second Reading debate on the Betting Levy Bill, 5 December 1960, (during which Arthur Lewis pressed hard and unsuccessfully for a similar levy on dog racing), Butler said there was unfinished business from the Betting and Gaming Act earlier in the year: 'the scheme for control of bookmakers is not complete without proposals for a levy', which was to be raised by a Horserace Betting Levy Board (called the 'Central Board' by Peppiatt). Peppiatt had found that there was general support in racing for a levy, including support from the bookmakers, though Butler accepted that the bookmakers might not *like* the levy. Nevertheless, they realised that they had a part to play in the racing industry, and a duty to pay the levy. The point of the levy was not to benefit any sectional interest, but to enable 'a great national sport and a great national industry' to help itself.

The Government's intention was to keep the new Board at arm's length from the Home Office, though Butler did not use such forthright words. (Indeed, nothing has changed in the intervening quarter century. The Home Office still believes that its intervention should be minimal, and that its job is primarily to administer what exists, rather than to play any active part in racing.) To preserve the Board's autonomy, Butler had added two independent members to the composition recommended by Peppiatt, and he announced that it would be left to the chairman and these two to resolve disputes with the Bookmakers' Committee, a second statutory body which was to be set up to represent the bookmakers. 'It does not seem to me,' he said, 'that the Home Secretary is well qualified to resolve it.'[8]

The Horserace Betting Levy Board's eventual composition, therefore, was three Home Office appointees, who were 'persons who have no interests connected with horseracing which might hinder them from discharging their functions as members of the Board in an impartial manner'; two were appointed by the Jockey Club, one by the National Hunt Committee, and the Chairman of the Tote and of the Bookmakers' Committee were members *ex officio*. This composition remains unchanged, except that, when the Jockey Club and National Hunt Committee merged in 1968, the Jockey Club took the third seat, which it said would be filled with someone especially appointed to represent the interests of the professional associations. Since the foundation of the Horseracing Advisory Council in 1981, the Jockey Club has allowed the HAC's chairman to take this seat, though at the time it was not easy to persuade the Club's diehards to give the seat up.

Butler was asked whether the levy constituted an hypothecated tax (the point which had been made in May by Enoch Powell), but in reply made the distinction (which some people might see as rather narrow) between *taxation* which 'should not be hypothecated for a particular purpose' and a *statutory levy* raised by some body other than the State. Patrick Gordon Walker, for the Opposition, disagreed: he disliked the loss of Parliamentary control of taxation and argued that, from the bookmakers' point of view, the levy would be a tax, even if raised by the Levy Board.

David Renton pursued the hypothecation point in summing up the debate. A statutory levy was acceptable 'in the quite unusual circumstance of the subject matter of the Bill' – by which he seems, however, to have been referring more to the extensive consultation that had preceded it than to the subject matter itself. He added the very important point, to which the Home Office has always adhered, that 'these are not public funds in the true sense of the word.' The Board's accounts would, therefore, not be scrutinised by the Public

Accounts Committee (in other words, they would not be subject to direct Parliamentary control) but the Home Secretary would approve levy schemes in principle, and the House would see a summary of the Board's annual report.

Opposition speakers made a number of other important points. Gordon Walker said that Labour supported the Bill, though 'with rather less enthusiasm than some of the racing interests'. Safeguards would be needed to protect some interests and 'to curb the somewhat exuberant attitude of the Jockey Club'. Racing interests tended to exaggerate the industry's virtues and tribulations. It was an agreeable, attractive, and in some ways democratic pursuit, but it was also 'one of the bastions of snobbery in this country'. Yet he was clear that British racing 'must not fall back internationally'. This was already happening: 'in part due to the rather self-satisfied complacency on the part of the racing authorities. . . we are not leading the way any more'. He also thought (quoting with approval *The Times* of 16 October 1960) that Peppiatt unfairly burdened the Tote, by comparison with the bookmakers. 'Frankly,' he said, 'I am fearful of the backstairs influence of the Jockey Club' (which, with the National Hunt Committee, naturally wanted the highest possible yield from the levy). 'It is one of the highest and one of the most haughty embodiments of the Establishment in this country.'[9]

George Wigg defended the Jockey Club (as he had done in a debate on the 1960 Act), though not wholeheartedly. He saw it as haughty on paper, but 'the idea that it is haughty and takes unto itself positive powers of direction is as far from the truth as it can be'. On the contrary, it was too diffident and 'does not provide the leadership that one expects'. He was worried by the large amount of money (£1,250,000) that Peppiatt thought racing needed, but he was in favour of the Bill, which was 'a triumph for what are, after all, the typically English virtues of common sense and compromise. . . It is an exercise in the political art by the Rt Hon. Gentleman [Butler], who is superb in this field.'[10] However, he did not think Ascot should be given any of the levy because it was so snobbish, and the Ascot office (which vets applicants for entrance to the Royal Enclosure) should be abolished.

Other MPs made far-seeing points: for example, Eric Johnson suggested, as he had done in the debate on the Peppiatt Report, that turnover might provide a better basis than profits for assessing the bookmakers' liability, and John Farr hoped the Levy Board would buy a stallion for the National Stud. Richard Stanley, who declared his interest as a member of the Jockey Club, made a wide-ranging speech in which he asserted (perhaps with truth) that vets' knowledge of horses was 'on a par with the knowledge of doctors in the eighteenth century'. His most important contribution was his exposition of the view that the Jockey Club and National Hunt Committee should control the spending of the levy. These bodies were '. . . the rulers of racing. Unless we alter the whole racing procedure, they must be the people to do the distribution. Such people as the representatives of the veterinary colleges and race courses can come before the Board and explain what money they want, but they must leave it to the ruling bodies of racing to distribute the money.'[11]

This quotation exactly embodies the thinking against which Wigg reacted so violently when he became second Chairman of the Board in 1967, and which his predecessor, Lord Harding, resisted much more diplomatically and quietly from the beginning.

At the Committee stage McAdden was again active in the book-makers' interest, and asked why the Government had not followed the Peppiatt recommendation that they should run the scheme for themselves. Renton replied that the change had been made 'for administrative reasons'. The Bookmakers' Committee would do a great deal: it would scrutinise the categories in which bookmakers had placed themselves, and would draw up the levy scheme, but it would not collect the levy. This would involve many matters of detail, for which working bookmakers were far too busy.

Some attempts were made to alter the composition of the Levy Board. The first, to have Scottish racing protected by one member of the Board being nominated by the Secretary of State for Scotland, was rejected on the grounds that all members of the Board were intended to be impartial. It is interesting to note, however, that although this was a very reasonable reply, the Board, has, nevertheless, generally made a point of having a Scottish member.

The second attempt was to reduce the Jockey Club's representation from two members to one. Gordon Walker noted that Peppiatt had recommended one, but that the Bill said two, and thought that the change must be the result of Jockey Club influence. He even went so far as to say: 'Somebody must have got at somebody. . .'[12] He would not accept the claim that the Jockey Club's representatives and the one from the National Hunt Committee would be impartial and represent racing as a whole.

It comes as a surprise to anyone familiar with Wigg's later attitude to the Jockey Club that he again defended it on this occasion. The Club, he said, was not above criticism (and the more one knew about it the more one found to criticise); it was so bad at public relations that its telephone number, and that of Weatherby's, were not to be found in the directory, but no one questioned its integrity.

At Report and Third Reading, many of the arguments repeated those already heard in Committee. One interesting new insight emerges from Chuter Ede's remarks about the Jockey Club, which he said would certainly be a beneficiary from the levy schemes. The origins of his dislike of the Club may well lie in the incident he recounted on this occasion, when, as Chairman of Epsom Urban District Council, he had been called before the Stewards and informed that, if the roads on Epsom Downs were not widened, the racecourse would lose its licence. Some years later, it had fallen to him to summon the Stewards and inform them that the Cabinet considered that certain major races would be better run on Saturdays than during the week. However, he had invited co-operation, whereas the Stewards had given orders, and the contrast had plainly rankled ever since.

Even at Third Reading, McAdden did not give up. He deplored the speed with which the Bill had gone through the Commons, and believed that it should have been committed to a Standing Committee, instead of a Committee of the whole House: 'where one knows that, no matter what one says, the steam roller will come into operation and people who never heard any arguments will come in and bring the weight of their votes to bear. . .'[13] He also regretted the lack of Parliamentary control over the levy. An outside body he said, was being given 'the right to levy an unknown amount of taxation upon a body of Her Majesty's citizens'. He saw the setting up of the Levy Board as the result of machinations over the years by the Jockey Club and the Racecourse Betting Control Board, for which the Peppiatt Committee had been a mere cover: 'The Peppiatt Committee was set up merely to give, if I may quote Mark Twain, an air of verisimilitude to an otherwise bald and unconvincing narrative.' Wigg, as a member of the RBCB, naturally had to refute this allegation. Having done so, he could not resist a parting shot: 'I would remind [McAdden] of some of the things that are being said in the pubs and clubs at present. They are very unpleasant. It is suggested that the Government have now given increased pay to the police as a *quid pro quo* for the bribes that they will not now get from the bookmakers. I do not associate myself with that.' Nor could Chuter Ede, in the closing minutes of the Bill's passage through the Commons, resist a final dig at the Jockey Club:

> In giving this Bill a Third Reading, we are making one of the big steps in the English social revolution which has been going on through the life-time of every one of us here. Who would have thought at the beginning of this century that we should see stewards of the Jockey Club and people interested in horse breeding in this House watching the passing of a measure which would transfer from the pockets of the proletariat money which would go to the upkeep of their sport and the race courses and breeding in which they take such delight? This, indeed, is the most curious but the most striking example of the way in which we now all accept the benefits of the Welfare State.[14]

The bookmakers' Inner Cabinet, which had last met on 7 December, two days after Second Reading, next met on 21 December, the day after Third Reading and Report. On the whole, the bookmakers were dissatisfied with the Bill, and some members of the Inner Cabinet now felt that the Joint Committee should refuse to collaborate with the scheme. Another was disappointed and disgusted by 'a dictatorial piece of legislation'. It was infuriating, he said, that the Government had ignored the recommendations of the Peppiatt Committee after all the Joint Committee had done for so long. He thought the Jockey Club must now be running the Government, and would advise bookmakers' associations to refuse any co-operation. It looked as though the levy would simply go up year after year. Other members, however, though agreeing that they had been badly treated, thought that the dangers of non-co-operation were great for bookmakers generally, and it was this view that eventually won the day.

Scott and 'a friendly MP' had a meeting with the Home Secretary and W. H. Stotesbury (one of his officials) on which Scott reported at the 36th Inner Cabinet meeting, on 24 January 1961. He had been very impressed by Butler's friendliness. Butler had suggested that they should get their spokesman in the House of Lords to ventilate their views, and made it clear that he had no intention of dealing with any other association but the Joint Committee. He apologised if the transfer of responsibility for the administration of the scheme from the Bookmakers' Committee to the Levy Board had caused the Joint Committee to lose face in the eyes of its members, but that result had been unintentional and the decision made on the grounds of economy. Taking up two of the points which had been raised by McAdden in the Commons, Butler said that he did not intend, whilst he was in office, that racing should receive anything like the £3 million asked for by the Jockey Club, and that, if bookmakers wanted on-course bookmakers to be exempted, he thought they should put this provision into a levy scheme. In the light of these remarks, Scott told the Inner Cabinet that in his view they should seek amendments in the Lords for Parliamentary control of the levy, as this was the only way in which they could expect any help from the Home Secretary. They should also seek an amendment saying that the levy would not exceed £2 million a year. In the event, however, no amendments of substance were made in the Lords.

Meanwhile, the Racecourse Association was continuing its efforts to raise money. The bookmakers' main Committee, on 23 July 1961, heard that the RCA was hoping to charge off-course bookmakers £100 per annum per shop by way of commentary fee. To this request the bookmakers replied that in that case they would instruct Extel and the London and Provincial News Agency and the Press Association to cease supplying the commentary to off-course bookmakers. The RCA responded, though not until some months later, by issuing similar instructions to course executives and seems successfully to have called the bookmakers' bluff, since at the 42nd Inner Cabinet meeting on 1 April 1962, they decided to negotiate with the RCA over a sliding scale of charges.

The Horserace Betting Levy Board in action

The Betting Levy Bill received the Royal Assent on 28 March 1961, and came into effect on 1 September, with Field Marshal Lord Harding of Petherton as the Board's first Chairman. *The Times* had said on 20 March: 'The Betting and Gaming Act, 1960, the Betting Levy Bill and the adoption of overnight declarations make the new season on the flat the most revolutionary and momentous in the history of racing in Great Britain.' ('Overnight declarations', which, after much discussion, had at last been introduced at the beginning of the 1960 flat season, meant that trainers had to decide a day ahead which horses they were going to run, instead of leaving it to the last minute. The change was beneficial but expensive, because it entailed the employment by Weatherby's of special staff and the installation of extra telephones, etc.) The legislation would have a bigger impact, *The Times* continued, than the introduction of the Tote on the finances of racing, and in 1962 there should be five times as much money for distribution from Tote and levy as ever before. A new approach to doping would also be available once the Duke of Norfolk's Committee had reported to the Jockey Club.

The Board took over the distributive functions and many of the assets of the old Racecourse Betting Control Board (reconstituted as the Horserace Totalisator Board on 1 September 1961), leaving the Tote to operate pool betting and to make an annual contribution to the Levy Board, to be determined by the Board before the beginning of the levy period, after consultation with the Tote. The Board's statutory purposes were the same as those of the RBCB, the improvement of breeds of horses and the improvement of horseracing (which had been its original objectives in 1928), and 'the advancement or encouragement of veterinary science or veterinary education' which had been added in 1934. Its funds, apart from the Tote's contribution, would derive from a scheme proposed annually by the Bookmakers' Committee. The scheme's terms would be determined by the three Home Office appointees if they could not be agreed by the board as a whole (which, of course, included the Chairman of the Bookmakers' Committee), and then forwarded to the Home Secretary.

The annual levy scheme was required by the Act to consider (1) the need for contributions by bookmakers; (2) their capacity to pay; (3) the Tote's capacity to pay. The scheme recommended by the Bookmakers' Committee for the first levy period, 1 April 1962 to 31 March 1963, was accepted by the Board without amendment, but the second and subsequently many others were disputed.

The outline of the schemes has altered considerably over the years. Perhaps the most significant change was introduced in the seventh period (to 31 March 1969), when assessment based on the number of shops a bookmaker operated was replaced with a charge on turnover (a possibility which had frequently been mooted, in Parliament and elsewhere, and which the bookmakers had always feared), as well as a charge based on net profits. The thirteenth scheme (to March 1975) was the first to be based entirely on turnover.

The new Board carried on making grants to racecourses, in much the same way as the RBCB had done, though with the important difference, that, unlike the RBCB, it did not have to forward 'agreed claims' to the Home Secretary for approval and authority to pay. It

was also made clear that the Levy Board would not necessarily continue the old practices beyond the interim period, which it needed
to think out its own policies and priorities, and to assess the extent
of racing's needs. In addition, the Board took over from the RBCB
the financing of overnight declarations. It agreed to finance the Race
Finish Recording Company's patrol camera unit, and its first major
innovation was to finance the recommendations (relating to the
taking of samples and setting up of a research laboratory) of the
Duke of Norfolk's Committee on Doping, which reported on 10 April
1961. The Jockey Club and National Hunt Committee were also
actively considering how levy money might best be spent, and had
set up a committee under Lord Derby to sift advice on the subject
and ensure that the hopes of individual groups did not obscure the
picture of the ultimate prosperity of racing as a whole.[15]

Harding's appointment as first Chairman of the Levy Board was
in many ways an inspired one. He had joined the Army in order to
be able to have a horse and had ridden chargers in the First World
War; later he had enjoyed polo and pig-sticking in India and ridden
in occasional 'bumper' (amateur) races, and he was on friendly terms
with several of the leading figures in racing.

The Board started from scratch, in some offices, empty except for
a telephone, lent by Captain E. T. (Buster) Graham, the Secretary of
the Tote, who had spare accommodation above his own offices.
Graham even took the minutes of the Board's first meeting, and this
set the tone for the friendly relationship between Tote and Board
which lasted through Harding's period in office. He saw the relationship as one of co-operation between two more or less independent
bodies which needed to consult closely in order to ensure that the
Tote paid the maximum contribution to the levy, without endanger-
ing its viability as a separate business. Dealing with the Bookmakers'
Committee was more difficult and four of Harding's six levy schemes
had to be settled by him and the two other Home Office appointees,
Sir Denys Hicks and Mr T. D. G. Monro. Neither of them knew
anything about racing, but Hicks was an eminent lawyer who had
been President of the Law Society the year after Sir Leslie Peppiatt,
and Monro was a desirable Board member, both as a Scotsman and
an accountant.

Harding soon appointed another soldier as Secretary, Major-General Sir Rupert Brazier-Creagh. Brazier-Creagh (known affectionately
as 'bunsen burner'), who dropped his decorations and military rank

from the second annual report onwards, did much to get the Board on its feet, before leaving in November 1965 to look after stud interests in Ireland. He was succeeded by another soldier, Brigadier 'Sam' Waller, who later became one of the casualties of the Wigg era, though he stayed on in racing on the staff of the Racecourse Association.

Harding's was never a full-time job (it was turned into one later by Wigg) but it took him an average of three or four days a week, as well as visits to racecourses on Saturdays. Often he and Brazier-Creagh held their meetings with the Jockey Club at racecourses.

Relations with the Jockey Club seem to have been generally cordial, perhaps because Harding 'spoke the same language' as Major-General Sir Randle Feilden and others at the Jockey Club. Harding was sometimes urged to take a stronger line, but he realised that he was dealing with a self-perpetuating body and it would be no use trying to beat it over the head. In any case, Harding had never been in favour of confrontation.

But there were some bones of contention, the main one being the right to decide how the Board's money was to be spent. Harding believed in full consultation, but could not agree with the Jockey Club that the Board's function was to act as a collecting agency for the Club. In the end Harding was determined to be master in his own house and, to its credit, the Jockey Club seems eventually to have understood and accepted this, though of course once Wigg was appointed it made the disastrous mistake of reverting to the earlier line. Harding had also to resist the Jockey Club's natural wish constantly to extract more levy from the bookmakers.

Indeed, he never tried to maximise the levy, except indirectly, by improving racecourse amenities in order to produce higher attendances which, in turn, would produce higher betting turnover and therefore more levy. However, it is interesting, especially in view of Wigg's later success in maximising the levy, that as early as 1964 the Tote offered inducements to courses to race on seven days which would otherwise have been blank, in order to increase its own turnover. In subsequent years it continued to express concern about evening meetings (which caused higher expenditure and yielded lower turnover), blank days, the desirability of spreading fixtures evenly over the week, and the clashing of major meetings. Its representations seem to have had some effect, since the Levy Board's sixth report, for 1966-7, says that the 'Bonus Day' scheme 'whereby the Board agrees to grant £1,500 towards prize money to courses which fill certain blank days in the four winter months was extended to cover seventeen fixtures in the period covered by this report.'[16] Harding agreed that the Levy Board should contribute to prize money, because he liked the Irish model, where the same Board raises the money and spends it, and because it did not solely benefit owners, but trickled down through the system. (This 'trickle down' theory is one with which a great many people disagree, perhaps more now than in the 1960s, because they believe trainers and jockeys and lads ought to be able to make a proper living without relying on the vagaries of prize money.) In 1963, £69,000 was allocated for the improvement of prize money in prestige races on the flat and £227,228 was spent on raising minimum values. It was too late to influence the values of the Classics for 1963, as entries had closed in 1961, but £73,000 was allocated in 1964.

Betting tax

It was not long before the question of betting tax reared its head, as the bookmakers had always feared it would. The Chancellor of the Exchequer, Reginald Maudling, had stated in reply to a Parliamentary question on 11 December 1962 that he had asked Customs and Excise to look unto the problems associated with a general Betting Duty. On the following day Customs and Excise wrote to Archie Scott (as he reported to the Inner Cabinet's 45th meeting on 20 December), drawing attention to the Chancellor's reply and asking for a meeting with the bookmakers, to discuss the form the duty should take and the method of its collection.

C. H. Blake, who wrote the letter, can hardly have done so in any very happy spirit. The memory was fresh in Customs and Excise of the fiasco of Winston Churchill's tax on turnover, the details of which have been admirably recorded by Christopher Hood.[17] Indeed, the tax had passed into Departmental legend: on 21 July 1949 Sir William Croft had made it clear in evidence to the Royal Commission of 1951[18] that Customs and Excise could not view with any enthusiasm a renewed attempt to impose Betting Duty, and that it would be a pointless exercise unless off-course cash betting were first legalised. That condition had now been met, but there is no reason to suppose that the Departmental mind had been changed in other respects.

At the 46th meeting of the Inner Cabinet, on 3 January 1963, it was agreed to accept the invitation to meet Customs and Excise, when it would be important to stress the dangers of the tax, namely that it would drive betting underground and have a bad effect on horse racing, and at a meeting of the main Committee on 23 January it was reported that a letter had been sent expressing these two fears. It was also agreed that a deputation of bookmakers and other racing interests should call on the Chancellor, that the financial committees of the three main political parties should be approached, and that meetings with Customs and Excise should be continued. (Similar meetings were being held at this time between the Tote and Customs and Excise.)

The bookmakers did not succeed in getting an interview with the Chancellor. Robert Mellish, MP, after meeting a member of the Inner Cabinet, had telephoned the Chancellor's office and found that his view was that if he saw one deputation he would lay himself open to see every interested body in racing. He suggested instead that he should meet Mellish and perhaps have a written brief.

A memorandum on the tax was duly sent to the Chancellor in February 1963, in which the bookmakers protested against the bettng tax, because it would affect the racing and breeding industries; it would also cause people to bet illegally in order to avoid the tax, and so would defeat the objects of the Betting and Gaming Act, 1960. So far as racing was concerned, the efforts made over the last four years to get betting off the streets would be wasted, and illegal betting would lead to less levy. On the other hand, it was not difficult for betting to go underground, and if it did so, bookmakers would not lose the adherence of the public, who would still wish to bet, even if it were illegal.

That was not the end of the matter. Maudling said in his Budget speech on 3 April 1963 that he would like to introduce a tax on betting, partly because it was an area whose potential contribution to ever-increasing government expenditure could not be ignored, and partly because it was unfair to tax some forms of gambling and not others. On the other hand, past experience, especially that of Sir Winston Churchill, 'enjoins in any prudent Chancellor the need for great caution in this field'.[19]

There were also political difficulties. It had been pointed out to Maudling by colleagues, as well as by the bookmakers, that it would be a mistake to take any action which would impair the improvements produced by the 1960 and 1961 Acts. Furthermore, the levy was still very new, it had been difficult to bring in, and it was too soon to impose any further measure on the bookmakers. Maudling's speech showed that he had seen both these objections; he also said that the studies made by Customs and Excise had thrown up practical problems about creating an enforceable system. It was difficult to estimate the total turnover of all kinds of commercially organised betting; figures of £700 million or more annually had been suggested, but Maudling was anxious to tax the net expenditure by the public, which might be about £100 million. For all these reasons he was confining himself, at this stage, to having further studies made. (He may also have been influenced by a remark in Harding's statement on 23 January 1964, announcing the Levy Board's first modernisation scheme, that a tax on betting would be a disaster for racing in its present state.)[20]

In his 1964 Budget speech, when he announced a twenty-five per cent tax on fixed-odds betting on football pools, Maudling made rather similar remarks about the distinction between turnover and net expenditure, and the need to tax the latter. He now thought net expenditure somewhere between £100 million and £150 million per annum, and he would have liked a tax on stakes, which would yield £10 million or £12 million, but he was still deterred by the practical difficulties. On this occasion, Wigg agreed that the tax should be on net expenditure, but he changed his mind after Labour were returned to power a few months later.

The Chancellor announced his intention to impose the Duty in the autumn of 1965, and it was not opposed by the Conservatives, though in November 1966 they did complain about the method of collection, which caused expense for racecourses and practical difficulties for bookmakers. When the impending duty was first announced, the Levy Board and the Bookmakers' Committee had expressed considerable concern about its likely effect on the levy, and on the whole racing industry, but in its sixth report (to March 1967) the Board said that, after the Duty's initial adverse effect on the volume of betting, the levy was approaching its expected level. The Tote expressed apprehension, though this was within the context of a more general fear about the amount it was likely to be able to contribute to racing.

Harding's policies

It is clear from the story so far that Harding went into a situation fraught with politics. Indeed, he seems to have done so with his eyes open, and with the intention of enjoying it.

He realised from the start that the Jockey Club would have difficulty in accommodating itself to the fact that the Levy Board, a creature which it had itself called up, was now a second, and potentially rival, centre of power in a world which the Club had dominated without self-doubt for two hundred years.

Fortunately, Harding was in many ways an admirer of the Jockey Club. He thought the justification for its existence was that, however little its members knew about finance, or the business of running racecourses, they really knew about racing. Thanks to Harding's quiet approach, the Club was nursed into a number of innovations. However, it continued to regard the fixture list, which was plainly of direct interest to the Levy Board, as exclusively its concern, and Harding made little progress on that front.

But on others he was successful. It is a remarkable fact that, although Wigg, his successor as Chairman, is commonly seen as the great innovator in British racing (and must surely be seen as its dominating personality for many years), most of the innovations usually credited to him really started under Harding. Like the dates of the Kings and Queens of England those of Levy Board Chairmen are useful, but often distract attention from continuing processes. For example, it was clear from the beginning that all technical matters must be treated together; Sir Raymond Brown became Chairman of Racecourse Technical Services in March 1970 and the firm gradually grew as the requirement increased. (Its house in Wimbledon was so aligned that it gave a good enough view down the road for the cameras to be tested there.) Similarly, co-operation with the Jockey Club over security grew out of joint concern about stable security, and seems to have proceeded quite smoothly, though when Racecourse Security Services came to be set up in the Wigg era, it caused terrible trouble between Jockey Club and Levy Board, as we shall see in a later chapter. Improved travelling allowances for horses were paid from the Board's first years, and it covered the costs of the photo finish and camera patrols, anti-doping measures and starting stalls, and continued to pay for overnight declarations. Even the introduction of a turnover element in the assessment of bookmakers' liabilities had been mooted as early as the third levy scheme, though not introduced.

Within the Levy Board there were some stormy issues, like the setting up of the Racing Information Bureau, which Harding favoured, but many activities were non-controversial, notably the veterinary research – though of course there has always been dispute about *how much* should be so spent on this, particularly as much of it does not directly benefit racing.

However, buying stallions and taking over the National Stud were more controversial, though tremendously enjoyable for those few members of the Board who were directly involved. (The National Stud had been established at Tulley, Co. Kildare, in 1916, when Colonel Hall-Walker (later Lord Wavertree) presented his forty-one thoroughbred broodmares to the nation, on condition that the Government bought the stud farm.) The first stallion purchase, twenty-one shares (stallions are conventionally divided into forty shares) at £3,000 each in Counsel in June 1962, has never been seen as a good buy, but at least the principle of buying stallions could be justified under the Board's duty to improve the breed, even if the choice made in this case was not particularly good. Indeed, once the Board had decided not to establish breeders' prizes, it could think of no other way to improve the breed.

The intention to take over the National Stud from the Ministry of Agriculture, with which the then Minister, Christopher (later Lord) Soames was perfectly happy to co-operate, fell much less obviously within the terms of the Act, and the Home Office officials who had to advise whether the takeover could have fallen within Parliament's original intention suffered some anguish, but it went through smoothly, and the transfer was announced in Parliament on 20 February 1963. Shortly thereafter, the Stud's breeding policy was abandoned and the mares sold. In 1964 the stud at Gillingham (where it had been transferred in 1943) was also sold for £120,000 and a new stud of 512 acres and the adjacent Heath Stud at Newmarket were leased from the Jockey Club.

The extension of the Board's interests to include the National Stud seems to have been one of the few occasions in the Harding years on which the Home Office took a really close interest in the Board's affairs. Although its reports frequently refer to approval having been obtained from the Secretary of State for some course of action, and it is true that the Board's budget was, in Harding's days, examined at the Home Office, there seems in reality to have been minimal interference. This, of course, had been the intention of the 1961 Act.

There was much discussion in the Board's early days about the desirable balance between the various headings under the general objective of 'the improvement of racing', such as race course amenities, prize money, the integrity of racing, and so on. There followed plans to categorise courses and a new realisation (foreshadowed in the Ilchester Report of 1943) that there were too many of them. (There were at that time seventy-one courses, counting Newmarket as two, compared with sixty today. They ranged from the very highly regarded courses like Ascot, Cheltenham and Newmarket itself to small, rather obscure, ones, like Ludlow and Fakenham, which had, and still have, devoted local followings.) Harding decided that something must be done and published a list of twelve courses (which would be allowed to appeal) from which Levy Board support would be withdrawn after the end of 1966. This led to 'a blood-red row with Harry Rosebery' at the Jockey Club rooms, because Musselburgh, Lord Rosebery's favourite course, was one of those threatened. The row ended when Rosebery was called away to answer the telephone and shouted from the other end of the room 'I can't go on with this. I haven't got a long enough spoon.'

In the end four courses were closed; two went out of business in the interim period and six, including Musselburgh, were reprieved.[21] Lord Harding was convinced that it was the threat of closure which made Lord Rosebery, and others, set about putting their houses in order, so that it was no longer necessary to close them.

The Levy was not altogether easy to administer. The Board's second annual report (covering the first Levy Scheme to 31 March 1963) shows that the Bookmakers' Committee had hoped that it would yield at least £1,250,000, but that it had, in fact, raised only £892,617. The Bookmakers' Committee thought the second scheme should be much as in the previous year, the Board disagreed, and the scheme was determined by the three Home Office appointees. Meanwhile, although the Board had not completed its assessment of the need, it was already satisfied that the figure of £3 million, put to Peppiatt by the Jockey Club, was much too low.

Operating the scheme was difficult, partly because of its novelty and partly because a substantial minority of bookmakers did not co-operate. Defaulters could be pursued through the courts, or by objecting to their licences; the latter method was cheaper and easier, but since licences were issued by many different authorities all over the country, and since many of them would require oral evidence of objection, this too was impracticable for the Board. It was then agreed with the Home Office that the simplest way to ensure payment would be for bookmakers to attach to their applications for renewal of licence the Board's certificate of discharge or of exemption from the current levy. Even this, however, could not be implemented without legislation, as it was held to be beyond the Home Secretary's legal power to achieve it by Statutory Instrument. However, an Order was made on 26 April 1963, efffective 1 January 1964, containing the rather weak requirement that a bookmaker applying for renewal of his licence 'must state whether or not he had discharged all the liabilities to which he may be subject by way of levy under the Betting Gaming and Lotteries Act, 1963. (This Consolidating Act had replaced those of 1960 and 1961.) Discussions were held with the Home Office on 6 November 1963, concerning proposed amendments to the Act 'to strengthen the Board's hand in ensuring that a proper return is received from Bookmakers under the Levy'. There was clearly a need for some strengthening of the Board's powers, since in 1963/4 it had difficulty in obtaining payment from no fewer than 3,000 of the 11,500 bookmakers registered with it.

George Wigg expressed a widespread feeling, though his figures may not have been exact, when he said in the debate on the 1964 Finance Bill, that in the previous year, out of about nine thousand bookmakers, 4,477 had produced returns certified by accountants, which showed that they were making less than £1000 per year profit, and so were liable for only £50 levy. This, said Wigg, was laughable. 'Nobody in his sense would stay in bookmaking unless, if he did not have a Bentley, his wife had a mink coat.'[22]

The Churches Council on Gambling[23] noted that there had been much talk of a Tote monopoly in 1963, because it was so widely believed that bookmakers were evading the levy. The Council itself was neither for nor against a Tote monopoly, except in so far as it might produce the same benefits for racing as could only be obtained from a levy on a much greater volume of betting with bookmakers. If a Tote monopoly were to reduce the desire of the Government and the racing authorities to increase the volume of betting, the Churches would be well-pleased.

According to the Council, there had been a great increase in the number of licensed betting offices, to a grand total of 14,388 at 1 June

1963. As might have been expected, they were not merely catering for people who had been accustomed to bet before the 1960 Act but were attracting new customers as well, and, as many Members of Parliament had feared, big capital had come into betting. The Council was able to note, in its report for 1964,[24] that, although there was no national campaign against betting shops, there was widespread and spontaneous local opposition, perhaps partly as a result of the Council's own efforts. During the year the licensing committees, which in 1963 had refused very few applications (according to the report for 1963) seemed to have tightened up over the issuing of new licences.

During the 1962-3 season racecourse attendances, which had been going down for seven or eight years, declined more drastically. Early in 1963 the Board therefore employed publicity consultants (Patrick Dolan Associates, a subsidiary of Batten, Barton, Durstine and Osborn Ltd (BBDO)) to 'ascertain the reason why the public are ceasing to attend race meetings, although the public interest in horse-racing appears to be as great as ever'. *The Times* (22 February 1962) had speculated that betting shops might account for the drop in attendance in the cheaper enclosures and the *Financial Times* of 19 June, having noted that attendances had fallen from about six million to about five and a half million in ten years, said racecourses and on-course bookmakers were holding an enquiry into how other activities were reducing the attractions of spending a day at the races, and reported general agreement in racing that courses' first need was an injection of capital – for example, Goodwood needed £900,000 for a new stand. *The Times* of 10 December thought the levy had come in the nick of time.

The great value of the BBDO report, as of so many reports by outside consultants, was that it confirmed priorities already established by the Board, notably the need to modernise racecourses and to attract new racegoers. Racing must no longer present itself as the 'sport of kings' or of very rich gamblers, nor expect to repeat the rocketing attendances of the immediate post-war days when people were starved of entertainment. 'Television was introduced, hire purchase expanded, more people began to buy their own cars and travel further.' Out of every £1 spent, 1s 4d went on tobacco, 1s 3d on drink and only 4d on entertainment. There was ever-growing competition for what is nowadays called the 'leisure pound'.

The answer, the report continued, lay in reducing the number of racecourses, and improving the facilities and management of those that remained: prize money should be increased (and the 'trickle down' theory was endorsed) but not at the expense of improving amenities. Racing should no longer be seen purely as a sport. 'By treating it as an industry we can provide realistic solutions.' BBDO agreed that betting shops reduced attendances, though they could not quantify the extent, but placed more emphasis on the effect of live television. The solution lay in managements' hands. 'They could either charge the contractors sufficiently so that it does not matter whether attendances fall or not, or else review television rights so that attendances are maintained.'

The whole question of bookmakers was a major matter of policy, which lay outside the report's scope, but BBDO saw no justification for a large area of the best positions on most racecourses being taken up by bookmakers and thought they should be moved from their customary pitches between the stand and the rails. In new racecourse buildings their pitches should be behind or under the stands, not in front of them. However this recommendation produced no more result that have numerous others to the same effect.

Meanwhile, even before the report had been commissioned, the Board, after consultation with the Turf Authorities (the Jockey Club and the National Hunt Committee), had embarked on the mammoth task of working out priorities for modernisation; in April 1963 the first twenty racecourses selected were announced, and Harding said the country could not support more than sixty courses.[25]

On 11 April 1964 *The Times* again discussed racing's problems. In France, it had become a business, in America an entertainment, but in England, against the odds, it had remained a sport, even the sport of kings. But it was not the sport of the people. Attendances had fallen, for which television, betting shops and intensive competition from other sports were commonly blamed. But racing was slow to move with the times; its paternalistic system of control was out of date and had delayed such improvements as the introduction of starting stalls. Drastic action was needed, perhaps by a combination of Admiral Rous and Dr Beeching.

However, the paper added, though spectators were staying away, the number of owners and of horses in training was increasing, showing anything but a lack of confidence. The Racehorse Owners' Association put the annual cost of keeping a horse in training at £1,084, so that, with a horse population of eight thousand, owners were spending £8 million, and had won £3,200,000 in 1963, nearly a third of which they had contributed themselves. Furthermore, many big races were being won by foreigners, which encouraged them to pay high prices for top quality animals, which were then exported. (*The Times* did not make the point that racing cannot have its cake and eat it. High prize money brings foreigners to compete for it – so, of course, do other factors, like prestige – and without foreign participation, and consequent loss of some of the best bloodstock, there will not be a buoyant blookstock market.)

In the fourth annual report the Board was decidedly optimistic: 'it is the Board's belief, and this opinion is shared by many within the Racing Industry, that the climate has noticeably improved. There is a much more confident air about the future of racing and the steady drop in attendances noted over the past ten years has been arrested. Much remains to be done but a good start seems to have been made.'[26] This optimistic tone persisted in subsequent reports: in the one for 1965-6 the Board said 'the image of racing as a sport, entertainment and industry is steadily improving'.[27] The following year the tone was more guarded, because attendances were down at the majority of courses.

By now Harding had laid solid foundations for the Levy Board's future. Perhaps his greatest remaining achievement was to put flesh on the bones of co-operation with the Jockey Club and National Hunt Committee, by approving major plans for the modernisation of Newmarket's Rowley Mile. This was naturally a project close to the Jockey Club's heart, since Newmarket was racing's headquarters and its courses were the Club's property. At the same time, there were heart-searchings among some members, who feared that by accepting Levy Board finance to any great extent the Club would be putting itself in pawn. Furthermore, it was thought that the rather hastily prepared scheme of modernisation could be improved if more time were available.

Other members urged that the Club should go ahead immediately. By early May 1967 it was known that Harding's resignation as Chairman was imminent and there was no knowing what attitude another chairman might take. Towards the end of 1966 it had became known that Wigg might succeed Harding, not a prospect which the Jockey Club would have faced with equanimity. In fact a deal was swiftly agreed, which benefited both parties, since, in part return for a grant to modernise the Rowley Mile, the Jockey Club reduced the National

Stud's annual rent from £5,000 to £1 and increased the lease from 99 years to 999 years. Thus the new arrangement removed any embarrassment the Levy Board might have felt at having spent large sums of public money on erecting buildings at the Stud on land which it did not own, since the new 999-year lease was for practical purposes the same as freehold. At the same time, those members of the Jockey Club were appeased who had feared too close a bond with the Board.

Harding resigned in May 1967 to become full-time chairman of Plessey (the story that he consented to stay so long at the Levy Board in order to keep Wigg out is fictitious) and after a long interregnum, during which Sir Denys Hicks acted as chairman, Wigg was appointed in November, Viscount Head having at first accepted, but then refused, the appointment. There followed a period of upheaval in British racing, particularly in the relations between the Levy Board and the Turf Authorities.

Notes

1 Royal Commission on Gambling, *Final Report*, vol. I (Cmnd. 7200), July 1978, para. 9.14.
2 Home Office, *Report of the Departmental Committee on a Levy on Betting on Horse Races* (Cmnd. 1003), April 1960, para. 19 (The Peppiatt Report).
3 *Ibid.*, para. 24.
4 *Ibid.*, para. 41.
5 624 H.C. Deb., cols. 68 and 70, 23 May 1960.
6 *Ibid.*, cols. 87-88.
7 *Ibid.*, col. 93.
8 631 H.C. Deb., cols. 877 and 879, 5 December 1960.
9 *Ibid.*, cols. 886, 888 and 892.
10 *Ibid.*, cols. 900 and 901.
11 *Ibid.*, cols. 913 and 959-60.
12 632 H.C. Deb., col. 440, 14 December 1960.
13 *Ibid.*, col. 1222, 20 December 1960.
14 *Ibid.*, cols. 1223, 1225 and 1229.
15 *The Times*, 17 April 1961.
16 Horserace Betting Levy Board, *Sixth Report: 1st April 1966 – 31st March 1967*, London, 1967, p. 17.
17 C. Hood, 'The Development of Betting Taxes in Britain', Public Administration, 50, summer 1972, pp. 183-202; *The Limits of Administration*, London 1976 'Case Study Number Three: Taxing the Gambler', pp. 169-89.
18 Royal Commission on Betting, Lotteries and Gaming, *Report* (Cmd. 8190), 1951, paras. 788-92.

19 675 *H.C. Deb.*, col. 465, 3 April 1963.
20 *The Times*, 24 January 1964.
21 *The Times*, 10 July 1964.
22 694 *H.C. Deb.*, col. 1506, 7 May 1964.
23 Churches' Council, *Gambling – Why?*.
24 Churches' Council on Gambling, *Annual Report*, 1964.
25 *The Times*, 5 April 1963.
26 Horserace Betting Levy Board, *Fourth Report: 1st April 1964 – 31st March 1965*, p. 15. (The report was published very late, on 21 February 1966.)
27 *Ibid.*, *Fifth Report: 1st April 1965 – 31st March 1966*, p. 12.

V
The Wigg years / 1
Relations with the
Jockey Club and bookmakers

Lord Wigg (he received his peerage on leaving Harold Wilson's Government, in which he had been Paymaster-General) became Chairman of the Levy Board in November 1967, just before his sixty-seventh birthday. Lord Harding had resigned in May, and in the long interregnum, during which the Prime Minister, Harold Wilson, and Home Secretary, Roy Jenkins, tried to find a successor, Sir Denys Hicks, the Deputy Chairman, had acted as Chairman.

As Paymaster-General Wigg was a Minister without portfolio, and, in accordance with custom, his duties were not published in any detail. He was very close to Wilson, who gave him general directions to liaise with the security services, which Wigg interpreted as an instruction to be available for consultations if required, but not to interfere. However, recollections of the impressions he made on the 'intelligence community' are mixed. Some officials may have been grateful to have a Minister who took a close interest in their affairs, but in some quarters his influence was resented.

In addition to these shadowy duties, Wigg, although never a member of the Cabinet, would be invited to attend Cabinet meetings from time to time, and often attended meetings of the Defence and Overseas Policy Committee. The reasons for his leaving the Government are complex. On the one hand, as he makes clear in his autobiography, he was becoming increasingly disenchanted with the Prime Minister's conduct of affairs, and disapproved of the extent to which Wilson relied on advice from Mrs Marcia Williams (later Lady Falkender).[1] Furthermore, he welcomed the opportunity to occupy a commanding position in the world of racing.

On the other hand, Wilson himself may have been tired of receiving intimate advice from two sources, and the unpopularity which Wigg had incurred in some sections of Whitehall may also have weighed with him. In that case, the availability of the Levy Board would have provided him with the ideal opportunity to move Wigg out of the Government, into a position for which he was supremely well suited. Whatever the Prime Minister's thoughts, it is clear (from an interview with Wigg in January 1983, which was 'on the record' at his request) that he offered Wigg no choice. If he did not accept the Levy Board, he would still not remain in the Government. However, Wigg recalled that he had made the condition that he must have amending legislation. Exactly what he had in mind is not known, but he probably knew of the difficulties Harding had been having in collecting the levy, and he had himself said in the Second Reading debate on the Finance Bill of 1964 (7 May 1964) that many bookmakers must be greatly understating their profits. It seems likely, therefore, that he wanted improvements in the machinery of assessment and collection to be introduced by law.

Richard Crossman's diary supports the view that the offer of the Levy Board was a great opportunity, which Wigg would miss for ever if he did not take it now. It also tends to support Wigg's recollection that he was given no choice. Crossman records the Prime Minister's words: 'Anyway, I think it's the right time for him to move on', and continues: 'This confirmed the impression I'd got that afternoon from Trevor Lloyd-Hughes that George didn't really want to go and had to be pushed, but in a nice favourable way. . . "George's going will be a great relief, you know," he [Wilson] added. "He was becoming a great early morning pressure on my telphone, as you very well know."'[2] However, later in the *Diaries*, Crossman records that Wilson was missing Wigg, and wanted someone as confidant and adviser.[3]

Wigg was certainly one of the dominant figures of the British turf, though some would say that the Duke of Norfolk and Major-General Sir Randle Feilden were his equals. In the upper reaches of Whitehall he was necessarily seen as *the* dominant figure, for he was not merely the Home Secretary's appointee but the Prime Minister's (although this does not mean that he was given any greater consideration at working level in the Home Office than was due to any other Chairman of a statutory body). He also had a great knowledge and love of racing, which could not fail to impress those who dealt with him. Until he became Paymaster-General racing had been his hobby (otherwise he seems to have had few activities outside his work) but once in office he found that racing, too, began to be part of his work.

For example, he was involved in Crossman's decision (as Minister of Local Government and Planning) automatically to 'call in' (for consideration by the Minister) any applications for racecourse development, and in 1964 he sat on a committee to examine the possibility of introducing a tax on betting.

Under Wigg the Levy Board changed enormously from the body created by Harding. The latter had been a part-time chairman (though he had had to give three or four days a week to it), whereas within the year Wigg arranged, with the support of the Board, to become full-time, which was reasonable in view of the heavy load of work he placed upon himself.

The consequential increase in his salary (from £4,800 to £6,000 a year) provoked a hostile question by Arthur Lewis in the House of Commons on 27 February 1969, and a comment from Jack Logan in *The Sporting Life* of the following day that Wigg was worth double his pay. At £6,000 a year he was getting substantially less than he received as a Minister, yet 'even the most ignorant critic must know that he has been working the clock round for months since he first took office to rescue the Turf from bankruptcy'.

The characters of the Board's first two chairmen were quite different, for Harding, though firm, had believed in gradual change and the need to avoid confrontation. Wigg, on the other hand, was a man of enthusiasms, even obsessions, such as his successful determination to save Epsom and Walton Downs, which Stanley Wootton gave to the Board in 1969, on a 999-year lease at a peppercorn rent. He was also a man of feuds: one of his great interests was defence, and he had frequently sniped at the Duke of Norfolk (who took a great interest in the Territorial Army) – and sometimes agreed with him – long before they clashed as representatives of Levy Board and Jockey Club. He also enjoyed his enmity with Lord Mancroft, Chairman of the Tote during the last few months of Wigg's reign and formerly a Conservative Minister, who had not exactly invited friendship by his famous remark about Wigg's beloved Royal Army Education Corps, that it was 'the only unit of the British Army entitled to include the General Election of 1945 among its battle honours'.

Wigg had the great advantages of having been a member of the Racecourse Betting Control Board from 1957 to 1961 and of the Tote Board from 1961 to 1964, and of being an acknowledged expert on racing. He also inherited a Levy Board which Harding had built up into a confident body, able to assert itself against the Jockey Club. But Wigg was hampered by fiery likes and dislikes and by class-consciousness. These handicaps, of course, contributed to the epic rows which erupted in all directions (though a reading of the Board's bland reports barely betrays them) once he had taken office.

The differences with the Jockey Club and Tote had rational bases, but were complicated by Wigg's character and prejudices, so that institutional and personal factors became indistinguishable. Wigg believed the Tote to be inefficiently run, as well as hampered by legislation and the fixture list, but if he had got on better with Mancroft (Chairman, 1 May 1972 to 30 April 1976), and his predecessor, A. W. ('Sabre-tooth') Taylor (Chairman for two years from 1 May 1970 and formerly Deputy-Chairman of the Commissioners of Customs and Excise), these convictions would have been far less strong. (He seems to have go on much better with Sir Alexander Sim, who was the Tote's first Chairman, from 1961 to30 April 1970.) Similarly, Harding had sometimes had to take a strong line with the Jockey Club, but he had done it quietly. Wigg, on the other hand, would not realise that backwoodsmen could not be rushed. He did not want to turn the Club into a subsidiary company of the Levy Board, only to trim its wings, but he wanted to do so at top speed.

He thought the Jockey Club had been lamentably slow in adopting, for example, starting stalls and safeguards for jockeys, and in sorting out the Pattern race system (which, he believed, developed far too slowly after the Duke of Norfolk's report of 1965) and that it was inefficient over security. (The Pattern will be discussed in detail later. It is a system of classifying the major races, according to distance and the age of the horses entered, in order to avoid overlaps, and so lessen the risk of inadequate fields. The system started in England, and was later extended to France, Ireland, Germany and Italy.)

At the same time, Wigg hated the Duke of Norfolk's social power, a power so great in Wigg's eyes that it could frustrate with the mere implied threat of social ostracism any fumbling moves into the twentieth century attempted by the Club's more enlightened members. Without Wigg's extraordinary mixture of energy, dedication to work and determination to get his facts right, many of the changes for the better in British racing might have been achieved far more slowly or perhaps not at all, but they were achieved at the cost of lasting antipathies, and even hatreds. These, however, were at the personal level, and have not impaired the renewal of good relations between

Levy Board and Jockey Club. That was the main task which Wigg's successor, Sir Stanley Raymond (chairman, 16 November 1972 to 21 January 1974) set himself, as did Sir Desmond (later Lord) Plummer (chairman, 22 January 1974 to 30 September 1982) and Viscount Leverhulme (Senior Steward of the Jockey Club, 1973-6).

Wigg also had friends: Lord Goodman was adept at restraining him; Sir Denys Hicks he called 'my man of peace'; Sir John Astor was a long-standing friend who had been his 'pair' in the House of Commons on days when they both wanted to go racing; he was very close to that other gad-fly of the Establishment, Phil Bull; he lunched alone with a surprising variety of people who might have been thought his enemies, and even got on well, or at least had a love-hate relationship, with his constant sparring partner, Sir Randle Feilden. He was a genius at press relations, despite his habit of ringing editors, and indeed anyone else he wanted to talk to, at extraordinary hours and at great length. A host of lesser mortals, like jockeys needing rehabilitation after falls, were grateful to him and even some of those members of the Jockey Club who detested him also respected him, however unwillingly, and still do, for pulling the Club into the twentieth century.

Wigg supported the Bill which set up the Levy Board, and while he was its Chairman he served it devotedly, but later he turned against it. He said in a Debate in 1974, and again to the Rothschild Commission, that he had changed his mind because he had been converted against hypothecated taxation, but one can at least speculate that this was not a complete account. His change of heart may also connect with his dislike of the Jockey Club, which he saw as responsible for the very existence of the Levy Board, as a result of its threat to block the Betting and Gaming Bill in the Lords if nothing was given to racing.

When his first three-year term was drawing to its end, the Home Secretary (by then Reginald Maudling) and even the Prime Minister (Edward Heath) were told of the unhappy state of the Board itself, as well as its poor relations with the Jockey Club. But Wigg had done so much for racing that it was not difficult for Maudling, with whom he was on friendly terms, to re-appoint him, though only for two years, to Wigg's great disappointment. He left the Board on 15 November 1972, though he seems to have continued to see its papers unofficially. Very soon he turned poacher by becoming President of the Betting Office Licensees' Association when it was set up in

November 1973. BOLA was, and remains, largely associated with the major bookmakers' interest, so that his reception was a doubly remarkable about-turn, in view of the concern for the small man that he had demonstrated throughout his years at the Board. He remained active as President, and behind the scenes as well, until he died on 11 August 1983. For example, he played a useful part in the campaign of 1982-3 to save the Grand National, and steered the bookmakers to victory in a levy scheme, when it would have been politically unwelcome to the Board to have the scheme determined by the Home Secretary.

Despite Wigg's kindnesses to individuals, the Levy Board was an unhappy ship under his command, though things seems to have improved greatly in 1972, when Miss Margaret Meades, who had joined the Board from the Home Office in the previous year, became secretary, in succession to Lt Colonel P. M. Victory (secretary 1969-72). He was determined to run everything himself, which led to very mixed relations with his staff, whom he sometimes worked impossibly hard, and to unsettling changes of personnel. Yet he could be charming, and retailed fascinating gossip about politics: one colleague reminisced: 'despite everything, you had to love the old devil'.

The confusion, at least in the early years, over who was responsible for what, both within the Board and between the Board and the Jockey Club, caused uncertainty in the industry at large, and the report on the Board, which Wigg himself commissioned from the Economist Intelligence Unit in October 1968, pointed this out, although it managed not to mention the Jockey Club by name. This particular remark by the EIU cannot have pleased Wigg, though in the main the report said what he had hoped for, in recommending a streamlined organisation in which four departmental heads would report directly to the chairman, who would also become chief executive. The Board, however, although generally dominated by Wigg (only a few members stood up to him, notably Lord Kilmany and Lord Crathorne, whom Wigg respected, probably because he had resigned over Crichel Down in 1954), was reluctant to have him as chief executive, and he had to be content with the formal role of chairman.

Wigg was no conciliator, though he had political skill amounting to deviousness. Nor, however, did the Jockey Club always show itself the master of *finesse*, and some members were thoroughly insensitive in their dealings with him. The Club's fear of a man who was so quintessentially not one of themselves may have contributed as much as did Wigg's own failings to the bad relationship between Club and Levy Board, which persisted for some years after his departure. (Perhaps one of the real achievements of Lord Rothschild's Commission was at long last to clear the air between them.)

Wigg's first meeting with the Turf Board (a joint body of the Jockey Club and the National Hunt Committee) has passed into legend. He recalled that he was summoned to Portman Square, where the Board was assembled at a kidney-shaped table, with one chair in the centre for 'old George'. Feilden, as Senior Steward, expounded the Jockey Club orthodoxy (from which Harding had gradually weaned the Club) that it was the Levy Board's responsibility to collect the levy and the Jockey Club's to spend it. For good measure, the Duke of Norfolk warned Wigg that he must never talk to the press about racing without prior consultation with the Club. Wigg rose to the occasion with a forceful reply ('expletives deleted' as President Nixon would say) and told the Stewards that he would do as he liked; if they wanted to see him they must come to his offices in Southhampton Row. He would never come to them again.

The problems of communication which naturally followed this disastrous meeting led eventually to the formation of the Joint Racing Board. This body formalised the link between the two institutions, which in Harding's day had been informally maintained through the Turf Board. The latter, consisting of representatives of the Jockey Club, the National Hunt Committee and their representatives on the Levy Board, continued in existence, in order that the Turf Authorities' members of the Board shoud be properly briefed.

The meeting had many other consequences. One of the earliest was that Wigg would not co-operate, beyond providing some facts and figures, with the Committee which the Jockey Club set up in September 1967 under Sir Henry (later Lord) Benson to examine the organisation and financing of racing, and whose report will be discussed in detail in a later chapter.[4]

But Wigg did not spend all his time battling with the Jockey Club. Much of it was spent in dealing with the Home Office, where the settled life of Division E1, now known as E3, the section of General Department which dealt with racing (but which also had bewilderingly miscellaneous other responsibilities, covering, among other things, the Church, provincial taxis and summer time), came to an abrupt end with Wigg's advent. Thereafter he was constantly telephoning or writing (for example, about the conditions under which the Levy Board should participate in the Joint Racing Board), with the result that a disproportionate amount of official, and ministerial, time was spent on racing. Furthermore, Wigg never shared the Home Office view that the levy was not taxpayers' money; as a Parliamentarian (and a cautious man) he was naturally interested in accountability. However, the difference may have been more apparent than real, since the Home Office came to the same conclusion by a different route: the money might not be the taxpayers', but the Levy Board was a statutory body, of whose affairs the Home Office could not wash its hands.

Fortunately for Wigg, he was liked at the Home Office. Several of the senior officials who dealt with racing did not understand the industry and were not interested. Some of them saw it as the preserve of the aristocracy and the working class, with no room for middle-class officials like themselves; some were opposed to gambling, and had austere views on life in general, so that they had little sympathy for the Levy Board and its activities. (As Sir David Renton once said in Parliament, the bookmakers' runner who had covered the Home Office in the old days had been there largely for the convenience of Messengers and Ministers. He did not think the civil servants had been much interested.) Nevertheless, they liked and respected Wigg, surprising as this may seem in view of their disapproval of his success in raising gambling turnover. It seems that they were won over by his down-to-earth appeal (though one, at least, was baffled by his archaic army slang) and enjoyed the contrast with the Jockey Club, whose representatives the officials thought stupid, and invested with an objectionable aura of privilege.

Wigg did not ask the Home Office to undertake detailed work like vetting the Board's accounts, but he did insist on general approval of its activities and specific approval of any new activity. Since he contended that the Board had been acting *ultra vires* since its foundation, because it had failed to obtain approval of its schemes from the Home Office, he obtained from the Home Secretary (James Callaghan) an Instrument of Approval retrospectively ratifying everything it had done since 1961, and thereafter sought specific approval, as he was bound to do, of such activities as owning racecourses, participating in the Joint Racing Board, or selling the National Stud property at East Grinstead, which, once the stud proper had moved to Newmarket, existed only as a farm supplying fodder to Newmarket at much more than the market cost.

A further example of Wigg drawing the Home Office closer to racing, exactly what it had *not* wanted to do when the original Acts were passed, was to get through Parliament an amending Act (Horserace Betting Levy Act, 1969), whereby the Home Secretary himself, instead of his three appointees on the Board, would determine disputed levy schemes.

The seventh and eighth levy schemes – bad relations with the bookmakers

When Wigg joined the Board in November 1967 he was warned that the bookmakers were discontented because they had only one seat on the Levy Board, but that informal relations with them were good and useful. However, relations quickly deteriorated because of the disputes over the seventh and eighth levy schemes, and the 1969 Act which the disputes made necessary. So bitter were the disputes, particularly that over the eighth scheme, that the wrangle had looked like going to court, and the Home Office could not allow the Levy Board to be without income from the bookmakers until a decision was reached.[5]

The seventh scheme had, as we have seen, changed one of the bases of assessment from the number of shops owned to turnover, which it was hoped would 'result in a more equitable levy as between large and small businesses'.[6] In other words, the larger firms would have to pay significantly more than in the past. As *The Economist*[7] had robustly put it, the bookmakers had been rumbled, as the turnover figures made a mockery of their past contributions: they and their apologists would, in the future, have to think up more convincing arguments to counter demands for a proper levy.

The heart of the bookmakers' quarrel with Wigg and the Levy Board lay not in the shift to turnover as the main basis of assessment, but in the Board's and the Government's refusal to retain in the 1969 Act the clause of the 1961 Act (and later the Consolidating Act of 1963)[8] which stated that, in determining a disputed levy scheme, the three Home Office appointees must pay heed to the bookmakers' capacity to pay. Indeed, the bookmakers themselves had proposed the shift to turnover in September 1967, though it may well be that the larger firms did not agree, or had not yet realised the bad consequences that would follow for themselves. The agreement to work towards a scheme based on turnover had been reached before Wigg joined the Board, following meetings between the bookmakers and representatives of the Board of Customs and Excise. Wigg met the Bookmakers' Committee for the first time on 14 December, when he congratulated them and supported the turnover proposal.

The Levy Board papers show that the seventh and eighth schemes were continuing bones of contention throughout 1968. In October there is the first mention of a leak from the Board or from the Bookmakers' Committee (leaks became one of Wigg's obsessions) in relation to an article by Clive Graham[9] which was extremely well-informed on the collection of the seventh levy. By now, the Board's minutes show, 4,514 bookmakers were fully paid up, but 4,300 had not returned their forms of declaration, and 707 were in the pipeline. By November, opposition to the scheme is confined to 'several large bookmaking firms' and those whose businesses combine on- and off-course betting. A letter printed in *The Sporting Life* on 18 November 1968, from Cyril Stein, the Chairman of Ladbroke's, was quoted at the Board, repeating the statement in Ladbroke's annual report, that his firm would not pay a levy based on turnover. The letter also refers to unavailing meetings with Wigg, which led Wigg to confirm that he had indeed had confidential meetings with leading bookmakers, of which it appears fellow-members of the Board had until then known nothing.

With respect to businesses combining on- and off-course betting, Wigg said the decision to subject such concerns to the turnover charge had not been taken lightly. However, it had been done in the bookmakers' own interest, in order to force them to split their businesses, so that the Chancellor could be pressed to create a Betting-Duty differential in favour of the on-course operators, which in turn would create a stronger on-course market on which to base the Starting Price. He recognised that it was too late for bookmakers to split their businesses in relation to the seventh scheme, and there was no legal power to amend it retrospectively, but it might still be possible for the eighth. Meanwhile, the Board would look into any cases of hardship under the seventh scheme, though the offer may not have been of much practical value, since the last thing a bookmaking business can do is admit that it is a hardship case.

Meanwhile, Wigg had reported in October 1968 that he had taken the bookmakers' opposition to the eighth scheme, as expressed by the NAB, in hand through solicitors. He expressed regret to the Board that 'unfortunately there was no one bookmaker or group of bookmakers in positions of authority to join in the discussion and carry the bookmakers'. He also thought (and had said at the July meeting) that the whole wrangle was the bookmakers' own fault for accepting higher deductions on than off course (on course the bookmakers, by agreement with the Racecourse Association, recouped betting duty by a standard deduction of 1s in the £1, but off course it varied from 6d to as much as 1s 3d).

In December Wigg played his trump card when he announced to the Board that the Home Office was to sponsor the amending Act, referred to above. In fact, he had been urging the Home Secretary (James Callaghan) ever since 1 June 1968 to introduce amending legislation to remedy the flaw which the bookmakers had found in the 1961 Act, whereby the Bookmakers' Committee could release a bookmaker from the duty to pay levy by refusing to put him in any levy category. (He had also been trying, unsuccessfully, to persuade Harold (later Lord) Lever, the Financial Secretary to the Treasury, that the Government should undertake a general enquiry into all forms of gambling.) In his letter of 1 June he told the Home Secretary that he believed the number of recalcitrant bookmakers to be small, and that the number of those who wished to settle was growing rapidly. To Fred Peart (Lord Privy Seal) he wrote on the same day that Feilden had agreed, if need be, to help convince the Tories of the need for legislation. In a subsequent letter to Callaghan (24 July 1968) he admitted that it would be possible to retrieve the Board's financial position by insisting that the Tote paid its debt to the Board. But the flaw would still remain.

Callaghan was initially reluctant to promote legislation, and thought Wigg should first test in the courts the bookmakers' claim that the eighth scheme was *ultra vires*. By 7 August, however, Wigg was able to write to Peart that Callaghan was being very helpful about the amending legislation and that he wished his officials to investigate with Peart's the possibility of including it in the autumn Parliamentary timetable, and on 5 September Callaghan finally agreed, though there was still some doubt about whether time could be found for a Government Bill, or whether a Private Member's Bill would be necessary.

At some point in the negotiations with Callaghan, Wigg exploded in the face of the Home Secretary's reluctance (though none of his letters records the strong difference of opinion), and it was at that meeting that, greatly to his officials' surprise, Callaghan agreed to the Bill. Perhaps no one but Wigg could have been so persuasive, and then, having obtained Government time for the Bill (and assistance with drafting it from Professor Lord Lloyd), have got it through an uninterested Parliament. But, thanks to the political skill with which he not only dealt with his own party but also prepared the ground with the Opposition, not to mention his continuing contacts with the Government, which may even have enabled him to have some influence on the composition of the Standing Committee which considered the Bill, the bookmakers were outmanoeuvred, though by the end of his period he was again on excellent terms with them.

Once Wigg had announced the impending legislation, the opposition on the Board seems to have died away, no doubt because the bookmakers diverted their energies to lobbying both House of Parliament, although unsuccessfully, as we shall see.

The removal of the safeguards in the 1961 Act, which required the Home Office appointees to have regard to the extent of the need for contributions, and the capacity of the bookmakers and the Tote to make them, provoked energetic opposition from the bookmakers, which will be chronicled in some detail below. The Levy Board view seems to have been that they were making too much fuss: in the past they had said they could not afford betting tax, but, given time, they had passed it on to the punters and adjusted their terms of trade, and they could do the same again.

In fact the safeguards were no more than common sense, and Elystan Morgan, the Junior Minister at the Home Office who was piloting the Bill through the Commons, assured the House that they would continue to be observed. The bookmakers, however, were indignant, because without the safeguards they would never have agreed to the principle of a levy, and they believed it questionable whether, without that agreement, Parliament would ever have authorised a levy or the formation of the Levy Board. Nor could they see why it was necessary to remove 'capacity to pay' from the Bill, if Morgan was able to give the assurance that it would, in fact, be observed. They also feared (as was stated during the Bill's Second Reading) that the absence of the clause would make it possible for a completely impossible scheme to be imposed, and for some future Government to use the bookmakers' inability to comply with it as a weapon against them. Nor, as Michael Rolfe pointed out in *The Sport-*

ing Life on 19 February 1969, did the bookmakers think that they and Members of Parliament were talking about the same thing. The individual bookmaker thought of 'capacity to pay' as meaning his own capacity, whereas Parliament tended to refer to the ability of the bookmakers taken as a group to pay the proposed levy.

The energy of the bookmakers' campaign against the Bill accounts for the sparseness of the NAB's records for the period, since most members of the General Committee came from out of London, and worked so hard combatting the Bill, both during the day and in the evening, that, as one veteran has put it, 'there was hardly time for a haircut or a bath'. However, the Committee's only relevant minutes (those for 16 February 1969) reveal that early in December 1968, as a result of a newspaper rumour that legislation was to be rushed through Parliament, a deputation from the Bookmakers' Committee had gone to the Home Office on a fact-finding mission, where they had been given an outline of the Bill's provisions. That had been a few days before its First Reading, and had been their first information of the draft Bill.

Shortly afterwards, the Bookmakers' Committee had enquired at the Home Office and been told that their January meeting would be soon enough to consider what amendments they would like to make, although Lord Wigg's information from the Home Office at that time was that the Bill would probably receive its First and Second Readings before Christmas. Although the Levy Board had already been promised a copy of the Bill in draft, a request for a copy by the Bookmakers' Committee had been countered by a senior Home Office official with the reply that he woould have to take instructions on that point. Because of this treatment by the Home Office, the Association gave the facts to the press through a meeting arranged with a Mr Manning of the *Daily Mail*.

The minutes continue that an attempt to slip the Bill through Second Reading before any opposition could be rallied had almost succeeded before Christmas, when few members were in the House, but fortunately for the bookmakers the House had failed to reach the Bill that night. Meanwhile, the NAB had seen MPs either at the House or at the offices of its Parliamentary Agent, including a meeting with two of the Opposition front-bench spokesmen, and the additional time gained by postponement had enabled more members of the Association to see their MPs, which had been of great value. The Association had also arranged luncheon discussions at the

House and had been able to brief fully those members who seemed willing to be helpful, and at short regular intervals information sheets had been posted to all MPs, as well as copies of *British Bookmaker* dealing with the Bill. (Their inexperience as lobbyists, not surprising when one remembers that their cause had been legal for less than a decade, is indicated by the fact that they invited Elystan Morgan to lunch in February 1969, and got a polite refusal from his Private Secretary.)

As the Bill was a Government measure with the Whips on, the best that could be hoped for was to have some amendments included, and during the Second Reading debate it came under strong criticism, particularly on lack of safeguards for bookmakers, including criticism from some of the Government's own supporters. When it came to the Committee stage, the Government had a majority (eleven Labour and nine Conservative MPs with a Labour chairman), and the Government still had the Whips on.

The majority notwithstanding, John Temple's amendment to re-insert the capacity to pay provision in the Bill was carried in Committee by nine votes to eight, as Michael Rolfe reported in *The Sporting Life* on 26 January 1969. This had happened because Arthur Lewis abstained, Timothy Kitson had 'rounded up a couple of Tory members from the corridor' and Marcus Lipton and William Hamling were absent. However, the Government was determined to have its way, and at the Report state the Home Secretary tabled an amendment, once again removing the safeguard; this was duly carried by 122 votes to 108 on 5 March 1969, despite the bookmakers' efforts to persuade Labour members to abstain. The Home Secretary's action, *The Sporting Life* commented,[10] was like using a political sledgehammer to crack a nut, and must expose the Government to ridicule.

Not all the press was as sympathetic to the bookmakers as was *The Sporting Life*. A hostile article in the *Guardian* read in part:

> The Scottish bookmaker Mr John Banks recently stated quite openly that running a betting shop was like having a licence to print money. So far he has purchased 40 betting shops and is open to acquire more.
> If that is the case, why should there be any doubt about the capacity of a betting shop proprietor to pay his levy on turnover? The levy has been changed to one on turnover rather than one on profit because of the difficulty of finding out what profits a bookmaker makes. The point is that if he has not the capacity to pay, should he be allowed

to continue in business? . . .
> The bookmakers have so far defeated everyone who has tried to do battle with them, from Winston Churchill as Chancellor of the Exchequer onwards. Now it appears they have Parliament on their side. Why not let them run the country? They could certainly give us a run for our money and would be on our side.[11]

Though defeated in the Commons the NAB renewed their efforts in the Lords. First they approached the Duke of Devonshire, reminding him that he had played a part in making the 1960 Act workable, and expressing the hope that he would ventilate the bookmakers' fears at Second Reading. They sent a similar plea to three other Peers, but despite their efforts the Bill was unopposed at Second Reading. Lord Mowbray tried to reinsert the safeguard at the Committee stage in the Lords, but eventually withdrew his amendment.

Thus the bookmakers had lost a great battle, but they had gained invaluable political experience. This they used to the utmost effect, as we shall see in the next chapter, in opposing the Horserace Totalisator and Betting Levy Boards Bill of 1972.

The aftermath

In July 1969 Wigg reported to the Board that the Home Secretary had confirmed the eighth levy. He saw this as an indication that the Secretary of State had accepted the Board's philosophy about the levy, hoped the bookmakers realised this, and looked forward to a peaceable future. Peace was, in fact, achieved, and in September the Chairman of the Bookmakers' Committee said that a new era in good relations with the Board had begun. However, collection of the eighth levy was slow, because extensive use was made of the appeals procedure and even the larger firms paid by instalments. (Later legislation introduced a new 'pay as you earn' procedure.)

The cash flow problem was compounded by the possibility that the Board would buy Epsom and Sandown Park racecourses. (Wigg had mentioned this to Sir Philip (later Lord) Allen, Permanent Under-Secretary at the Home Office on 1 February.) He wished the Home Office to persuade the Treasury that Levy Board borrowing should be treated as public sector borrowing, and therefore exempt from the credit squeeze that had been imposed on the banks. The Home Office strongly supported the case, but Allen was obliged to inform Wigg that the Treasury would not shield the Board from the squeeze.

Treasury consent would, however, be forthcoming for borrowings from non-bank sources.

For the remainder of Wigg's period the bookmakers seem to have been docile, though he himself was not fully satisfied with the degree of control the Board had over them.

A number of reasons can be found for the bookmakers' readiness to co-operate. First, Wigg's expansionary policy, introduced after the confirmation of the eighth levy, benefited them greatly, since it provided for a race every fifteen minutes, and so made possible virtually continuous betting. Secondly, he consented to put to the Home Office proposals made to him by a leading bookmaker in September 1970, whereby a new, unified, bookmakers' association would be created with financial assistance from the Levy Board. The Home Office would not agree to any such assistance, which it would be necessary to show would be conducive to the good of horse racing, though it did not completely close the door. It appears, however, that the bookmakers were unable to agree among themselves, and that no further proposals were made. Finally, the bookmakers' good relationship with Wigg must have been cemented when, in March 1972, he came out against the Tote Bill (the Horserace Totalisator and Betting Levy Boards Bill).

The Board's financial position was now sound, though it had to cut its coat according to its cloth. Wigg had warned in June 1969 that no contributions could be expected from the Tote for two years, while A. W. Taylor (chairman of the Tote) put his house in order, and in February 1971 he announced that it would be necessary to cut expenditure, as the Board's income was down by £450,000, owing to the Tote's lack of contributions. Nevertheless, the Board thought prize money should not be cut, and this, Wigg argued, endorsed his policy of expansion.

He returned to the expansionary theme in December 1971, when he referred to the need for more levy, to finance such activities as Racecourse Technical Services and the redevelopment of Sandown Park. He recognised that smaller bookmakers needed relief from levy payments, but thought the large ones should fund the increase, as they had benefited so markedly from the Board's expansionary policies. In February 1972 he added that he needed more money to pay for a security service, and that the Bookmakers' Committee had accepted his request for a levy yielding some £5 million. Earlier the Committee had questioned the prudence of increasing the levy, in

view of the impending Tote Bill, but Wigg had briskly said that that
was irrelevant.

Wigg and the Jockey Club

Wigg's relationship with the bookmakers was as nothing beside the
variable and often stormy one he had with the Jockey Club, but,
whereas he was eventually on excellent terms with the bookmakers,
by the middle of 1972 he was so disgusted with the Jockey Club that
he wanted never to think of it again.

There were many issues. We have already seen that his attitude
to Sir Henry Benson's enquiry was coloured by his antipathy to the
Club. One relatively minor issue was the now legendary speech
made by the Duke of Norfolk on 20 December 1969, attacking Wigg
and (later Sir) David Robinson; (the latter was at that time a very big
and successful owner). Another was the Jockey Club's Royal Charter,
which it obtained in February 1970. Major issues were the fixture list
('he who controls the Fixture List controls racing' is an old adage)
and the hot debate over racecourse security. Of course, there were
many other issues, but these give the flavour of the time.

The immediate background to the Duke's Ascot speech lay in
Robinson's speech at the Gimcrack Dinner on 9 December, when he
said that racing was an industry and should be run by businessmen.[12]
The Times, in a leading article entitled 'Making Racing Pay', compared
Robinson's approach with that of the Jockey Club, most fully expressed in the Benson Report's plea for a statutory authority which would
funnel back into racing far more of betting turnover than it had
received so far. Robinson, however, blamed the Jockey Club for
racing's parlous state, and proposed to demonstrate the new
businesslike attitude at Kempton Park, which he had recently
bought. 'Either racing puts its own house in order, and does so
quickly, or it finally passes into the hands of a willing receiver,'
Robinson had said – the receiver, in *The Times*'s view, being Wigg.[13]

Michael Phillips wrote in *The Times* of 17 December that Wigg had
fanned the flames when asked to comment in a BBC interview on
what Robinson had said, and had made things worse at the Bollinger
Luncheon a few days later, by comparing the Jockey Club to 'a well
kept veteran motor car, interesting for use on the occasional drive
if you have infinite time and patience and willingness to judge the
article by its original quality and value'. His reference to the Stewards

as a meritorious, hard-working and dedicated body did not really help!

The Duke's speech, which was certainly not delivered on the spur of the moment, was made in the unsaddling enclosure at Ascot on 20 December, where he spoke his mind for ten minutes over the public address system. *The Times* recorded that he first attacked Robinson's approach, and told him that he must not blame the Jockey Club if he failed at Kempton, though he wished him luck there. He then turned to Wigg.

> Lord Wigg, in his own wisdom, entered the realms of a platform which, if I may say so with respect, was badly chosen. He referred to the stewards of the Jockey Club being superb. He referred to the rest of the Jockey Club as being a veteran car.
>
> I have been a member of the Jockey Club for 36 years, and I served as a steward for 15. Therefore I suppose that in the eyes of Lord Wigg I have been superb for 15 years, and now I belong to that car.

Norfolk felt that the time had come for someone who was no longer a steward to give a lead. 'I will go on striving,' he said, 'for racing as I know it, and as it should be. It is high time that we pulled ourselves together, with one goal in mind.' (Later, Wigg obtained a tape recording of the speech, and insisted that the Duke had referred to 'racing as I *knew* it.')

Wigg was furious, partly because the Levy Board had paid for the public address system over which the Duke had made the speech. 'An irate Lord Wigg hopped from one foot to another in an audience which, if the ovation at the end was anything to go by, was behind the duke almost to a man.'

If Wigg interpreted the applause in the same way, it can only have enraged him further, but as usual he handled the press well, and the majority of the papers carried his riposte to Norfolk prominently. In a radio interview on 'The World This Weekend' Wigg said of the Duke:

> he acted as if he owned Ascot. He is but a Trustee. . . every reform put through either by myself or somebody else has been opposed by him.
>
> He and the Jockey Club believe that my function is the plebeian task of collecting the money. Theirs is the aristocratic task of spending it.

The Duke was a product of the horse and buggy days, 'the glamorous, expansive and rather comfortable times for dukes'. Wigg claimed to have listened with incredulity and great sadness to the Duke's speech, and as a result 'had a miserable day at the races'. He objected to the Duke using the meeting to harangue the crowd in political terms in front of the Queen Mother.[14]

The row was ended, though for Wigg it was never laid to rest, by a call for reconciliation (issued from his home, it was a Sunday) by the Senior Steward, Sir Randle Feilden, on 21 December. When the Duke died, Wigg paid generous tribute to him in the House of Lords, saying, in part:

> we quarrelled, and we quarrelled publicly. He believed he was right – I am quite sure I was; but it is that which makes me say what I want to say.
>
> Here was a man of great honesty of purpose who saw his duty and did it to the best of his ability. He never dissembled, and to such men much may be forgiven.[15]

The whole ridiculous episode was rendered even more farcical when it came out some years later that the 'veteran car' passage had been written for Wigg by 'a prominent public figure' (in fact Lord Goodman), and approved in advance by Feilden.[16]

The Royal Charter

Feilden was, of course, also intimately involved in the Jockey Club's acquisition of a Royal Charter. This was announced on 10 February 1970, when Feilden said that the Club was now in a much stronger position to approach the Home Secretary and seek legislation to set up a statutory racing authority, as had been recommended in the Benson Report. He added that the Club would seek the backing of all the other organisations in racing to bring about 'the most important change ever to have been sought in the history of racing', and that the Racehorse Owners' Association and Thoroughbred Breeders' Association had already pledged their support.[17] *The Times* reported Wigg as having been philosophical about the possible end of the Levy Board and of his own job.[18] (It may have been about now that Robinson told him he could always have a job running Kempton.)[19] He had commented on the Charter, *The Times* went on: 'The Stewards are facing the future and are facing a changed world. . . they are saying "we must face public accountability" and have chosen a Royal Charter as the way to do so.' On 26 February a question about the grant of the Charter was put down in the Commons for the Lord President of the Council by Roy Roebuck, MP, who remained a friend of Wigg until his death, and gave the address at his Memorial service.[20]

Wigg was perhaps not as philosophical as he made out. In a long letter to Sir Philip Allen, he had said that Felden had told him some months previously that the Club intended to apply for a Charter but that he had heard no more until he received a Personal and Confidential letter from Feilden in 10 February, saying that the Charter had been approved and was to be announced the same day. Wigg must have been taken aback by this short notice (which might have been longer but for the troubles over the Duke's speech just before Christmas) and must have been infuriated by a press release from the Racing Information Bureau on 10 February, which said that the Privy Council had first been approached two years earlier.

Wigg must also have been irritated that no one in the Home Office had told him what was happening, but the explanation is quite simple: the Privy Council Office's request for comment from the Home Office had not been circulated to the right division! It does, however, seem odd that Wigg had gleaned nothing from members of the Jockey Club, particularly as, according to the same press release, the merger of the Club and the National Hunt Committee was a prerequisite for the grant of a Charter, and must have been extensively discussed. On the other hand, it appears that some Club members were hardly aware that a Charter was in the offing, and they may not have connected it with the merger. One senior member recalls that Feilden told him in confidence of the application for a Charter. He asked if he could tell Wigg, but Feilden refused permission. Another remembers Feilden suddenly producing the Charter at a Jockey Club meeting, like Chamberlain producing the piece of paper which supposedly guaranteed peace with Hitler.

Wigg, understandably enough, made trouble. However, his main intention was to ensure that the Jockey Club would not be able to use the Charter (which gave it no additional powers) as a lever to obtain legislation to set up a new statutory racing authority of the kind recommended by Benson. In this dispute, the Jockey Club was no match for him. Nor was it anywhere near him in the other running battles, of which perhaps the most notable were those over racecourse security and the fixture list.

The row over security

Security had always been a joint concern of Club and Board, which seems to have originated in worries about horses being got at in racecourse stables and in transit from their trainers' yards. A Jockey Club committee, known as the FWP committee from the initials of its members, Fielden, Lord Willoughby de Broke and the Hon. J. P. Philipps, reported in April 1964, and made numerous recommendations on these subjects.[21] They included the proposal that Securicor should be engaged to guard racecourse stables, which was duly put into effect and paid for by the Levy Board, because there was no other source of funds. This arrangement caused some bad blood, because at least one senior staff member, and later Wigg himself, thought it had been foisted on the Board.

In December 1970 the Board decided that a review of racecourse security should be undertaken, probably by a senior police officer. A year later the Paton Committee on the suppression of doping reported,[22] and at about the same time Securicor were given notice of renegotiation of the contract, whose terms would depend upon the recommendations of the police officers, who by now were conducting the review (Chief Superintendent J. E. Watson, with Inspector T. Mather, both provided by the Chief Constable of Lancashire with the Home Office's agreement).

The real trouble seems to have started in January 1972, when the Joint Racing Board discussed the Watson Report. Feilden had not had time to read it, and in any case had assumed that Brigadier Henry Green, then in charge of Jockey Club security, would be involved in any further investigation. Nevertheless, he agreed to the Report's recommendation that a police officer of Chief Constable status be appointed to assess the report and agreed to be on the interviewing committee.

The committee interviewed candidates on 1 February 1972, yet at the Joint Racing Board on 7 February, Feilden suggested that a working party, to include an ex-judge and a business executive, be set up to report on Watson's study, a suggestion which Wigg refused, because it would be an enquiry into an enquiry. He went on to say that the present situation bore a striking resemblance to that of 1965, when delaying tactics by the Stewards had led to a contract being signed with Securicor and the cost being borne by the Levy Board. (On the same day, William Hickey wrote in the *Daily Express* that it was likely that Harold Prescott, aged 58, Assistant Chief Constable of Lancashire, would be appointed head of racing security.)

Feilden seems to have been the victim of a major misunderstanding, since he was obliged to reply that he had only that morning realised, on reading the minutes of the Anti-Doping Committee, that the Committee had recommended a review of Watson's report. Even worse, he had thought that he had been interviewing people who might conduct an investigation, not candidates for appointment as Chief Inspector of security. Wigg, who seems to have linked the questions of the appointment and the proposed extension of the forensic laboratory without any protest from Feilden, then asked if he should withdraw the offer of appointment to Mr Prescott, and so put into abeyance the extension of the laboratory. To this Feilden said that in his view the Selection Committee had not even agreed that the job should go to Prescott, and Wigg replied that no police officer of Prescott's calibre would accept anything less than a permanent job. At this point it was decided that, in the absence of any progress or agreement, the discussions should continue at the next meeting.

Meanwhile, the story broke in *The Sporting Life* on 8 February 1972, the day after the meeting. The paper said that the Levy Board and Jockey Club had clashed head-on, and then reported that, having said 'words fail me', Wigg had proceeded to issue a long statement (which repeats, thought at greater length and with additions, the account given above). He would not confirm that Prescott had been selected, but did say that 'the police officer selected made it clear that he would not come on any other basis' than a permanent appointment 'and it would be nonsense, in my judgement, to suppose that he could be willing to come on any other basis'. Wigg added, rather darkly, when asked if he would object to an ex-judge looking at racecourse security: 'I would object to an ex-judge, but I would be very much in favour of having a judge with powers to call witnesses and take evidence on oath looking into racecourse security in all its aspects over the last ten years.'

Feilden's counter-statement (also in *The Sporting Life*, 8 February 1972) said that the Stewards had complete faith in Brigadier Green and Securicor, and did not think a new service would necessarily be more effective, particularly as there had been no recorded instance of a horse being interfered with in a racecourse stable since the present arrangement had been introduced. *The Sporting Life* commented that the two bodies now appeared to have totally opposite views of the efficacy of the present security system. Wigg evidently believed that 'the racing scene is not as lily-white as Sir Randle and the Jockey Club would have the public believe'. He must be basing this view on Watson's report, but 'Unfortunately no one has seen fit to release this document for publication'. The paper added on 11 February that one suggestion was that the report had not been published because it was libellous. 'Be that as it may, snippets keep leaking out.'

On 12 February *The Sporting Life* reported a Jockey Club statement expressing shock that extracts of the Watson Report had been leaked to the press, and refuting the allegations made. In response to the claim that a more professional approach was needed, it also revealed that the Club's Special Investigation Department was staffed by thirty-two former police officers, all with CID experience, and none ranking below Detective-Inspector.

At the Levy Board meeting on 21 February, the discussion continued, complicated by failure to agree the minutes of the previous meeting, so that two sets had to be prepared. Wigg had already assured Feilden on 18 February that the Levy Board had no wish to control Racecourse Security Services (RSS), three of whose six directors would be appointed by the Jockey Club as well as three of its seven guarantors. Nevertheless, the Club's members of the Board reported that the Club (here they were presumably referring to the generality of members as well as the Stewards) was really worried about RSS, since, if it went through as it stood it would be 'tantamount to the stewards abrogating their traditional responsibility for disciplinary matters'. However, by the end of the meeting the Board had agreed to set up RSS and to run down Securicor's services as rapidly as possible.

On the next day there appeared a Levy Board statement,[23] which seemed to say between the lines that the Board was going ahead with its plans, whether the Club liked them or not. It recognised that there was an acute problem of personal loyalty for Feilden, who was at the same time Senior Steward of the Jockey Club and a member of the Horserace Anti-Doping Committee, whose unamimous recommendations the Board was backing. It went on that the central issue was to bring together the activities of the forensic laboratory and of the security forces on and off course. This would strengthen the Stewards' role and provide sound organisational and administrative backing, to enable the Jockey Club to carry out its traditional disciplinary tasks. The RSS was therefore to be set up, under the full-time direction of Mr H. Prescott. The Board would not control RSS but it would consider plans to extend the laboratory, at a cost exceeding £100,000, and to extend the camera patrol.

Thus a trivial, yet fundamental, dispute came to an end. It was trivial because the agreement eventually reached was sensible and has worked well: there was no need for it to generate great sound and fury, and if the Levy Board Chairman had been a man less abrasive and less feared by the Jockey Club, it probably would not have done. Furthermore, Prescott, on whose appointment Wigg had been so determined, resigned in December 1974, and his successor, D. A. Corbett, in February 1976; the latter was replaced by Brigadier Henry Green, who had been the Jockey Club's Chief Security Officer before the trouble began. Now he returned as Director of Security for RSS, and remained in office until September 1977. So, in the end, the Jockey Club laughed last.

On the other hand, the conduct of the negotiations again illustrates Wigg's skills: his grasp of facts; his ability to present them in a favourable light; his use of the Home Office when necessary; his carefully nurtured relations with the press; his gift of making his opponent look a fool – it is difficult to imagine anything more farcical than Feilden thinking he was interviewing candidates for one job and then finding out that he had been interviewing for another; his forcefulness in debate and as chairman; his ability to carry the bookmakers with him (since it was they who, indirectly through the levy, were to pay the additional costs); above all, his determination to achieve his ends, and his generosity once he had gained his point. The obsessive energy that he lavished on this, and every other, issue proceeded from a deep conviction that his proposals were the best for racing, to which he was devoted; but a lesser man, and one not burdened with his hatred of people whom he believed to occupy high positions solely because of class advantage, might have served racing better.

The issue was fundamental, because it was about power. The Jockey Club's fear of the new arrangements was in part reasonable, if it is reasonable to regret the loss of power, because the Club did undeniably have to share its responsibility for security, once RSS was set up. Reasonable doubts were backed up by the irrational feeling of some members that anyone not directly employed by the Club might turn out to be a crook, and Wigg's deviousness only strengthened these feelings. The Club was, in fact, being offered a good deal, since it retained a substantial measure of control over the new body, while all its funds come from the Levy Board, but their perceptions of Wigg's personality and character prevented most members from seeing that the deal was good.

Some other achievements

There can be no doubt that Wigg did great things for racing, and that in the end the establishment of RSS was one of them. Another major achievement was to get criteria established for the fixture list, though at the cost of another battle with the Jockey Club. The criteria provided for at least two fixtures a day (even if courses had to be 'bribed' to arrange them on unpopular days), with races at quarter-hour intervals, so that people spending the afternoon in a betting shop would not lose interest between races. This pleased the bookmakers, because it increased turnover; it improved the Levy Board's finances, because increased turnover produced more levy; and it pleased the Treasury, because it produced more tax.

Perhaps Wigg would only have been willing to turn racing into a tax-raising machine for a Labour Chancellor. Be that as it may, his determination, unlike Harding, to maximise turnover (here lies the origin of MOLMOT – maximisation of levy through maximisation of turnover – the catchphrase of the big bookmakers a decade later), though popular with the bookmakers, naturally appalled the Home Office since in thrusting opportunities upon people to bet it ran directly against official thinking at that time and pointed up the Government's traditional dilemma. On the one hand it wanted the tax revenue, on the other it believed that people's propensity to bet should be allowed reasonable outlets but not encouraged to grow.

Wigg also succeeded, in 1970 (in association with Feilden and Lord Ward of Witley, the President of the National Greyhound Racing Association), in achieving a lower rate of tax for on-course punters than was paid in the betting shops. He was not against Betting Duty in principle, indeed he claimed that his brief from Wilson had been to raise both levy and tax, but he was against too high a duty or too abrupt increases in its rate, and led several deputations of protest to the Chancellor from 1969 onwards, taking with him the bookmakers and Feilden on at least one occasion. One of his reasons for advocating a moderate rate of tax was that increases would lead to illegal bookmaking, with consequent loss of revenue to the Board.

Wigg's other achievements included the modernisation of the Levy Board's scheme of subsidies to racecourses (though, again, he antagonised the Jockey Club by insisting that it, and Weatherby's, be subjected to an Organisation and Methods study), and the doubling of prize money during his period in office.

A major achievement was the success of his scheme to acquire United Racecourses, the owners of Epson and Sandown, and later to buy Kempton Park, which secured these 'lungs of London' for racing in perpetuity. United Racecourses came before the Levy Board on 28 April 1969, and the Board resolved to purchase the two courses and to borrow up to the equivalent of £3 million in Swiss francs for the purpose. Events then moved rapidly; the Home Secretary saw no objection in principle to a takeover bid, and on 2 May *The Times* reported that shareholders in United Racecourses had been offered 25s a share, and on 6 May it noted that a revised offer of 30s had been recommended to shareholders by the board of United Racecourses. This offer the shareholders accepted with alacrity, and to fund the takeover the Levy Board borrowed £1,500,000 in Deutschmarks. (As we have seen, Wigg had been assured in advance that Treasury consent would not be withheld.)

Shortly afterwards the Home Secretary had signed an Instrument of Approval, after great heart-searchings by the civil servants, who also consulted the Law Lords, over whether Parliament could possibly have intended the Board to own and operate racecourses. The Instrument allowed it to do so through a holding company; the Board must not itself take part in day-to-day management, nor acquire further courses unless they were viable propositions, as Sir Philip Allen informed the Board in a covering note on 4 June. By February 1970 all the shares in United Racecourses had been acquired, at a cost of £1,381,198, and in January 1971 the Board agreed in principle to the modernisation of Sandown, at a cost of £3 million. The Board realised that it could never recover such a sum, but saw the expenditure as being for the general good of racing.

In September 1970 Robinson offered Kempton to the Board for £800,000, the price he had paid for it, largely because he had been refused development permission. The Board's solicitors (Goodman Derrick) and accountants (Deloitte's) both advised that it was a good buy, and the Home Secretary gave his consent.

Conclusions

During Wigg's period, all the important ideas (except the Benson Report, which Wigg scotched) seem to have come from the Levy Board: the Jockey Club was either neutral or on the defensive. Wigg dominated the Joint Racing Board, even when Feilden was in the chair, just as he dominated his own Board, and did most of the talking at both. By maximising the levy he accelerated racing's trend from being primarily a sport to primarily an industry. It must sometimes have seemed, to friend and foe alike, that he was driven by demons, whispering that he had too little time for everything he wanted to do. He chose to do things the hard way, or perhaps was compelled by his strange mixture of prejudice and conviction, and he never let go. A good example is his last letter to *The Times* (16 September 1982), in which he complimented the Jockey Club, as he had done so often over the years, on its administration of the rules of racing. But the racing industry, he continued, in the words of the Rothschild Commission, was 'hopelessly addicted to subsidy' and this had come about because the Club 'has maintained positions which have enabled it to exercise decisive power without regard to the economic consequences'. The Levy Board in recent years had accepted the Club's domination and had spent its income on excessive grants towards prize money and interest-free loans to Jockey Club courses.

Expansion is the key-word to describe Wigg's years at the Levy Board and examples could be multiplied of the creative policies he pursued, often, it must be remembered, building on Harding's foundations. But the remaining question to ask is: 'Why did he do it?' What motivated this passionate out-pouring of energy and determination?

The answer is complex. It is true that, though he became an officer himself, he disliked the 'officer class'. He thought it morally wrong that racing should be run by a private club, so exclusive that it cut itself off from ninety-five per cent of the available pool of talent. But his most fervent belief was in the 'common man'. He was fond of quoting Colonel Rainboro's speech to the Levellers at Putney in the autumn of 1647: 'Really I think the poorest he that is in England hath a life to live as the richest he. And therefore truly I think, Sir, it is clear that every man that is to live under a government ought first by his own consent to put himself under that government; and I do think that the poorest man in England is not at all bound in a strict sense to that government that he hath not had a voice to put himself under.'[24] Wigg's was not a threatening kind of socialism. The case he had made to Bevin for the continuation of racing during the war was that a man must have *some* opportunity to exercise judgement and choice, and often the man who went to the factory with his spam sandwich in the morning, and worked there all day, had no other opportunity for decision than to choose the horse on which to stake his sixpence. If the Jockey Club could only have seen that a man who would say that could also be turned into an ally, it might have directed more of its energy towards the process of self-modernisation which was beginning in the mid-1960s, instead of letting it drain away in sterile self-defence.

Of course, it is tempting to see the clash between Wigg and the Jockey Club in symbolic terms. Wigg was a first-generation member of the power élite: in his lifetime he had wielded more power than most members of the Jockey Club. Against him stood the ranks of a much older élite (though many of its members came from families quite recently recruited to it), with power deriving from different sources. He could never come to terms with them as a group, though he could get on well enough with some individuals.

At the end of his life Wigg came to think of himself as a High-Tory socialist, whose guiding principles were duty and stability, just as they were of many of his enemies. But both he and they found it impossible to see the common ground because he, though a member of the Labour Party oligarchy, was at heart a man of the people.

Perhaps it is fitting that his posthumous bust has been placed in the Paddock area at Epsom, and not in the Members' Stand.

Notes

1 Wigg, Lord, *George Wigg*, London, 1972. Wigg's dissatisfaction with Mrs Williams is confirmed by Woodrow Wyatt [Chairman of the Tote since 1976) in his *Confessions of an Optimist*, London, 1985, p. 307.

2 R. Crossman, *The Diaries of a Cabinet Minister*, vol. II, London, 1976, p. 564, entry for 9 November 1967.

3 R. Crossman, *Diaries*, vol. III, London, 1977, p. 227, entry for 17 October 1968.

4 Jockey Club, *The Racing Industry: Report of the Committee of Inquiry* (Benson Report), London, 1968.

5 *The Sporting Life*, 28 February 1969.

6 Horserace Betting Levy Board, *Seventh Report: 1st April 1967 – 31st March 1968*, London, 1968, p. 10.
7 *The Economist*, 23 December 1967.
8 Betting, Gaming and Lotteries Act 1963.
9 *Daily Express*, 16 October 1968.
10 *The Sporting Life*, 28 February 1969.
11 *The Guardian*, 20 February 1969.
12 *The Times*, 10 December 1969.
13 *The Times*, 11 December 1969.
14 *The Times*, 22 December 1969, report 'Relations in racing reach the low tidemark' by Michael Phillips and another by a Staff Reporter.
15 356 *H.L.* Deb., cols. 656-7, 3 Febrary 1975.
16 Wigg revealed this strange fact in a letter to *The Times*, 4 November 1981, commenting on the paper's obituary to Sir Randle Feilden.
17 Racing Information Bureau, *Press Release*, 10 February 1970.
18 *The Times*, 11 February 1970.
19 Wigg mentioned this offer in the Centenary Supplement of the *Sporting Chronicle*, 29 May 1971.
20 796 *H.C.* Written Answers, cols. 405-6, 26 February 1970.
21 *The Sporting Life*, 17 April 1964.
22 *Joint Racing Board, Report of the Committee on the Scheme for the Suppression of Doping (The Paton Committee)*, London, 1971.
23 *The Sporting Life*, 22 February 1972.
24 Wigg, *George Wigg*, p. 355.

VI
The Wigg years / 2
The Tote and
the bookmakers' lobby

Relations with the Tote

Whilst Wigg's relations with the bookmakers improved, those with the Tote began quietly, but regressed through bad to catastrophic. The Tote's contribution for the seventh levy period (to 31 March 1969) was determined by the Board as one and a half per cent of on-course cash and on- and off-course credit turnover, the turnover of the off-course cash betting subsidiary being assessed for levy in the same way as the bookmakers'. The one and a half per cent was accepted by Sir Alexander Sim, the Tote's chairman, in March 1968, though he would have preferred to wait and see what the budget contained. His fears were well founded, as on 25 March Betting Duty, which had been first imposed at two and a half per cent the previous October, was increased to five per cent. The Tote's report for the year to 31 March 1968 records its fear that any increase in Betting Duty could seriously affect the turnover forecast in its estimates. This would be further affected by the new Selective Employment Tax (SET) promised for September 1968, which it thought would cost the Tote £150,000 in a full year. In 1967-8 the Tote had paid £922,832 Duty, and only £677,368 levy.

In 1969 Sim had not been able to produce firm proposals for the Tote's contribution under the eighth scheme, and the Levy Board again determined it at one and half per cent. Meanwhile, turnover had fallen significantly during the seventh period (1968-9); Betting Duty, at five per cent, had taken 24.89 per cent of the Tote's revenue and its levy contribution fell to £437,147, after which the Tote was £374,838 in deficit on the year's operations. Its eighth annual report pointed out that the 1969 Budget proposal of 'an excise duty on off-course betting premises based on three times the rateable value of those premises' as well as increased rates of SET, would still further affect results.¹ (Iain MacLeod had unsuccessfully moved an amendment to the Finance Bill, to exempt the Tote from the new Duty.)²

A paper produced by the Tote on 29 September 1969 shows that to cover SET and meet the two an a half per cent betting duty imposed in 1966, it had had to increase its deductions from fifteen per cent to twenty per cent of losing stakes. This increase had caused Wigg to write to James Callaghan, who was then First Secretary of State at the Department of Economic Affairs, on 20 October 1966, saying that he had pointed out to Roy Jenkins (Home Secretary) the political unwisdom of sanctioning the increase. Subsequent correspondence between officials shows that both the Home Office and the Department of Economic Affairs had indeed been consulted. However, the Home Secretary considered that he had no power to intervene, and in any case he saw no reason to do so.

Wigg's letter to Callaghan should be read in the context of a memorandum by Sir John Astor to Roy Jenkins, of which he sent a copy to Wigg for comment on 13 October 1966.³

Astor argued the case against opening betting shops for evening racing at present, in order not to upset the greyhound organisations. The only way, he believed, to please the Treasury, racing, and the public was to organise betting under Tote-only conditions. Having rehearsed the bookmakers' arguments against Tote monopoly, and his own counter-arguments, Astor concluded:

> The decision whether to open betting shops during evening racing should be taken against the background that eventually under a Tote Monopoly, it will be possible to regulate hours of betting, but that under present conditions it would be very difficult to enforce closing before racing.
> The claim of the bookmakers that Tote-only betting is unable to satisfy a large public demand for various types of betting cannot be substantiated.
> Tote-only betting would, in some respects, alter the pattern of betting, but once firmly established, and with nation-wide coverage and modern means of transmission and collation, the Tote would give a service which would be to the general benefit of all concerned.

The memorandum is important for three reasons. It helps to show that Wigg was closely involved with people in racing while he was Paymaster-General; it demonstrates that the Tote monopoly movement, in which Astor had played a leading part in the 1950s, was not dead. Finally, Astor's reference to modern means of transmission and collation, which now exist, show how far-sighted he was.

The Tote's paper continues that, in order to meet the increased five per cent Betting Duty, it had had to increase its deductions again, this time to 23.5 per cent on win, place and forecast pools, and 25 per cent on the jackpot, daily double and daily treble. Tote prices had become less competitive with those offered by the bookmakers and turnover had fallen from £40 million to £31 million since the Duty had come in. The trend, the paper went on, was bound to continue. 'From 1962 to 1967 the Tote produced approximately one-third of the Levy Board's income, though handling only about 1/25th of the country's betting', but thereafter its share of the levy had declined sharply.

As it was a non-profit making statutory body the Tote thought it should be exempt from Betting Duty. Further, since its activities were confined by statute to horse racing,the Board was unable to cover overheads when there was no racing, by accepting bets on dog racing, football, etc. The Tote had informed the Chancellor that its future was in jeopardy. It had also informed the Home Secretary, James Callaghan, whose Under-Secretary, Elystan Morgan, replied on 8 September (after a two-month interval) on behalf of the Home Secretary (who was 'unavailable'), that officials were urgently con-sidering these difficult and intractable problems and felt that there were no obvious solutions which would suit both the Tote and the Government. However, it was common ground that the Tote's activities must be enlarged.[4]

On 29 September, the same day as the Tote's paper, Chapman Pincher had reported in the *Daily Express* that the Tote Board was expected to resign after an emergency meeting to be held in London. The passage is interesting, because it illustrates how so relatively unimportant a body as the Tote might affect a Minister's fate: 'If this does happen, [i.e. if the Board resigns] it will create a serious situation for the Home Secretary, James Callaghan, as it could provide the Prime Minister with a final reason for dropping Callaghan when the Cabinet is reshuffled shortly. Callaghan was warned of the Tote's desperate situation last July, but did nothing. Mr Callaghan blamed the situation in Ulster for his inability to deal with the Tote's problems.'

On 6 November 1969 *The Sporting Life* reported that, after a meeting between Callaghan and the four Tote Board members, an official statement had been issued declaring the Government's 'determined aim that the Tote should continue and become economically viable'.

The contribution for the eighth period (1969-70) fell to £412,933 on a turnover of £27,528,880. Nevertheless, the Levy Board again set the contribution for the ninth period at one and a half per cent but, since the new appeal procedure introduced in the 1969 Act applied to the Tote as well as to the bookmakers, the matter was referred to the Home Secretary. He confirmed the one and half per cent but added that the amount might be reduced by some or all of any deficit occurring in that period. The Tote continued gloomy about its prospects and thought it would gain little from recent tax changes. The 1970 budget had repealed the new duty on off-course betting premises with effect from 30 April 1970, but had raised off-course Betting Duty to six per cent, though leaving it unchanged at five per cent on course.

From the Levy Board's papers it becomes clear that the Tote had not, in fact, been able to pay its contributions. On 28 August 1969, Wigg reported that he had written to Sim two days earlier, asking him when the debt of £864,295, due on 31 March 1970, would be paid, to which Sim replied on the same day that he had absolutely no idea. The discussion at the Board meeting appears to have been amicable and Wigg expressed understanding of the Tote's difficulties. He also tabled a draft letter to Sir Philip Allen, asking him to obtain the Home Secretary's views as to what should be done about the Tote debt. Either, he wrote, the Home Secretary must make a decision or 'my Board must seek a remedy through the Courts. The latter alternative is unthinkable, for the spectacle of one Statutory Body sueing another as a result of policies approved by the Home Secretary has only to be stated to be rejected.' Very little of this seems to have leaked into the Press, though the always well-informed Chapman Pincher did report in the *Daily Express* of 12 September 1969 that the Tote was in trouble, crushed by taxation, and asked whether it could pay its levy dues.

In the event the Home Secretary decided that the Tote should contribute nothing in the ninth period (1970-71). Nevertheless, the Levy Board again proposed one and half per cent for 1971/2; Arthur Taylor, the Tote's new chairman, thought the contribution should be nil; Wigg believed that one and a half per cent was fair, as the Tote could make a reasonable profit if only it were well run, and the Levy Board's and the Tote's accountants were in disagreement over projections of the Tote's expected loss in 1971-2. Wigg also argued that the Levy Board's demand would strengthen the Tote's hand in its continuing battle with the Home Secretary for legislation which would make it viable (such as the power to accept bets on other sporting events than horse racing). However, Taylor stuck to his guns and again appealed to the Home Secretary, who decided that the contribution to the tenth levy should be one and a half per cent, but should be payable only to the extent that the Tote's financial surplus for 1971-2 exceeded £250,000. This decision caused the Chairman of the Bookmakers' Committee to suggest that the tenth levy might prove difficult to collect from the bookmakers, as they would be unhappy about the Tote's advantageous position.

The Board continued to needle the Tote by yet again proposing one and a half per cent for the eleventh levy, 1972-3. Taylor again appealed, and the Home Secretary fixed the Tote's contribution at £75,000: this was presumably a nominal contribution, intended to save face all round. It may be that nobody expected it to be paid, since the Tote's report for 1971-2 shows that it had paid only £41,758 in 1970-1 and still owed £465,505.

On 1 May 1972 Taylor was succeeded as chairman by Lord Mancroft, whose father, by a strange chance, had been the Minister to see through the Commons the 1928 Act, setting up the Racecourse Betting Control Board.

There followed a major battle with the bookmakers to extend the Tote's powers by legislation. There was concern in the Home Office about the Tote's finances and the Home Secretary (Reginald Maudling) favoured a Tote monopoly, as did some of his officials. During Taylor's last year as chairman, the Government, with the Opposition's support, and despite some opposition in the Cabinet, had introduced a Bill[5] (which initially also had Wigg's support) whose most important provisions were to allow the Tote preferential rights in applying for betting office licences, that is, to operate as a bookmaker, without demonstrating to the licensing authorities that there was a local need; it would allow the Tote to take bets on other events than horse racing; and it would allow the Levy Board to lend money to the Tote and guarantee its debts.

Wigg had told the Home Office in August 1971 that he was in favour of legislation to bolster the Tote, though he had warned that any legislation would be controversial, because of the bookmakers' likely response. Nor, he pointed out, would allowing the Tote to operate as a bookmaker automatically make it viable. It lacked the necessary managerial skills,and bookmakers could lose money as well as make it. At present the Tote could sue for debts, which it would not be able to do as a bookmaker.

An alternative to bookmakers was essential, if only because bookmakers' terms were often bad. But the Tote should not be subsidised by the State: instead the Levy Board should be empowered to make grants to it, or to guarantee loans for schemes approved by the Secretary of State. With these new powers, and a new Board, the Tote could be viable within a year. Ideally, he thought then, and was to repeat in the future, the Tote would be handed over to private enterprise. Indeed, at one time he even seriously proposed that the Tote should buy William Hill's, the bookmakers, with money provided by the Home Office for the purpose.

Without the Tote, Wigg said, racecourse attendances would fall, and courses would suffer from the loss of the admission charges paid by its employees. It was not the case, as the Tote often complained, that it had been paying too much levy, but that the bookmakers had been paying too little.

The Times (9 February 1972), in an article by Christopher Morley, Financial Editor, said that the tottering Tote 'had appealed for a blood transfusion to the Labour government Home Secretary, Mr Callaghan, and its board had threatened to resign en bloc in the face of Labour inaction. But the Tote's future was not seriously in question until the brave new commercial world of Tory policy was ushered in [by Heath's 1970 Government], with its catch phrase of not supporting the lame ducks of business.'

The Tote's life was still at stake, Morely continued, no longer because of the 'lame duck' philosophy – though some backbenchers were still using that phrase in relation to the Tote – 'but because, in the face of a government decision to revitalise the Tote, the bookmakers have moved in for the kill'. The bookmakers feared that if the Tote had a preferential right to open betting shops (a right which the 1960 Act gave it for the first year of the scheme, but which it had not been able to exercise for lack of capital, as Taylor said in a letter to *The Times* of 11 February 1972), the licensing authorities would revoke hundreds of existing licences; nor, they argued, did they contribute to the levy in order to allow it to subsidise an inefficient competitor.

The bookmakers, with their expenses guaranteed up to a reputed £100,000 by Cyril Stein, chairman of Ladbroke's (though in fact the campaign cost much less) lobbied MPs energetically. The operation was expensive, since many of the bookmakers had to come specially to London, where they stayed at the Dorchester Hotel, and there were many MPs to be approached. Being relatively new to lobbying (though they had had some experience in 1969) and perhaps still bemused by their new-found legality, the bookmakers were sometimes thought to be a little heavy-handed, but their major coup was to retain Brian Walden, Labour MP for Birmingham, All Saints, as their Parliamentary adviser at a fee of £3,000 per year.[6] He was appointed in May 1972, quite late in the campaign, having already taken a prominent part in the Parliamentary proceedings. Though he was not a lifelong devotee of bookmaking, his interest in the subject had caused two leading bookmakers, independently of one another, to 'spot' him as a reliable adviser and he took the task very seriously, though he would not lobby MPs or arrange social events. Mark Carlisle, the Junior Minister at the Home Office responsible for the Bill, was in any case convinced by the bookmakers' arguments (he had the advantage of knowing Eric Barber, one of their leaders, from the Altrincham Conservative Association), but Walden added greatly to their effectiveness, and seems to have gained universal respect for the manner in which he presented their case.

The 1972 Act and the bookmakers' lobby

The new legislation was first discussed by the National Association of Bookmakers' General Committee on 21 November 1971. It was reported that the Bill had been given its First Reading in the House of Commons on 12 November, without any prior notice having been given to the bookmakers' representatives. (Nevertheless, the Bill can hardly have come as a complete surprise. It must have been known that there was grave concern in the Home Office about the Tote's finances, and it would have been reasonable to suspect that something was likely to be in the wind.) Stress was laid on the need for immediate action in view of the timetable for the Bill (Second Reading, 29 November, Report Stage in January or February 1972). There was unanimous agreement on specific opposition to clause 3, depriving licensing justices of their power to refuse licences to Tote betting shops on the grounds of want of public demand, and to clause 5, giving the Levy Board power to assist the Tote by way of grant, loan, guarantee or otherwise. There were also reservations about clause

1, authorising the Tote to act as a bookmaker and to bet on a wide variety of events, and fears were expressed about the vulnerability of racecourse bookmakers in the event of the Tote acting as a bookmaker on course.

It was suggested that bookmakers should withhold their levy payments unless an undertaking were given by the Levy Board that bookmakers' levy money would not be used to finance the Tote, but this was not agreed because it was thought that the threat of illegal action would rally support to the Government for its Bill. Nor was it agreed that the Bookmakers' Committee should refuse to consider the twelfth levy scheme until the Bill's implications had been discussed with the Home Secretary, because the twelfth levy was too far ahead to be used as a bargaining counter at this urgent stage. Nobody supported the proposal for 'withdrawal of labour' by bookmakers on-course. It was agreed that an immediate meeting with the Home Secretary should be requested, that action should be taken to induce Lord Wigg to declare his attitude towards the Bill and that a meeting with him should be requested before he attended a meeting of the Home Affairs Committee of the Labour Party in the following week. The NAB was also to request a meeting with the Home Affairs Committee and would lobby MPs at luncheons arranged for the purpose by letters from the National Association to all MPs and by members of affiliated Associations who were writing to their local MPs. Magistrates should be alerted to the significance to them of clause 3. Amendments to the Bill would be tabled and press publicity arranged.

The chairman was authorised to form a London-based Bookmakers' Action Committee to campaign against the Bill in whatever ways it thought best, and the Action Committee was to give all bookmakers' associations the opportunity to identify themselves with it, so that bookmakers could be seen to be speaking with one voice.

The BAC set to work with tremendous energy. On the very day it was set up, and again on 4 December, extensive information was sent out to MPs. The first priority was to persuade as many back-benchers as possible (many of whom might otherwise have had little or no interest in racing) that the Bill was inequitable. Thanks to the BAC's efforts, there was also considerable Press coverage, in general newspapers as well as the sporting press, and numerous letters were written to the press by punters. As early as 9 December 1971, Walter Terry, political editor of the *Daily Mail*, reported that powerful lobbying had produced considerable opposition to the Bill among Tory backbenchers and that Maudling was to argue out concessions with them at a private meeting on 13 December. This was a meeting of about fifty members of the 1922 Committee, at which, according to Simon Hoggart, Maudling said 'the Bill is no joy to me.'[7]

At the same time, the BAC was busy briefing bookmakers throughout the country on the threat poised by the Bill, and drumming up funds to pay for the campaign. Many bookmakers contributed to the fighting fund, but a sizeable number did not, either because their heads were in the sand or because they reckoned someone else could pay. The most conscientious bookmakers not only contributed but also wrote to and met their MPs. Much of the day-to-day work on this side – assembling briefs for the bookmakers – giving advice on approaches to MPs – telephoning – and placing advertisements in the appropriate journals – was carried out by Harold Hodgson, Secretary of both the NAB and the BAC.

The BAC gave a series of lunches for small groups of MPs during December and January. On the whole the results were good, though not all the press comment slavishly followed the bookmakers' line, and some press coverage was positively anti-bookmaker. For example, Joe Ashton, who was later a member of the House of Commons' Committee on the Bill, and consistently opposed the bookmakers, published an article headlined 'Why bookies are trying to eat their way into our hearts'.[8] He recorded, with disapproval, that every MP had been invited to a 'slap-up' meal. Tories had been asked to the Mirabelle Restaurant, at £7 per head, and Labour MPs to the Hyde Park Hotel, at only £4. (Hoggart adds that this discrimination provoked protests from Labour Members!) However, despite some MPs' misgivings over the bookmakers' heavy-handed approach, it was, on the whole, far from ineffective.

This phase of the campaign ended with two receptions at the House of Commons, on 1 and 2 February, and on the 2nd *The Sporting Life* carried an article by Gus Dalrymple with the cheering headline 'The Bookie fellers who fight for British justice'. The Bill's Second Reading followed immediately afterwards on 3 February, and it is hardly surprising that Maudling acknowledged the weight of feeling against the Bill, though he insisted that its spirit would be closely adhered to.

Introducing the Second Reading debate, Maudling said that the Bill's intention was to enable the Tote to compete fairly with the bookmakers. The huge increase in off-course betting in the 1960s had worked against the Tote, and the 'wholly unfair amount which the tote had been compelled to pay towards the levy in the early years had left it without any working capital to expand and modernise and make its operations more efficient.'[9]

However, while the Tote would be able to bet at fixed odds on any sporting event, its pool betting would be confined to horses, unless the Home Secretary's approval were obtained. Maudling had no intention of allowing the Tote to engage in football pools, but in other respects its commercial decisions would be left to its own Board. For example, until it had experience of bookmaking it might wish to make agency arrangements with bookmakers to manage its off-course operations.

As we have seen, Clause 3 released the Tote from the need to prove local demand before opening a betting shop. However, the Home Secretary accepted that the clause as drafted might appear to limit the powers of the licensing justices, and he undertook to introduce a Government amendment in Committee.

Maudling was obliged to acknowledge that clause 5, which empowered the Levy Board to assist the Tote by grants, loans, guarantees or otherwise, went too far, and would have to be thrashed out in Committee. He was, in other words, prepared to meet the bookmakers' fears that their money (which was, of course, really the punters' money collected by the bookmakers) would be used to sustain their ailing rival. They were, it is true, prepared to sustain it themselves, but in ways that they themselves could control.

There was a good deal of concern over a number of aspects of the Bill. Members, on both sides of the House, reproached the Home Secretary for having failed to consult bookmaking interests in advance, and pointed out that if he had only done so, he would have been spared the necessity to re-draft clauses 3 and 5. John Page's pithy comment that 'A nationalised bookmaker is likely to be as successful as a milk-drinking crocodile'[10] seems also to have reflected a substantial body of opinion. The failure to consult is, indeed, puzzling, and Maudling must have regretted it. It may have been caused by mistaken advice from officials that the Bill would be easy and non-controversial, and there may have been some misguided intention to try to pre-empt the bookmakers' counter-measures by taking them by surprise.

Brian Walden, who already took a great interest in the subject, long before he was retained by the bookmakers, joined in the attack on the Home Secretary: 'The amiability of his character and the plausibility of his manner distribute around him a rosy, enervating glow, which sometimes masks the contradictions of what he says'[11] Walden was 'a great sympathiser with the Tote', but he believed that it should not be allowed to bet at starting price, nor to use bookmakers as its agents. He was particularly opposed to the 'iniquitous' clause 3.

The bookmakers were not short of friends in the House, but their enemy, Joe Ashton, was also vocal, and commented very unfavourably, as he had done in the *Sheffield Star*, on their efforts to brainwash members with hospitality.

These, and numerous other, contributions at Second Reading showed that the Bill, to which Maudling had agreed because he had been told that it would be quick and easy, was going to be nothing of the kind.

Once Second Reading was over the bookmakers devoted much attention to the devising of amendments for the Committee stage. At the NAB General Committee on Sunday 27 February 1972 the chairman reported on the Action Committee, and said that support from bookmakers throughout the country had also been impressive. MPs had been intensively lobbied inside and outside the House, and meetings with the Home Secretary, the Under-Secretary of State at the Home Office, permanent Home Office officials and Tote Board representatives had been held. With the assistance of Cyril Stein and his firm (Ladbroke's), whose help from the beginning had been invaluable to the Action Committee, a memorandum supported by figures had been produced for the Home Office, to show how the Tote could be made viable with the help of bookmakers by popularising the jackpot, that offer being conditional on the Tote confining its operations to pool betting. The pressure had resulted in the Home Secretary promising to amend clauses 3 and 5. The most serious remaining threat was clause 1, which would make it legal for the Tote to bet at SP and Board prices on a racecourse.

The Action Committee had drafted amendments for the Committee Stage and Association members who were constitutents of MPs on the Standing Committee would be asked to see them. Another meeting was to be sought with the Home Secretary to discuss possible amendments and on 28 February there was to be a meeting with representatives of the Racecourse Association to enlist their help to defeat any move to introduce racecourse betting shops run by the

Tote.

The bookmakers must have been greatly encouraged in their already vigorous campaign when Wigg came out against the Bill. He announced this change of heart at the Levy Board on 20 March 1972, and 'went public' in an interview with *The Sporting Life* on 29 March. At the Board he had said that it would be wrong to allow the Tote to operate as a bookmaker, and to write off its debt to the Board. In *The Sporting Life* he amplified these points, and said that he had at first contemplated resigning in order to fight the Bill in the Lords, but had then decided to talk to *The Sporting Life* instead, having informed the Home Secretary, to whose generosity in raising no objection he paid tribute.

He believed that the Tote could not be run as a statutory body. Either it should be wound up or handed over to private enterprise: in that case all bets, whether placed on or off course, should be taxed at the on-course rate. He went on that the Tote was already losing £250,000 a year: the Bill would not be help to a lame duck: 'It is an attempt to inject life into a dead duck.' Bookmaking required good management (which, by implication, the Tote had not got). The Bill's purpose might be to give the Tote freedom, but that could well turn out to be 'the kind of freedom suffered by the canary when it is out of its cage and finds itself attacked by the sparrows'. The Tote would presumably open betting shops in lucrative areas, where there were ten shops already, all competing with each other. But when the canary appeared, the ten sparrows would join forces against it. If the Tote improved its terms of trade to compete with them it would go bust; if it did not, it would get no business.

In those days Wigg still believed that the right way to finance racing was through the levy, which he always insisted was punters', not taxpayers', money.[12] Later, as we have seen, he changed his mind, and decided that the levy was a tax, and undesirable, because hypothecated. Formerly, he had been in favour of the Board making loans to the Tote, but in his *Sporting Life* interview he made it clear that he was now opposed to anything of the kind: 'there was a vast difference between making a loan to a venture that was ultimately going to prove a success and providing money collected with the goodwill of the bookmakers for a venture which he believed could never pay.'

The bookmakers' pressure continued in the period immediately before the committee stage. Late in March the bookmakers had written to Francis Pym, the Government Chief Whip, complaining that the Committee's composition was biased against them, and had naturally received a dusty answer. On 11 April Michael Rolfe (who – under his real name of L.V. Wyles – was a member of the Bookmakers' Action Committee) reported in *The Sporting 'Life* that the Magistrates' Association saw no reason why the Tote should not apply for betting office licences in the same way as bookmakers. The Association had passed a resolution deploring the Government's amendment to clause 3. This amendment brought back the 'demand' provision, but only to the extent that the Tote could be refused a licence if demand were already satisfied in the area by other offices operated by the Tote.

The Committee sat fifteen times, from 20 April to 22 June 1972, though it could have covered the ground in half the time but for Arthur Lewis's interminable speeches and endless amendments, which occasionally showed a flash of political insight but were very often inconsistent, off the point, and valueless as part of a serious inquiry. He was given an extraordinary amount of rope by the Committee Chairman, but Mark Carlisle rebuked him several times. On one occasion he said: 'I noticed that at one stage during his speech, he said that he had persuaded himself that he was right in what he was saying. What I am not sure of is whether that is a compliment to the power of his oratory or whether we ought to sympathise with the standard of his intelligence.'[13] At the final sitting, Carlisle insisted that Lewis had not changed the form of the Bill one iota.

It is not clear why Lewis filibustered as he did, unless he hoped to prolong the sittings so long that the Bill would not pass during the current session. Like everyone else, he knew that the legislation was urgent, if the Tote were to be kept alive at all, and he may have judged that the Government's timetable would be too tight for it to be reintroduced during the following session. In any case, his behaviour must have seemed a high price to pay for democracy.

From the beginning the Minister, Carlisle, and the bookmaker's main champion, Walden, adopted consistent, though flexible positions. At the Committee's second session, on 25 April 1972, hints of a deal began to emerge. Walden said that the bookmakers would not object to the Tote being given preferential tax treatment if it dropped its aspiration to enter the SP market and confined itself to pool betting. W. R. Rees-Davies introduced a new concession, when he said that the Tote needed at least the opportunity to open on-course betting shops (the NAB had been running them for some years and passing the profit to the racecourses after deductions for its own administrative expenses), and that 'as part of the general deal, the bookmakers do not object to giving the Totalisator this opportunity on the course.' (This concession had been suggested by Charles Layfield, and seems to have been one of the decisive factors in converting Ministers to the bookmakers' point of view.) The real difficulty, Rees-Davies went on, was clause 3, because demand was already totally satisfied. He doubted whether the Tote had the necessary expertise for bookmaking, but could see no reason in principle why it should not enter that field by buying an interest in an existing firm.

On 1 May Lord Mancroft succeeded Arthur Taylor as Chairman of the Tote. Mancroft had declared himself firmly in favour of a Tote monopoly in debates in the House of Lords on 19 May 1966 and 13 March 1967. He had insisted not only that a Tote monopoly would benefit the industry but also that, although there were no more crooks among bookmakers than among butchers or bakers, the criminal elements in racing could not operate without bookmakers. As he put it in 1967: 'Most of all the departure of the bookies would be a great advantage to the chief constables' and 'The simple method is to nationalise the betting offices and put the bookmakers' staff in to run the Tote monopoly'.[14]

Mancroft's appointment was obviously not popular with the bookmakers. Nor was Wigg pleased. They were already on poor terms, partly because of Mancroft's remark about the Royal Army Education Corps, and partly because as a junior Minister at the Ministry of Defence, he had sometimes had to refuse Wigg information which he very much wanted. Relations were not improved by Wigg's attempt to vet Mancroft's annual report, nor by a confusion over the Tote's accounts for 1971-2, when Mancroft had snubbed Wigg by refusing to give any information without first consulting his Board.

The question of the Tote's debt also continued to come before the Levy Board. Wigg thought the Tote's headquarters in Euston Road should be sold and its operations concentrated with those of Tote Investors Ltd in New Bridge Street. Euston Road had not been used to capacity for a long time, and the sale proceeds could have been put towards the debt to the Board, though Wigg said nothing could be done until the Tote Bill was through.

Wigg's feud, as it became, with the Tote, naturally continued after he had moved to BOLA. One of his shots had been prepared long in advance, for, whilst still at the Board, he arranged for the terms of reference of the Select Committee on Nationalised Industries to be extended to include such bodies as the Tote; it duly covered it in its second report[15] which in the event was broadly favourable.

On 11 May the line-up of forces in the Committee on the Tote Bill crystallised with Walden's declaration of a probable financial interest: 'I shall probably be associated with the National Association of Book-makers. . .'[16] He amplified the bookmakers' readiness to co-operate with the Tote: 'The bookmakers' point of view is clearly that they are prepared to ensure the viability of the Tote by all means which stop short of the Totalisator becoming an SP bookmaker. Similarly, the Tote has no reason to wish to diminish the number of book-makers, least of all the number of bookmakers on course, because the Totalisator does not want a weak on-course market.'[17]

At the next sitting (18 May) Carlisle moved towards the book-makers' position by reminding the Committee that the Bill merely gave power to the Totalisator to become a bookmaker if it wished. As the sittings progressed, Carlisle seems to have become increas-ingly doubtful about the wisdom of the Tote's entering bookmaking, though of course he never said so in so many words.

Walden saw little merit in the Government's amendment to clause 3, which would have allowed the Tote one shop in an area before having to prove demand, and would no longer have allowed any shop to be opened simply with a Certificate of Consent from the Levy Board. As Walden put it: 'The Minister is giving the nursemaid's defence of her illegitimate child – that it is only a little one.'[18] In response to a question from Rees-Davies, and with the Minister's permission, Walden went on to give some details of what the NAB was prepared to do for the Tote, though the confidentiality of the proceedings precluded his indicating the Tote's response. The book-makers, he said, were prepared to give a guarantee to operate their jackpot for the Tote; they were prepared to turn over the profit from on-course betting shops, for the racecourse and Tote to divide between themselves; but they were not prepared to allow the Tote into SP betting. This was not because they expected their profits to suffer, but because they feared what some future Government might do to make the Tote viable, if a Conservative Government was pre-pared to go so far as this Bill.[19]

Walden and Carlisle were agreed that a meeting between the Tote and the NAB was urgently necessary. Carlisle confirmed that he had passed on to the Tote the NAB proposals which Walden had brought to him, and emphasised that the negotiations themselves were no responsibility of the Home Office. (It does, however, seem extraordinary that no direct negotiations had been arranged, when one remembers that the NAB had made its initial proposals as long before as the previous December.)

On 23 May Carlisle showed himself even more conciliatory than hitherto, and hinted that if the Tote decided that it could remain viable as a pool betting agency, it might not need clause 3. In that case the Minister would consider writing safeguards into the Bill with regard to the implementation of clause 3 and was 'quite prepared to look at this matter again on Report in the light of any developments that may occur between now and then'.[20]

Thus the stage was set for the Government's eventual climb-down, whereby clause 3 was passed but its coming into force made subject to a Commencement Order, which has never been made.

But the deal was not yet clinched, and Walden feared that the Tote might be dragging its feet so that it would get its Bill, and thereafter be able to disregard the bookmakers' offer and go into SP betting on its own account. This led him to show his teeth: if the Tote really was unwilling to negotiate seriously, he would not be deliberately obstructive, but, on the other hand, the Bill could not be guaranteed an easy passage in either House. Walden was able to make play with the fact that he was also a member of a much more important Committee, that on the Finance Bill. An amendment to that Bill had been tabled which would improve the Tote's tax position, but Walden was no longer in a mood to help: 'I was sympathetic to that Amendment and intended to speak to it, but I shall not hand the Tote that and this Bill on a plate without negotiation.'[21]

Carlisle was able to confirm that 'full and frank' discussion had taken place between the Tote and the bookmakers, and that a further meeting had been arranged, which assurances no doubt placated Walden.

Indeed, although the Bill had not been much altered in its marathon Committee stage, the bookmakers were now in an extremely strong negotiating position. A working party of bookmakers and Tote representatives was at last set up late in June to look in detail at ways in which the Tote could be helped, still on the assumption that it would not move into bookmaking. The working party was chaired by Gordon Wasserman, an able young civil servant, who had been brought in to work on the Bill when it began to run into difficulties.

Wasserman was convinced, having visited New York to study pool betting there, that an efficiently run Tote could live off pool betting, if it played on its strength, which was its ability to make long odds more frequently than could the bookmakers. The bookmakers also, of course, wanted to confine the Tote to pool betting, but the Tote itself was still determined to move into the SP market, partly because the Jockey Club had encouraged its bookmaking ambitions and thereby emphasised its inability to make money otherwise. Thus the least co-operative members of the working party were the Tote's representatives.

The bookmakers were ready to subsidise the Tote, or to run its operations on an agency basis, for an annual fee to the Tote of at least £1 million. This would not have been an act of charity, since instead of laying off among themselves, they could have saved staff and reduced their commercial risks by laying off into the Tote pool. (If a bookmaker stands to lose a considerable amount if a certain horse wins, he 'lays off' the risk by backing that horse with another bookmaker, or with the Tote.) They also believed that a properly-run Tote could make really large profits, comparable with those of the French *tiercé* and they would have been prepared to invest in the necessary electronic equipment, with a terminal in any betting shop which wished to have it.

Cyril Stein, and the other bookmakers on the working party, did their best for the Tote, but achieved little, probably because, as Walden had surmised at the Committee stage, the Tote was not prepared to forgo SP betting, and so would not negotiate seriously until after it had achieved its Bill. Once the Bill had received the Royal Assent on 2 October, the working party seems to have fallen apart.

However, the bookmakers achieved victory for themselves, since their readiness to support the jackpot and allow the Tote to operate betting shops on course seems finally to have persuaded Ministers to make the dreaded clause 3 subject to a Commencement Order. The Tote's financial behaviour may also have told against it.

An example was given by William Fanshawe, who pointed out in the *Sporting Chronicle* on 2 August 1972, under the headline 'Money Well Spent', that the on-course tax had just been cut from five per cent to four per cent and the Tote had discovered that its forecast loss for 1971/2 had turned into a reasonable profit. Yet instead of using the tax cut to consolidate its financial position the Tote was passing the benefit straight on to the punter, by reducing its deductions from the pool by one per cent.

After all this extra-Parliamentary activity, the debates on Report and Third Reading in the House of Commons were an anticlimax. Carlisle, in introducing the amended clause 1, said that the Tote's better results and the lower on-course tax made Levy Board subsidies unnecessary. However, the Board would still have power to assist the Tote's operations on racecourses where it could not expect to be viable, and the Tote's debt to the Board would be written off. Walden, who had been in touch with the Minister in the interval since the Committee stage, declared his financial interest, and said that the new clause 1 was satisfactory to the bookmakers. He congratulated Carlisle for having facilitated talks between them and the Tote, but other members rather spoilt the cosy atmosphere. Arthur Davidson, who had led for the Opposition in Committee, pointed out that the result was a victory for the bookmakers, however much Carlisle and Walden played it down, and J. R. Kinsey asserted that the House owed it to Arthur Lewis that the Tote's good results had become known while the Committee was sitting. 'The Hon. Gentleman proves that it is a long ill wind that blows nobody any good.'[22]

Carlisle was unable to give details of the Tote's accounts, since they had not yet been laid before Parliament, but understood that they would show a modest profit. He also denied knowledge of any agreement between bookmakers and the Tote Board. Indeed, there appears to have been none. What had impressed Ministers was the bookmakers' readiness to make concessions, rather than the Tote's acceptance of them.

Carlisle gave Walden further, relatively minor, concessions and then moved on to clause 3. He justified the Commencement Order on the grounds that, first, the current discussions with the bookmakers might lead the Tote no longer to want clause 3, and secondly, that it would be wrong to give the Tote a statutory advantage over other bookmakers if it chose to go into the SP market via an agency agreement. However, he added, if it decided that it could not do without that market, and could not make a suitable agreement, so that it needed to go it alone, a future Home Secretary might activate clause 3. Thus the Minister was giving the Tote a broad hint that it would be well advised not to try to set up its own SP betting shops, a warning which it chose to ignore.

Norman Fowler, who himself had written a Bow Group pamphlet on betting,[23] quoted the influential Revd Gordon Moody, of the Churches' Council on Gambling, on the possibility of an agency agreement: 'such an agreement could give bookmakers a hold over the [Tote] Board. If I were a bookmaker I think I would not want the Totalisator to die, so long as it remained a nice little thing, and I could pat it on the head and, while pretending to feed it, take a regular supply of titbits out of its mouth.'[24] Fowler asserted that the Government's emphasis had shifted from competition between Tote and bookmakers to co-operation between them, a point which both Walden and Carlisle answered unconvincingly, and believed that there should therefore be an overarching control mechanism for gambling.

In his winding-up speech, Carlisle said that the Bill's main point was clause 1, which allowed the Tote to operate as a bookmaker, as well as to conduct pool betting, on any sporting event, at home or abroad. (He could hardly say anything else, now that so much of the original Bill had been lost.) He concluded with another, under-standably sour, attack on Arthur Lewis: 'All that his opposition has done is to cause a great deal of unnecessary work for many people who might well have been spared it.'[25]

Conclusion

The emasculation of the Tote Bill was indeed a famous victory for the bookmakers. It illustrates what can be done by a lobby which has widespread grass-roots support, combined with effective central organisation, pertinacity, money and good advice. Not only could the bookmakers mobilise their members throughout the country, but they understood the importance of bringing pressure to bear on the Government, and of doing so at several levels.

They created interest in their case and opposition to the Bill among backbench MPs on both sides of the House; they briefed Members extensively and showed them hospitality, too much of it for some of their targets; they went on deputations to the Home Secretary (Maudling) and the Minister of State at the Home Office (Carlisle); they had a seemingly endless supply of well-drafted Amendments; and in Brian Walden they employed a first-class advocate. Their campaign is a text-book example of how a determined group can achieve its ends.

Harold Macmillan once said – 'never take on the Roman Catholics or the miners'. He might have added – 'never take on the book-makers'.

Notes

1 Horserace Totalisator Board, *Report and Statements of Account for the Year 1 April 1968 to 31 March 1969*, London, 1969, para. 13.
2 *The Sporting Life*, 12 June 1969.
3 Sir John Astor has kindly allowed me to quote this document.
4 Exchange of letters reported in*The Sporting Life*, 30 September 1969.
5 The Horserace Totalisator and Levy Boards Bill, 1972.
6 Walden's initial contract was for £3,000 per year, for five years. It was later changed, by mutual consent, to £5,000 per year on an annual basis, instead of a five-year term.
7 Simon Hoggart, 'A fall at the committee fence', *The Guardian*, 11 May 1974.
8 *The Sheffield Star*, 18 February 1972.
9 830 *H.C. Deb.*, col. 700, 3 February 1972.
10 *Ibid.*, col. 783.
11 *Ibid.*, col. 742.
12 See, e.g., Wigg's letter to *The Times*, 15 March 1971.
13 *H.C. Deb.*, Standing Committee G, col. 294, 11 May 1972.
14 281 *H.L.Deb.*, col. 18, 13 March 1967.
15 Select Committee on Natonalised Industries, *Second Report: the Horserace Totalisator Board* H.C. 344, 4 May 1977.
16 *H.C. Deb.*, Standing Committee G, col. 288, 11 May 1972.
17 *Ibid.*, col. 297.
18 *Ibid.*, col. 336, 18 May 1972.
19 *Ibid.*, cols. 342-3.
20 *Ibid.*, cols. 390 and 392, 23 May 1972.
21 *Ibid.*, col. 555, 15 June 1972.
22 842 *H.C. Deb.*, col. 1385, 7 August 1972.
23 N. Fowler, *A 'Policy for Gambling*, Bow Group Memorandum, London, December 1967.
24 842 *H.C. Deb.*, col. 1421, 7 August 1972.
25 *Ibid.*, col. 1439.

VII
The Jockey Club

The Jockey Club's origins are lost in the mists of the eighteenth century. According to the leading authority on its history, it was first mentioned in print in 1752. Originally it was no more than a group of noblemen and gentlemen who were interested in racing (in those days the word 'jockey' had not acquired its modern meaning, but signified an owner as much as a rider).[1] Gradually it extended its control from its headquarters at Newmarket to cover the whole country, and became the supreme power in the racing world. It was, and remains, author and administrator of the rules and has power, if not of life and death, then certainly of livelihood or indigence, over anyone professionally engaged in the sport. It may also, by 'warning off', forbid undesirables, who may have no professional connection with the sport, to set foot on any racecourse.

The social composition of the Club has not changed very markedly since the eighteenth century. The members are, on the whole, upper class, and many are rich, and they are still served by Weatherby's, the firm of hereditary 'civil servants' which they have employed as agents for over two hundred years.

But, fortunately, not everything has remained unaltered. One event from which one might date the change in the Jockey Club's thinking, which has indubitably occurred (however much its critics may insist the contrary), is its appointment, as far back as 1942, of a committee (the Racing Reorganisation Committee) presided over by Lord Ilchester: 'To consider the whole future of racing in general, and in particular with reference to the encouragement of Owners and the greater comfort and convenience of the Public'.[2]

The report, presented on 3 February 1943, was wide-ranging and far-sighted, but on most of the recommendations action followed very slowly, and on some not at all.

Shortage of money may in part explain racing's failure to follow through. Paradoxically, however, even if there had been plenty of money, the Jockey Club and the racecourses might not have felt any particular need to spend it. The racecourses, as Roger Mortimer has pointed out,[3] seem to have been quite content to subject their patrons to what would nowadays be seen as intolerable conditions, and many of the leading members of the Jockey Club were so rich that they had not yet realised that racing's underlying financial condition was unsound.

This false sense of security was in a way understandable, because after the war racing was extremely popular. After the years of austerity, people were grateful for any leisure amusement, and racing was one of the few available. It was less easy to realise that, as prosperity spread, education improved, and leisure opportunities proliferated, the public no longer needed to accept the poor conditions on racecourses. At the same time some big owners and breeders, pushed by such men as Lord Crathorne and Lord Kilmany, were becoming worried that British racing was losing its traditional supremacy and being replaced by the French, who were winning British races and buying some of the best British bloodstock, as well as having much higher prize money than existed in Britain. It was only by the mid-1950s that the anxieties of these different interests, racecourses on the one hand, and owners and breeders on the other, crystallised into a general feeling that something must be done about racing's cash flow. Without racing's post-war popularity notice must surely have been taken more promptly of Ilchester's recommendations.

The Ilchester Committee had realised, as long ago as 1943, that there was strong demand for change. There were five interests to be considered, those of the breeder, the owner, the public, the racecourse executives and the race horse. All were dominated by the question of finance.

The report acknowleged that racing had become less attractive to the general public than in countries where the sport was newer. Taking first the breeders, the Committee rejected breeders' premiums – 'we are unable to support these bonuses' – taking the view that the breeder should be satisfied with the market price at the time of sale (the suggestion had been that a percentage of prize money should be allocated to the breeders of all winners). The Committee thought owners made too great a contribution to stakes, and that their other expenses must be reduced. For example 'The closing of entries long before the time of running entails many wasted entries', 'Prizes are at present built up largely from contributions by the owners of horses' and they believed that if an objection to a winner or placed horse had been upheld, under Rule 173 (as it then was: the numbering has since changed), the offender should not necessarily be placed last: these are all familiar staples of the 1980s! They also recommended transport allowances, similar to those made by the Racecourse Betting Control Board in the past, and that they should cover travel by road as well as rail, a reminder that in those days horses very frequently did travel by rail. Presents to trainers and jockeys should be standardised at five per cent for each: to give more would become an offence (except in the Classics), unless permission had been obtained from the Stewards of the Jockey Club, in races with not less than £1,000 added for the winner.

The Committee recognised that owners had a right to free admission to the Members' Stand, and added the admirable idea that an owner whose entrance fees and forfeits in any year amounted to, say, £200, should be entitled to a season ticket for the following year, which would admit him free to all Members' Enclosures, whether he had a runner or not. That idea came to nothing (though big owners do get some concessions from the Racecourse Association), but the Committee's suggestions that the Stewards would benefit from closer contact with owners and that some appropriate machinery be set up was followed by the foundation of the Racehorse Owners' Association, in 1945, only two years after the report. Thus the ROA was in a sense the child of the Jockey Club. Yet the Association has always been looked at a little askance by some members of the Club, perhaps because the necessity of its existence is all too lively a reminder that ownership now spreads far beyond the original magic circle.

Turning to the public, Ilchester made a recommendation which has often been repeated since, without result, namely that a special enclosure should be made for bookmakers between the Members' and the Grand Stand, and between the Grand Stand and the Silver Ring. (The Silver Ring is the next enclosure to the Grand Stand, which in turn is next to the Members' Stand. It is furthest away from the winning post and therefore cheaper.) The view from the cheaper stands should be improved: 'in these days of mechanical appliances for moving earth, artificial embankments do not constitute the same difficulty as they did in the past.'

The Committee was concerned about Tattersall's Committee's

jurisdiction over disputed bets and thought that it should be confined to bookmakers on course. 'It matters little to the Starting Price bookmaker whether he is warned off the Turf or not' and 'these Starting Price offices make no contribution to racing'.

The Committee hoped that admission charges could be reduced. Grand Stand admission charges varied enormously; before the increase in Entertainment Tax in 1942 they ranged from 15s (including tax) to £1 15s. It was essential to maintain 'a just proportion' between the charges for the various enclosures: 'To make admission to the Grand Stand too cheap would be to flood it with the more noisy and undesirable elements who now confine themselves to the cheaper stands. This would at once put a stop to any hope of attracting the type of public for whom we are hoping to cater by more comfortable surroundings and conditions.' That remark must ring bells with many modern racecourse committees and managers!

The Committee also, rather diffidently, suggested evening racing, which might attract a new public, and it recommended a sliding scale of allowances for apprentices. But it rejected overnight declarations. There were obvious disadvantages to owners and trainers. Moreover, it would encourage the stay-at-home backer – 'a person who contributes nothing to the business of racing nor to its finance'.

The Committee again showed its openmindedness in recording the suggestion that owners' transport overheads might be reduced if there were seven races a day. The Committee had no definite opinion, but thought the idea worth considering.

Almost every paragraph of the report strikes a chord in the mind of today's reader. For example, it looked closely at watering, a subject 'upon which opinions are sharply divided, but it is admitted on all sides that to give satisfactory results this must be done with great care. . . the whole course should be watered evenly, both side to side, and for its whole length.' It is still a matter on which opinions are sharply divided; one has only to recall some trainers' protests about watering at the Curragh before recent Irish Derbies.

In many respects the Committee was ahead of its time: it realised that racecourse management was often poor, though it did not go into the subject in any detail, and the Jockey Club did not study it systematically until it appointed Sir Rex Cohen's committee in November 1968.[4] In others it was more in tune with the spirit of the age: for example, it did not recommend any increased liaison between Weatherby's and the press. 'There are occasions, however when delays are unsuitable; whilst in others, the uncertainties of the laws of libel intervene to make explanations impossible.' (The reference must be to disciplinary cases.) Nor was the Committee at all keen on loud-speakers on courses, except for announcements of jockeys, etc. before a race, and the result and prices afterwards. 'It was made clear to us however, that any form of audible broadcast during the progress of a race can only lead to confusion, a point on which the judges are unanimous.'

The Committee thought 'particular care must be taken in the appointment of local stewards', and that stewards' secretaries should be given more powers, 'now that they have proved their worth.' They did not, however, go so far as to say that they should have a vote. Forty years later that is still a burning question.

In the section on the race horse the committee argued against valuable races for two-year-olds early in the season, which 'not only tempted an owner to force a two year old, but encouraged breeders to aim at producing sharp and early horses, against the best interests of the breed of race horse generally'. Yet again, the Committee touched on a seemingly eternal theme, when it urged that owners be encouraged to keep horses longer in training, 'by the provision of races with substantial prizes for horses of four years and upwards'.

Perhaps the most important section of this seminal report was that on finance. The Committee believed that some racecourses, which it did not name, were redundant and should be closed. It noted that most courses were owned by shareholders who expected dividends, or public bodies which expected some contribution to their funds. Only five of the forty seven courses under the Jockey Club's jurisdiction (jumping courses were controlled by the National Hunt Committee) were run on a non-dividend basis. The course whose whole surplus could be put back into racing was the ideal: 'We feel that something can be arranged on these lines for the attainment of our objects. We seek to acquire on fair terms the control of a selected number of racecourses which would be taken over. We have examined the organisation which would be necessary to operate such an undertaking, and are perfectly satisfied that it will fit readily into the present system of horse racing.' In that passage (commonly attributed to Lord Portal) lies the germ of Racecourse Holdings Trust, through which the Jockey Club now owns nine race-courses (including two at Newmarket) on a non-profit-making basis.

Lord Ilchester's report gives a sharp insight into a bygone world.

But it is also the same world as our own, where many of the issues are still much the same. We may be accustomed now to loudspeakers and helicopters, but watering still excites passions. What is remarkable about the report is that it covered, in only twenty pages, such a wide range of subjects. There is nothing surprising in Lord Ilchester and his colleagues having authoritative views on two-year-old races – that kind of question was traditionally the real business of the Jockey Club, and so remained for another twenty years. But the committee also addressed itself, with equal care and seriousness, to such questions as catering; it realised that the general public must be considered, and it saw that the end of a major war (still over two years ahead when it reported) would be the right time to make fundamental changes. In helping the Jockey Club to make the transition into the post-war world, it began the process of coaxing it into the twentieth century.

Immediately after the war, pressure for modernisation came, not from the mass of ordinary racegoers but from press men whom most members of the Jockey Club hesitated to regard as social inferiors.

There was an influx of reporters who were no longer prepared to kowtow to the Jockey Club, and who sometimes criticised the rulers of racing in a way they had never experienced before. 'Suddenly,' one of them recalls, 'the press room was full of Old Etonions', whose shared class background, coupled with enough money to tide them over if an aggrieved member of the Jockey Club tried to get them dismissed by their editors, meant that they could treat the Club on equal terms.

Some of them, like Clive Graham and the Gilbeys, had started before the war, but they were joined by such men as Philip Clifford (who had been a part-time racing writer before the war) and Tom Nickalls. The latter started work on *The Sporting Life* even before he left the Army, and served on it with distinction until 1968. He was, and remains, a generous man who never picked quarrels, but he had been a brother officer of Lord Willoughby de Broke and at school with many members of the Jockey Club, and saw no reason to pull his punches. He had also ridden horses all his life and had a formidable knowledge of breeding.

It was because men like Nickalls could not possibly be dismissed as ignorant, nor as having class 'chips on their shoulders', that the Jockey Club took notice of them, however reluctantly, just as it did of Harding in the 1960s. Their influence cannot be quantified, but they certainly helped to acclimatise the Club to the new egalitarianism of the post-war world.

The Jockey Club in the 1950s

Though change was in the air, neither Ilchester's report, nor Old Etonion press men, brought it about rapidly, and the Jockey Club in the 1950s retained its essential characteristics of two centuries earlier. It was a group of friends, many of whom were substantial owners and breeders, who not only thought they were the natural rulers of racing but actually were. Nobody now would devise such a body from scratch, but after two hundred years of evolution the Club understandably did not consider any other body taking its place. Indeed, it would still be hard to devise an alternative.

There was no reason in those days to 'broaden the base' of membership. That idea was first seriously floated in the report of a committee chaired by Lord Howard de Walden in 1964. There was no need to court the public by taking in people from lower social classes, nor to find members who had particular skills in such fields as finance, the law, or accountancy. Nor was there any need to cultivate Members of Parliament: in that much simpler world the Club could rely on automatic access to both Houses of Parliament, especially the Lords, and virtually complete coverage of the élites that governed British society. Membership was the ultimate social accolade, and still seems to be the only present for 'the man who has everything' (and a few women since December 1977).

What members knew about was horses, and how to frame races to test them, and the administration of the Rules of Racing. They had an especial affection for their own courses at Newmarket, and many of them enjoyed betting with bookmakers. There was no real doubt about their overall integrity, though some members smiled privately at the peccadilloes of their friends.

However, the Jockey Club was slow to press for a new financial deal for racing. It is true that it had played a large part in setting up the Racecourse Betting Control Board in 1928, and Lord Ilchester's report had shown that much more money was needed, but even in the early 1950s it still seems not to have realised how bad the industry's condition was, and therefore had not promoted its needs in any detail. Perhaps part of the explanation of this early lack of vigour also lies, as one senior member has suggested, in the fact that most influential members of the Club were at that time very rich, and regarded breeding and racing horses as other people might regard breeding labradors. They felt no incentive to get a higher level of prize money, and some members may have been inhibited by their attachment to betting with bookmakers from pressing for a Tote monopoly. Such a solution, for which, as have seen, Sir John Astor and some other MPs had been pressing energetically since 1951, would otherwise have been the obvious target, especially as the Jockey Club had for so long been accustomed to the Racecourse Betting Control Board as the source of such outside subventions as racing needed.

However, as we saw in Chapter II, by the mid-1950s it had become clear that the Government intended to legalise off-course cash betting, and the idea soon became widespread that the bookmakers would then be required to make a 'financial contribution to racing'. (The word 'levy' did not immediately come into general use.) The Jockey Club thereupon began negotiations with the Home Office and the bookmakers, in which it made it clear that it would not be satisfied unless *all* off-course betting (on horses) was made subject to levy. In due course the Peppiatt Committee accepted the principle of the Levy, though it thought racing could make do with £1,250,000 annually, rather than the Jockey Club's suggested £3 million, and the Horserace Betting Levy Act was passed in 1961.

Autocracy and Democracy

The exclusiveness and autocracy of the Jockey Club have been widely commented upon, but it was also, in its own way, democratic. The Club was small, with only about fifty-seven members, six of them honorary, in 1967, just before the amalgamation with the National Hunt Committee, and the business was straighforward enough for all important issues to be presented to the members at general meetings, of which there were then eleven a year. Many members took no very active part in the meetings (Lord Howard never spoke at all until he became Senior Steward) but if the Stewards sensed that the feeling of the meeting was against a proposal, they would withdraw it. Now, with only six meetings a year, the greatly increased membership (115 in 1987, plus eleven honorary members), the increased complexity and volume of business, and the consequent growth of the committee system, far more work is necesssarily left to the

Stewards and the committees, so that the general meeting has become correspondingly less important.

In the 1950s (and of course later) the Jockey Club seems to have been peopled with larger-than-life characters, like the Duke of Norfolk, Lord Rosebery and Lord Sefton, who was so removed from ordinary people that he is reputed never to have signed a cheque in his life. Younger members, who today would not feel intimidated by their seniors in the Club, and in any case, if they are keen and able, can quickly gain influence by being put on to a committee, then stood in awe of such figures. And well they might, for woe betide a new member who sat in the Duke's chair, or ventured to speak at a meeting before allowing a year or two to go by after his election.

The Duke of Norfolk was perhaps the most interesting of these figures. He had a nice sense of humour, though it surfaced slowly, but he had been a Duke since the age of eight, and had been seldom crossed; even at Oxford, where he was never an undergraduate but attended a crammer's, his tutor would habitually say of the often absent Duke 'Let us wait a little longer for Norfolk', no doubt to the chagrin of the students who shared his tutorial, and may have got less teaching than they would have liked. The result of this lifelong deference was that, as one of his friends has sadly remarked, 'he pretended to be older than he was, that was why he died so young'. (He died at the age of sixty-six, in 1975.)

Stories abound which show that the Duke was not afraid to present the image of the archetypal backwoodsman – indeed, it seems unlikely that he ever considered his image at all. Another side to the picture is, however, presented by a man who admired him, Peter Willett, the eminent journalist, authority on breeding and, since 1981, member of the Jockey Club. Norfolk, he says, in a rather double-edged sentence, 'was a patient listener, and resilient in argument in the open spaces between his own rock-hewn prejudices',[5] but he had judgement and common sense, and his conviction that deference was due to his high rank was balanced by his unswerving devotion to duty. Willett also points to his 'prudent wisdom'. Someone had urged that the rules for admission to the Members' Enclosure at Ascot should be eased, to which Norfolk replied 'How would you like it if all and sundry were allowed into your club?'; yet within a year he had changed the rules.[6] This is a splendid example of the ability of the English upper class, an ability which endlessly frustrates the political Left, to maintain its position by appearing to bend before the wind of change, and by actually doing so to an extent.

In the early 1950s some of the oldest members still thought of trainers more or less as upper echelon servants; there were very few whom they would invite to their houses on social terms, and Lord Rosebery reacted with an indignant 'You might as well tell a man what to pay his butler' to the proposal that training fees be standardised. A similar response may still be heard to the suggestion, on the face of it a sensible one, that Weatherby's should eliminate slow payment of trainers' bills by deducting them from the owner's account at source: 'That's always been a private matter, between owner and trainer.'

In those days the inner circle protected itself without a hint of self-doubt: any non-member of Newmarket race club using the Member's Stand at Newmarket had to have his voucher signed by a member of the Jockey Club (which resulted in some dreadful insults to distinguished people); Lord Sefton had no qualms about ordering the first Secretary of the Levy Board, Sir Rupert Brazier-Creagh, out of the paddock at Chester, because he had no formal right to be there; there was a very strong convention that women did not place bets; most owners knew their fellow owners' colours at sight: the world of racing, at least at the top, was uncomplicated, ordered, and, to the outsider, anachronistic. The Senior Steward served only a year at a time, as had been the custom for two hundred years, and had little chance to become expert in running the Club's affairs (it is even said that some of them were not particularly fond of racing) until 1965, when Major-General Sir Randle Feilden was appointed, and remained in office for eight years. (He had previously been Senior Steward in 1954 and 1961.) It may, of course, be argued that in those simpler times, before it became clear that racing was in a financially parlous state, the business was also simple; much of it could be done by the Senior Steward and one of the Weatherby family in a 'jug and bottle session' on the morning of race day. Nevertheless, it seem to have taken some time, as one would expect in an ancient institution, for the administrative system to catch up with new conditions.

Perhaps the Club's chief difficulty has been to separate, in its own collective mind, the various roles that it plays. On the one hand it is the custodian of the rules, and the administrative and disciplinary authority; on the other it is an exclusive social club, where members enjoy splendid facilities for a small subscription. In the past the social distance between the rulers and most of the ruled was so great that some members may not even have understood what power they wielded over lesser beings' livelihoods, and even if the Stewards' decisions were usually right, their attitudes must often have seemed insensitive, or even callous.

The two roles are not *necessarily* incompatible, but they lie uncomfortably together, so much so that one influential and far-sighted member believes that the social side should be allowed gradually to wither away (as was often suggested of hereditary peerages until Mrs Thatcher revived them) and that members should be elected solely for the contribution they can make to running the business of racing. Such a trend already exists, for new members are now seldom elected over the age of sixty and must be willing to do their share of administrative work. One unfortunate result is that some distinguished owners and breeders are aggrieved at having never been invited to join, because they are too old, or lack the time or ability to participate.

The method of election has changed with the demands of membership. In the old days it was assumed that no one would refuse the honour and a man would not be asked if he wanted to join, but simply elected and informed afterwards. If he was blackballed the candidate was, at least in theory, none the wiser. In the 1960s there was much discussion of how elections should be carried out, and what turned out to be a transitional system was adopted whereby, once a man's proposer and seconder were satisfied that their candidate would not be opposed, they would tell him that he was coming up for election. However, blackballing was retained, and there were at least two unfortunate occasions when the Stewards were convinced that a candidate would be unanimously elected, only to find him blackballed at the election, which had been expected to be a formality. In the 1970s blackballing was finally abandoned and election is now by consensus; it has also become not merely desirable, but essential, to inform individuals that they are under consideration since, now that membership is no longer merely a social accolade, there are some who cannot accept, because of the work involved. The Club's difficulties now are first, the age profile (partly the result of the amalgamation with the National Hunt Committee) which means that only about two-thirds of the members are able to serve on committees, and, secondly, the scarcity of potential new members of sufficient ability who can afford to give their time, unpaid, to the

Club's work.

It is never easy to pinpoint the beginning of movements in ideas and attitudes. If the Ilchester Report is discarded, because of its lack of results, then one might place the turning point in 1964, when Lord Howard first introduced the committee system (previously there had been only the Finance Committee and various *ad-hoc* bodies) which was much extended in the 1970s. On this interpretation, General Feilden (a man who got things done, and who no doubt benefited from not being an hereditary grandee in the Norfolk mould) might be seen as having consolidated the new system and having seen the need to bring the Club into the modern world, and Lord Leverhulme as a transitional Senior Steward who led the Club into a sustained period of adaptation and modernisation, which continues to the present day. This, however, is too simple a view.

The difficulty is to separate actions and attitudes. Some of the oldest members may still retain the social attitudes of fifty years ago, but most members realise that times have changed, and behave accordingly. My own view is that the dawn of that realisation may be found not in 1964 but at least as early as the mid-1950s, when the Club began to see that racing was financially in a parlous state. Thereafter there were two strands of opinion, with some people believing that increased subventions should be sought from the RBCB, whilst others saw the inevitability of a financial contribution from the bookmakers, and some seem to have fluctuated between the two views. Both bookmakers and Jockey Club soon saw that they were going to have to talk to each other, and did so fairly regularly from 1956 until the passage of the Betting and Gaming Act of 1960 and the Horserace Betting Levy Act of 1961. Both parties also talked separately, and sometimes at cross purposes, to the Home Office, and to the Racecourse Association, though the bookmakers always preferred to deal with the Jockey Club rather than with the RCA. It is this readiness to talk to all comers, in order to assure new sources of funds for racing, that marks the Jockey Club's induction into the post-war world. Without that experience the choice identified by Lord Howard's Committee in 1964 would not have presented itself so starkly; the choice, that is, between sticking to the Club's traditional role, or, by taking an initiative with the Levy Board, seeking to share the leadership of what was not not only a sport, but an increasingly complex industry. The Committee renounced isolationism and came down unanimously on the side of participation in the politics of racing, though the word 'politics' was not used. It has followed that path ever since, though sometimes with faltering steps.

But even before the complications of the modern world fully made themselves felt, the Jockey Club's traditional concerns posed their own complexities, as the story of 'The Newmarket Charter' shows.

The Newmarket Charter

The achievement of what came to be known as the 'Newmarket Charter' provides a good example both of the Jockey Club's ability to protect the interests of racing by limiting immigration from London and preserving Newmarket as a town primarily for horses, but also of its failure at that time to realise the necessity of maintaining effective relations with its natural allies, the trainers and breeders, who turned against the Charter and overturned the section of it relating to the acceptance of three thousand Londoners.

Both the post-war Labour Government and its Conservative successor believed that London's growth, both in area and population, required that people and industry be encouraged to move out into such counties as Sussex, Middlesex and Suffolk. Labour's thinking is expressed in the New Towns Act of 1946, which was directed to the establishment of completely new towns, whilst the Conservatives' Town Development Act of 1952 was concerned with the development of existing towns which could benefit from an injection of new blood, or 'overspill' from London.

During the 1950s the Government had discussions with county councils about the number of immigrants they could accept, and they in turn consulted their borough and district councils. Such a meeting was held by the West Suffolk County Council (WSCC) in Bury St Edmunds on 7 December 1960. It appears that Newmarket was excluded from the first agreement negotiated between the WSCC and the Greater London Council, though exactly why is not clear. However, the town did not accept exclusion for long; on 31 July 1961 the Urban District Council voted to join the WSCC scheme, and in August the Clerk to the Council agreed with the WSCC that three thousand overspill Londoners would be accepted, on condition that this figure might be reduced if 'integration' turned out not to work.

It now became necessary to decide where the Londoners were to be housed, and the issue became whether they should be concentrated near the town centre, or be placed more on the outskirts. The interested parties (the County Council's Planning Committee, the Newmarket Urban District Council (NUDC) and the Jockey Club, acting for the bloodstock industry) met on 15 November 1961 to discuss the linked questions of overspill and the natural expansion of the town for which provision must be made, even without over-spill. The Planning Department and NUDC contended that in order to provide the necessary housing it might be necessary to zone for residential use certain studs (Scaltback, Phantom, Hamilton and Moreton) near the centre of Newmarket. The Jockey Club disagreed, arguing that all the necessary development could take place in the Cheveley Park area, where seventy-five acres were available, though it conceded that one of the studs named by the NUDC, Scaltback, was not of great importance to the breeding industry, as it had not been used solely as a stud since pre-war days. The club also suggested that, as Brickfields Stud (three miles out of Newmarket on the Ely road) was in any case likely to be broken up by a proposed new by-pass, its remaining land might sensibly be used for housing development. This suggestion seems to have impressed both coun-cils, despite their preference for more central development, since in August 1963 it was decided that Brickfields Stud should be bought by the NUDC, with the agreement both of its owner, Andrew Johnstone, and of the Jockey Club. One thousand houses were to be built, and provision made for industry and commerce. Meanwhile the Jockey Club had accepted an overspill figure of three thousand which it was expected would lead to a total Newmarket population of seventeen thousand in 1981.

In January 1964 the NUDC lobbied the Conservative Minister of Housing and Local Government, Sir Keith Joseph, to put the scheme into effect. Joseph did not favour overspill for Newmarket, though he was impressed by the unanimity of the various parties who did. However, after the change of Government in 1964, his Labour suc-cessor, Richard Crossman, agreed (in a letter to the WSCC dated 23 March 1965) that Newmarket should be included. The NUDC approved the WSCC's overspill agreement on 19 July, and obtained the Minister's consent for a loan to cover the purchase of the land at Brickfields on 24 March 1966.

Meanwhile, early in 1965, the Jockey Club had discussed with the NUDC the possibility of building houses on Hamilton Stud, which the Club owned, instead of Brickfields. The Club was not anxious to sell Hamilton, but needed money to modernise the Newmarket racecourses, and it seems that the Club had not yet seriously considered the possibility, or desirability, of obtaining any significant sum from the Levy Board.

In August 1965, just after the WSCC's draft overspill agreement had been approved, the town map was reviewed, and the County Council raised its population projection for 1981 from the seventeen thousand agreed in 1961 to some twenty thousand, rising to twenty-eight thousand by the year 2000. In consequence more land would be needed and the County Planning Department proposed that Brickfields Stud, up to the line of the proposed by-pass, should be used for residential or industrial purposes; fifty acres of Moreton would be taken for industry; Hamilton should be used for housing; Southfields (which, like Hamilton, belonged to the Jockey Club) should be used for new training establishments; there would also be additional development on stud land to the north of the town.

The Jockey Club's attitude is well summed up in *The Report of the Duke of Norfolk's Committee on the Pattern of Racing*, which was completed on 29 June 1965 and published in August: 'Newmarket has a special place as the home and headquarters of racing in this country. In our view it has a special priority and must at all costs be maintained for the breeding, training and racing of horses. It may not, in the eyes of everyone, be considered a very accessible place, but it should be given a priority for the maintenance of our industry against any claims that may be made for housing or any other form of industry.'[7]

In the light of that paragraph, it is not surprising that the proposals dismayed the Jockey Club, which circulated a leaflet of protest to all WSCC members in late October 1965. The Clerk to the WSCC, Alan Skinner, replied that 'The eventual use of four studs, including Brickfields, from inside the urban area, out of some fifty studs situated in or near Newmarket, cannot fairly be said to represent a threat to the racing industry.'[8] He continued that, with the increase in traffic, it would no longer be suitable for horses to walk through the centre of Newmarket as they had always done.

These plans were unacceptable to the Jockey Club because they involved housing people on studs, and struck at the root of the Club's conviction that Newmarket was a town primarily for horses and for the people whose living depended on them. Nevertheless, General Feilden reluctantly agreed, later in November, that the Club would release Hamilton, because he could see no alternative.

On 30 November 1965, Eldon Griffiths, the Member for Bury St Edmunds, spoke in the House of Commons on the West Suffolk Town Expansion Programme. His main purpose was to urge the Ministry of Housing and Local Government to ensure that expanding population did not outstrip the social facilities that existing towns could provide, and he referred specifically to several towns in the constituency. Of Newmarket he said: 'town expansion is unfortunately bedevilled by disagreements. I regret to say that local political candidates have been trying to get into the act for partisan advantage.' He urged the Minister to do his utmost, as Griffiths himself had tried to do, to bring the conflicting parties into sensible agreement. 'There can be no future for Newmarket unless racing and the urban district council agree.'[9]

However, despite Griffiths' intervention, the Club seems very soon to have regretted its agreement to the Plan, and to have gone on to the offensive. It made strong representations to the Minister, actively supported by the Newmarket Trainers' Federation (NTF) and the Newmarket and District Stud Farmers' Association (SFA), so that the Minister called in (i.e. suspended) the Planning Permission and called a Public Inquiry. Shortly afterwards, in January 1966, the Jockey Club also founded the Newmarket Committee, which co-ordinated the views of groups opposed to overspill, including the owners, trainers, stud farmers, the British Bloodstock Agency and Tattersalls.

Despite these preparations, the Jockey Club realised that a public inquiry would inevitably lead to open acrimony and total loss of confidence between the racing industry and the District Council. The Club therefore sought an informal agreement and, after meetings between the Newmarket Committee, the WSCC and the NUDC, a compromise was reached early in April 1966, little more than a month before the inquiry was due, and embodied in the 'Newmarket Charter' which was signed on 27 April. The agreement stated that the population would stabilise at twenty thousand after 1981, a figure which included three thousand overspill; new housing and industry would all be sited at Brickfields, while Hamilton and the other studs would be saved.

The Charter, signed by representatives of the WSCC, the NUDC and the racing and breeding industries, affirmed the equal importance of protecting racing, offering wider employment prospects and seeing that the NUDC had sufficient finance and population to enable it to provide amenities at reasonable cost. The public inquiry into the change of land use at Brickfields took place without acrimony; on 25 July 1966 the Minister authorised an overspill agreement between the WSCC, NUDC and the Greater London Council. Details of the development were swiftly worked out, and adopted by the NUDC on 6 February 1967, though the agreement was not signed until 19 May 1967. Even then, according to one account, the signing was done in a hurry, to forestall councillors opposed to overspill who had just been elected to the Council.

This delay may have been the cause of the Newmarket Charter's eventual overthrow, because it allowed time for the opposition to overspill to organise. The Newmarket Society was formed in June 1966 (a time when preservation societies were being founded all over the country) by, among others, Hugh Sidebottom, a local farmer and keen racing man, and soon reinforced by important trainers, notably John Oxley. It played a significant part in focusing opposition on overspill, though it did not, as a society, adopt a policy of outright opposition until 1968.

The Society's original aims were to 'preserve and improve the amenities of the town', as it stated in the first issue of its *Newmarket Society News*, May 1967, and to this end it supported candidates for the annual elections to the NUDC. The operation was extremely successful, as the Society gained two seats in 1966, and by 1967 it had six councillors among its membership. By 1968 the Society controlled the Council; one of its members, Kenneth Kemp-Turner, who had come to Newmarket as recently as October 1966, and first joined the Council in May 1967, had already become chairman.

With Kemp-Turner's arrival in Newmarket the tempo of local politics changed. He was wholeheartedly opposed to overspill, unless, as he said in his campaign leaflet, there were safeguards for Newmarket people's rents, rates and jobs, and for the character of the town itself, and on that platform he successfully contested a seat in the municipal elections of 1967 which, until then, had been held by a Council member who had never had to fight an election in his eight years on the Council. Kemp-Turner was a man of unusual ability, who went on to become Chairman of Suffolk County Council after the amalgamation of East and West Suffok in 1973.

Some members of the Newmarket Society were affronted by Kemp-Turner's campaign, and some even disliked him. Immediately after the elections, the June (and last) issue of *Newmarket Society News*, edited by Geoffrey Wragg, a Councillor and assistant to his trainer father, Harry Wragg, reaffirmed its allegiance to the Newmarket Charter as the only possible basis for the expansion of Newmarket. Kemp-Turner, however, though still not opposed to overspill in principle, was so worried by the unanswered questions about its effects on the town that his attitude amounted to opposition in practice. His efforts divided the Newmarket Society. He himself always took pains to stress that, although a member of the Society, he was never a Society candidate, and two leading Council members, who were also members of the Newmarket Society, actively opposed his efforts during his first year on the Council to have the overspill agreement overturned.

Since the Society was not unanimously opposed to the Charter, Kemp-Turner founded the NEWE Group (Newmarket Expansion Without Entanglement) with the encouragement of a leading trainer, Bernard van Cutsem, and wrote its foundation advertisement, which appeared in the *Cambridge News* of 20 March 1968. It urged the absolute necessity to oppose overspill, by finding candidates opposed to it for the five Council seats which were to become vacant in May. The formation of this splinter group was necessary because at that stage the Newmarket Society was unwilling officially to oppose overspill.

Once candidates had been secured, Kemp-Turner and his friends persuaded the Society to hold a special meeting to discuss overspill. They forced a vote,and apart from the Chairman (Colonel Adrian Scrope), who abstained, and Geoffrey Wragg, who opposed, the vote against overspill was unanimous. (It appears to have been at this meeting that trainers and breeders first became vocal in their opposition to overspill.) Thereafter, Scrope resigned the chairmanship, Wragg declined to stand for re-election to the Council, and four of the five NEWE candidates were successful in the 1968 election. Thereupon the Charter was repudiated, the overspill agreement rescinded by mutual agreement with the Greater London Council, and Brickfield was eventually sold to Bovis Holdings.

Once overspill had been defeated, the NEWE Group was disbanded and the Newmarket Society died away, to the regret of those of its members who believed that the town needed a continuing Preservation Society. However, there may not have been many of these, since, although no copy of its membership list is available, it seems to have consisted largely of trainers and stud farmers. Indeed, one informant goes so far as to say that its membership was exactly the same as that of the Newmarket Trainers' Federation. If that is true, it is difficult to see why the Society should have been started at all, unless it was thought (as one participant believes) that the attempt to 'bring racing into the community' and to promote the view that the interests of Newmarket and of the racing industry were identical, would best be undertaken by a group not obviously limited to racing interests. On the other hand, if the Society was really a group of trainers and stud farmers, why were they not quicker off the mark? As General Feilden said in an address to the Newmarket Trainers' Federation and Stud Farmers' Association on 28 June 1966, if they had spoken up when overspill was first mooted in 1961/2, strong opposition might have killed the idea then.

Racing interests had good reasons to oppose overspill. They had always tried to preserve the supremacy of the horse in Newmarket. Now they feared that new industries would endanger the labour supply, by providing wage competition in an area where trainers and stud farmers had enjoyed a virtual monopoly, and these fears may not have been fully allayed by the Charter's undertaking that 'It is the intention that industrial and commercial development be carefully planned in relation to the present industries in Newmarket'. (The same point had been more straightforwardly made in an earlier draft, discussed by the Newmarket Committee on 6 April 1966: 'The Planning Authority will endeavour to see that [industrial and commercial development] will not compete in the same labour market as the racing industry.') It is, however, not altogether clear why trainers and breeders should have feared competition, since they did not recruit from the ranks of skilled or semi-skilled labour, nor even locally in the main.

There was probably also a general feeling against newcomers from London, especially if (as one candidate suggested) some of them might be black, and there were certainly doubts about the feasibility of simply halting the population at twenty thousand in 1961. Some people thought the Jockey Club had been naive to believe any such limitation was possible. One commentator even suggested that the Jockey Club actually wanted overspill, in order to obtain a good supply of stunted Londoners as stable lads!

One likely reason why opposition to overspill did not solidify until 1967 is that such bodies as the Newmarket Trainers' Federation had not clearly realised what was going on. The Jockey Club had handled the negotiations in 1961/2, when there had been little disagreement, whereas the revision of the town map in 1965, and the publicity given to the disagreements between the WSCC, NUDC and Jockey Club in the period leading up to the signing of the Charter in April 1966 and the public inquiry in May, naturally attracted more attention, and the Charter itself gave people a definite focus for discontent.

It is difficult not to feel sympathy for the Jockey Club, whose hard-won Charter was rejected by the people they believed themselves to represent. In the end the Club was disliked by both sides: by the Council, which felt that the Club should have stopped the Newmarket Society, and by the Society itself for having signed the Charter in the first place. The Jockey Club, on the other hand, had taken the view that it could not stop overspill, but only mitigate the harmful consequences to racing. To stop it altogether, it would have had to gain control of the NUDC,and it seems very unlikely that it would have wished to involve itself in local politics to that extent.

A cynic might suggest that the Jockey Club was the mastermind behind the Newmarket Society, and this interpretation is supported by remarks attributed to Robert Fellowes, the Jockey Club's agent in Newmarket, in *The Guardian* on 2 October 1982: 'It is said that not much happens in Newmarket without the Jockey Club giving its blessing. There were major convulsions about 15 years ago when the local authority wanted to introduce London overspill. It is reasonably fair to say we fought this singlehanded.' This statement led former members of the Council to believe that the Club, when it agreed to overspill, had secretly been working against it, and infuriated former members of the Newmarket Society, who felt that the Society, and not the Club, should get the credit.

It may be true that if the Jockey Club had sought to prevent the Newmarket Society from functioning it could have done so, and preserved the Charter. But there is no evidence, beyond the remark attributed to Fellowes, that the Club was playing a double game,and some counter evidence, in the form of contemporaries' recollections, that the Club had nothing to do with the Society's foundation or running. Indeed, the Club is said to have been distinctly 'huffy' when the Charter was overturned, and on 24 April 1966 Feilden wrote to Frank Christopher, the then Chairman of the NUDC, that he could do nothing about vociferous interests opposing overspill. This does not mean that the Club liked the idea of overspill; indeed, it was decided at a meeting at the Turf Board's offices on 21 January

1966 that if Newmarket were to be relocated in Cambridgeshire as a result of the Boundary Commission, the racing industry would have to think long and hard about allying itself with Cambridgeshire if the Cambridgeshire County Council refused to stop overspill. That decision, however, does not support the suggestion that the Club was secretly working against the agreement it had already signed with West Suffolk, but it does suggest that the Club would have welcomed a way out of the agreement, if an honourable one had existed.

It remains to be asked why the NUDC itself wanted overspill. The answer seems to be that the Council had a vision of a Newmarket which would be more than a thousand-horse town. It wanted to end the breeders' and trainers' wage monopoly, which to some small extent was already being breached by Sprite's caravan company; it needed money to improve derelict areas, like the Rookery, which is now a shopping centre, to provide housing for the natural increase in population, and to renew the sewage works. All this required more rate income, which might be expected from the new houses to be built on new stud land and from new industries; GLC subsidies would help with the new sewage works; services for a population of twenty thousand could be provided more economically than for twelve thousand; the Board of Trade would grant industrial development permits if the necessary labour could be shown to exist; and almost the only way a District Council could get loan approval from the Minister of Housing and Local Government was under the Town Development Act of 1952.

Not all the above points were universally agreed. For example, there was doubt about the net benefit to the NUDC of building more Council houses, and Mrs Oxley, one of the Newmarket Society's first councillors, alleged in a letter to *The Newmarket Journal* of 28 March 1968 that if overspill went through, the NUDC would end up paying £200,000 to the GLC. Nevertheless, the overall case was powerful, and may have been supported by political considerations. For example, some people would have favoured Bury St Edmunds becoming increasingly marginal as a Conservative seat.

Local political considerations are also relevant because West Suffolk was a small county, and there was some risk of its being integrated into East Suffolk, as indeed it was in 1973. An additional forty thousand Londoners might have decreased that risk, and would have increased the County's grant from central Government. All this explains the accusation of empire-building made against the Chairman of the WSCC.[10] There was also some feeling in Newmarket that local government needed to consolidate its position, or run the risk of being superseded. The fear has turned out to be justified, as Newmarket has lost it District Council to Forest Heath, and, having been told that it is too large to have a Parish Council, now has no local government of its own at all.

This case study illustrates both the strengths and weaknesses of the Jockey Club. It was strong on common sense and honourable dealing, on recognising the inevitable, on avoiding public fuss and coming to a reasonable compromise, largely through informal negotiation. It was weak on communication with the groups who later turned against the Charter, and once those groups had solidified their opposition to the Charter in the forum provided by the Newmarket Society, there was little the Club could do to prevent the destruction of the agreement which had been achieved with so much effort. But both the Jockey Club and the Newmarket Society wanted the same thing, the preservation of Newmarket as a town for horses, and it would be a churlish visitor to the town today who would regret their success.

While the saga of the Newmarket Charter ran its course, numerous changes were being introduced, many of them in collaboration with the newly established Levy Board. The Jockey Club's firmness in insisting that, whether or not there was a Tote monopoly, racing must gain some benefit from all gambling on horse racing had led to the formation of what was, in effect, a private tax-gathering machine.

Lord Harding, the Board's first chairman, understood perfectly that he was responsible for how the Board spent its money, but he also understood the nature of the Jockey Club. It could not be changed overnight, and there was no point in confrontation.

Thus, many of the changes of the 1960s started in a peaceful atmosphere, which was shattered, as we saw in Chapter V, when Harding retired in 1967 and was replaced by the enthusiastic and knowledgeable, but also abrasive, Lord Wigg. The Jockey Club did not know how to handle him, and he did not know how to handle the Club, though he thought he did.

Meanwhile, Lord Howard de Walden's report of 1964, when the Levy Board was only three years old, marks another important step along the Jockey Club's long road to modernisation.

The Jockey Club

The Howard committee

Lord Howard de Walden is the living embodiment of the change in attitudes which has enabled the Jockey Club to adapt to the modern world. He has served three times as Senior Steward, 1957, 1964 and 1976-9. When he retired in 1964 he thought of himself as the last of the old breed of Senior Steward, but when he returned in 1976 he was convinced of the need to modernise the Jockey Club and its image, and in September 1982 took part with relish and enthusiasm in the first 'in-depth' study of the Club on television.

In 1964, when he was near the end of his second term, he chaired a committee of the Jockey Club whose tasks were to analyse the various categories of Stewards' work, recommend any necessary reorganisation and enquire into the financial implications of its recommendations. The committee set out, with the Club's usual no-nonsense clarity, two diametrically opposed points of view about how the Turf Authorities (i.e. the Jockey Club and the National Hunt Committee) should go forward. The first view encompassed what was generally acknowledged to be the traditional business of the Jockey Club. Those who thought on these lines believed that the Turf Authorities could not be expected to run 'The Racing Industry', a term which had 'come into use when it was desired to impress the Government in dealings connected with entertainments tax and the taxation of betting. This is an inexact term which can be conveniently contracted or expanded in its interpretation.'[11]

The report went on that, however inexact the term, it undoubtedly included the sport of racing, and members of the Turf Authorities were primarily elected for their interest in the sport, and their qualifications to administer the rules from which their power derived. The committee said (perhaps with tongue in cheek?) that many of the members would be perfectly qualified to run an industry, but had not the time: in any case, public opinion accepted a sport being run by a private club, but might not think the same about an industry. Public opinion would probably be content to leave the Rules to the Turf Authorities, but would be more likely to opt for the Levy Board as the industrial master, because its control of the purse strings gave it a different kind of power from that of the Turf Authorities, which could more appropriately be wielded by a statutory body.

It followed from this view that the Turf Authorities should confine themselves to administering the sport, and offering advice about the

[163]

industry. According to the committee, this had been the Authorities' policy so far, and if they tried to extend their scope their power and prestige would be seriously at risk. Their lack of any wish to dominate the industry was demonstrated by the fact that they had delegated power to the Racecourse Association. Indeed, they had forced every racecourse to join, and so close had the redoubtable Mrs Mirabel Topham, the owner of Aintree, come to refusing, that Lord Howard had almost been faced with the embarrassment of having to ban the Grand National!

That was one view, that of the traditionalists. The opposite, or expansionist, one was that completely new conditions existed since the Government had set up the Levy Board. The industry was in a bad way, and a clash with the Board was almost inevitable about how to improve it. The question was whether the Turf Authorities or the Board, or both, should give a lead to the industry. According to the expansionist view, the Turf Authorities must take an initiative with the Levy Board, in order to run the whole business together. Otherwise they would be pushed aside.

Faced with these alternatives, the committee was unanimous that the Turf Authorities must take an initiative, and recommended that a joint board of the Jockey Club and National Hunt Committee be set up on 1 January 1965, to be known as the Turf Board. The Levy Board would be represented, and the professional associations (racecourses, owners, breeders and trainers) would be indirectly represented through an Advisory Council. The Turf Board would have its own Managing Director and secretariat. The Managing Director would almost certainly not have had experience of the administration of racing, but the committee proposed that the Assistant Managing Director should be E. W. Weatherby. On that assumption the committee did not consider that the secretary to the Board should also be a Weatherby.

The committee had considered Weatherby's position in some detail. In 1962 their services had cost the Turf Authorities £60,000, made up of the salary cost of those employed on the Turf Authorities' work, plus twenty-five per cent and a rental charge for the accommodation used. The committee considered that 'the institution of a Turf Board would impose no undue hardship on Weatherby's'. They would lose the top administrative post in racing, but would continue to provide the Registry Office and be secretaries of the Jockey Club and National Hunt Committee and of course their private business (stud book, banking, printing and Secretaryship of various race clubs) would not be affected.

The committee also recommended a number of measures of reorganisation to lighten the Stewards' work, of which the most important was the devolution of the Club's Newmarket interests to a Newmarket Estates and Finance Committee, to be supervised by a Jockey Club Agent, to whom the Clerk of the Course would be subordinate. The Newmarket interests would then be in a position relative to the Jockey Club similar to that of a subsidiary company.

The new emphasis on committee work would require the Jockey Club to broaden the base of its membership. More members in the thirty-to-forty age bracket should be elected, and a condition of membership should be willingness to serve on the Turf Board or on committees.

Significance of the Howard Report

This report marks a turning point, the point at which the Jockey Club realised that it must engage in the political game if it was to survive, and foresaw, three years before Wigg's time, the possibility of a serious clash with the Levy Board. It also pointed, in mentioning the duplication of work between the Jockey Club and National Hunt Committee, to one of the advantages of the amalgamation, which later was a condition of the grant of a Royal Charter. It reformed the internal administration of the Turf Authorities, did the groundwork for a modern committee structure, and saw the need for a more broadly based membership, if the new administrative tasks were to be successfully carried out. It also, although not exactly voicing dissatisfaction with Weatherby's, put the firm on notice that two hundred years as the supreme civil servants in racing did not guarantee another two hundred. The impression that a warning was being given may have been fostered by Brigadier S. H. Kent's appointment as Secretary of the Turf Board in October, and Manager the following January.[12] In the suggestion of an Advisory Council may be found the distant roots of the modern Horseracing Advisory Council.

By giving up control of racing to the Turf Board, one third of whose costs were paid by the Levy Board (the Home Office had not allowed Levy Board representatives to become normal members, but they were present by permanent invitation) the Turf Authorities in fact retained it, and by thinking in good time of devolving their Newmarket interests they paved the way for the Foundation of the New-market Estates and Property Company, when that became necessary (or so the Jockey Club thought) as a defensive measure against the possible depredations of Wigg or the threat of nationalisation.

The report also contains an irony. The autocratic figures of the 1950s and 1960s wanted to see the Jockey Club's power confined to administration of the Rules, while the liberal Lord Howard thought it essential to extend its activities through co-operation with the Levy Board. This extension, which began with the setting up of the Turf Board, is precisely what some of the Club's most bitter opponents object to. So Lord Howard, who represents the acceptable face of the Jockey Club, may have run great risks of bringing it under fire by extending its field of influence, rather than abating criticism by the reforms he pushed through. Conversely, the instinct of the die-hards may have been sound, that a body which did not purport to be representative of the industry as a whole, could best maintain its essential character, and stay out of the firing line, by sticking to the job it had always done, and leaving to newer bodies the new respon-sibilities created by the march of progress. This was exactly what Lord Wigg believed, so that by another irony his natural allies would have been the traditionalists!

The Jockey Club's process of self-examination continued with the Benson report of 1968. By then Wigg had taken over the Levy Board from Harding and his rooted objection to the Jockey Club, coupled with the Club's inability to deal with him, was beginning to create the very clashes foreseen by Lord Howard and his committee.

The Benson Report[13]

Sir Henry (later Lord) Benson was appointed by the Joint Turf Authorities in September 1967 to look into the financial requirements of the racing industry ('sport' does not appear in his terms of refer-ence) and how they might be met; to 'examine the organisation for the control of the racing industry, as distinct from the administration of the rules'; (this part of the terms of reference shows that the How-ard 'faction' was still in the ascendant) and to advise the Turf Authorities on an approach to the Government, setting out the indus-try's needs, and suggesting how the sums needed might be raised. The other members of the committee were the Marquess of Aber-gavenny, Sir Rex Cohen, and Major W. D. Gibson, with Brigadier

Kent as Secretary, and they reported in June 1968.

The Committee believed that the quality of British bloodstock was declining; racecourse attendances were declining; prize money was too low; the levy was wholly insufficient for racing's needs, and administration was hampered by the fact that no fewer than nine bodies had a hand in the industry's administration.

Benson himself was hampered by Wigg's refusal to provide any information beyond facts and figures. A statutory body, he averred, could not divulge anything about its future plans, and he obtained backing from Sir Philip Allen, Permanent Under-Secretary at the Home Office all through Wigg's period, for this, on the face of it, rather absurd view. Wigg's refusal did not prevent Benson from including the Levy Board in the list of those who had given evidence, to Wigg's great annoyance. When the report came out he read it avidly (having refused a preview, again after taking advice from Allen), but he refused to accompany Feilden to the Home Office to discuss it, presumably in order to reinforce his point that the report was solely a Jockey Club enterprise.

Wigg's disapproval notwithstanding, the inquiry was a timely project, conducted by the right man, since Sir Henry was an eminent accountant who looked after the affairs of several Club members. His uncle had been the first Chairman of Unilever, so there was a personal link with the future Senior Steward, Lord Leverhulme. He had the advantage of being an outsider, in that he was not an especially keen racing man, though he was subsequently elected to the Club in recognition of his services.

The report argued that low prize money meant that British horses were increasingly being trained and run in France, but few French horses were running in Britain. They were interested in only about six British races, and judging by their record in the Derby and Oaks had done well in them. Foreign-bred horses (not all of them French) had been placed first, second or third in the Derby and Oaks five times each in the twenty-one years 1919-39; in the twenty-one years 1947-67 they had been placed twenty times in the Derby and twenty-two in the Oaks.

The report showed that the cost of producing yearlings was rising at a much faster rate than their average sale price and added 'unless this trend is changed, breeders cannot be expected to continue to breed yearlings which will inevitably involve them in losses'. (This has turned out to be untrue: breeders continue undeterred, under the guidance of the extremely effective Thoroughbred Breeders' Association.)

Attendances had gone down significantly from 1958 to 1967, though less drastically at National Hunt than at flat meetings. The average for all meetings had fallen from 8,157 to 6,271, but at mixed meetings it had actually risen (a point to which the committee did not draw attention) from 5,888 to 6,674. The wages paid by breeders and trainers were on the whole lower than in agriculture, so that there was a steady drift of labour into industry, and racing was more heavily taxed than other industries. The plethora of administrative authorities had been added to by Wigg's refusal to serve on the Turf Board, except on terms of complete equality,and this had led to the setting up of the Joint Racing Board in April 1968.

The solution to the industry's problems, the committee believed, was to set up a new statutory body which would make a number of the existing Boards redundant. Notably, the Levy Board would be disbanded and all its functions taken over by the new Authority. This proposal might well have been acceptable to the Board under Lord Harding (though, of course, the Home Office might not have approved). Be that as it may, it naturally aroused Wigg's wrath, particularly as he cannot have failed to notice that members of the Authority would retire at the age of seventy. This effectively ruled him out (as Michael Philips noted in *The Times* on 30 July 1968), since he would be just on seventy by the end of his first term as Chairman of the Levy Board. Ironically, the report's recommendation was not far removed from the view to which Wigg himself eventually came, that racing should be run by a Jockey Club much reduced in size, which would swallow up the Levy Board and be accountable to Parliament.

The new Authority would consist of a chairman and three independent members appointed by the Home Secretary, four appointed by the Turf Authorities (two each for the flat and National Hunt) and one each by the racecourses, owners, breeders and bookmakers. It was thus an extremely subtle amalgam of the existing Turf Board, Levy Board and Bookmakers' Committee on the one hand, with Lord Howard's proposed Advisory Council on the other; the only major group omitted were the trainers, who, as persons licensed by the Jockey Club, were in a different category from the other groups. Furthermore, the Turf Authorities would almost certainly have been able to retain control of the new body. Even if the bookmakers and all four Home Office appointees went against them, the others would be unlikely to oppose them on any major issue.

Benson 'understood' that the Jockey Club and National Hunt Committee 'are at present considering the possibility of combining into a single body, which would thus be fully representative of both codes of racing'. (He was, of course, also aware that this amalgamation was being considered as part of the preparation for the acquisition of a Charter; indeed, the words 'fully representative' echo one of the Privy Council's criteria for the grant of a Charter.) The committee thought that the new combined body should have delegated to it the existing powers and responsibilities of the Turf Authorities, and (like Lord Howard in 1964) considered that its membership should be enlarged. An Executive Committee of twelve men, to be known as Stewards, would be elected by the membership as a whole, not self-elected, as they were then. There would be a continuing need for an experienced secretariat, which would best be met by appointing Weatherby's.

The Tote would no longer be a separate statutory body, but would be taken over by the new Authority, and have levy charged on its turnover, in the same way as bookmakers (who were at that time being charged on a mixture of profit and turnover) and in contrast to the inequitable treatment it had received hitherto. The Committee saw no reasonable prospect of a Tote monopoly at present; it might become feasible in the future, though probably not for at least ten years. The Authority would also subsume Racecourse Technical Services (owned and financed by the Levy Board, with three of its seven directors nominated by the Jockey Club, the National Hunt Committee and the Racecourse Association) and Racecourse Holdings Trust (partly financed by loans from the Levy Board and ultimately owned by the Trustees of the Jockey Club and of the National Hunt Committee).

The Benson Committee reflected the thinking of the more enlightened members of the Turf Authorities in its belief that each section of the industry should be represented by strong associations with written constitutions (which, it noted, the trainers lacked). The committee doubted also 'whether, at present the [Raceccourse] Association carries the authority which we think its position in the racing industry requires'.[14] This remark, once again, reflects Howard's thinking: he had strengthened the Association by obliging all racecourses to belong to it, but it still was not pulling its weight.

The new Authority would assume the responsibility for providing all prize money (on the Irish model, though the report did not say so) in return for which it would receive the income at present accruing to the Racecourse Association from the Commentary Fund,[15] and to racecourses from television, sound radio and cinema newsreel rights. Courses would also pay a fixture fee designed to cover all, or most, of the cost of services provided by the authority, and would no longer receive capital grants, save in very exceptional circumstances. However, as they would no longer be responsible for prize money, and would be allowed to keep half of any prize money raised from sponsors, they would still be substantially better off than before. If some racecourses were still in poor financial shape, they would be suitable candidates for acquisition by Racecourse Holdings Trust (there is an echo here of the Ilchester Report of twenty-five years earlier).

The committee made a number of other recommendations: bookmakers, again as in Ilchester, should be relocated, so as not to interfere with the public's view of the racing; members' enclosures should be opened to non-members without the need for a voucher signed by a member; racecourses should be graded; Sunday racing, and betting, should be allowed. (Sunday racing has recently been much to the fore, as we shall see in Chapter 10) The negotiation of television contracts would be taken over by the Authority from the Racecourse Association, since the Association had failed to negotiate block contracts with the BBC, and in any case higher fees could be earned and the international interest in some races more fully exploited. Finally, the committee was concerned about catering, as Ilchester had been. It understood that the Racecourse Association, the racecourses and the catering organisations had failed to discuss these problems in the past, and thought a working party should be set up at once.

All these were desirable reforms, but the committee's main concern, apart from setting up the new Authority, was to emphasise the inadequacy of prize money. On the flat it had amounted to £2,820,000 in 1967, but £6,085,000 was required. Now that the Duke of Norfolk's 1965 Committee had led to the establishment of the Pattern in Britain, and Lord Porchester's Race Planning Committee (1967) had continued its work, and extended it by locking the British Pattern into the French and Irish, it was possible to decide between the claims of the Pattern and non-Pattern races. (The international system of graded races, known as the Pattern, will be discussed more fully in Chapter 8.) The Committee concluded that the main prizes in racing should go to the Pattern races, with prize money averaging about £10,000. This would not be up to the French average of approximately £14,500, but it would be a great improvement. The committee took the point that the man in the street might think the prizes high, but that would be to ignore the heavy costs incurred by breeders, owners and trainers. Furthermore: 'The prize monies proposed cannot be compared with the large sums won by the public on the jackpot and the football pools, in which the effort involved is comparatively small, or with the monies now to be won on premium bonds where no effort at all is required.'[16] For other races, minimum values were proposed, according to the class and type of race.

The committee considered the proportion of prize money to the total cost of keeping horses in training to be quite inadequate. In 1966 it had been 40.3 per cent for all races (but only 32.6 per cent if Pattern races were excluded). Under the committee's proposal it would rise to 74.6 per cent (51.4 per cent excluding pattern races). The owners' contribution to prize money (24 per cent of the total on the flat in 1967) was also much too high.

Owners needed help in other ways. The Benson Committee, unlike Ilchester, favoured breeders' premiums, but only for the winners of Pattern races. Presents to trainers, jockeys and stable staff were still (as when Ilchester had reported) given at owners' discretion, usually at the rate of ten per cent each for trainers and jockeys, and anything between nil and five per cent for stable staff. The committee thought the element of discretion should be removed, and standardised deductions made at source by the Authority, at ten per cent for trainers, 7½ per cent for jockeys, and 2½ per cent for stable staff, the last to be distributed as the trainer thought fit.

The committee estimated that its recommendations would cost the new Authority £11,500,000 annually by 1970, against its forecast income of £2,690,000, leaving £8,810,000 to be found from a levy on betting turnover. Such a sum could be found by raising the levy to one per cent of turnover, but the committee hoped that the racing industry would succeed in persuading the government to fund the levy by reducing betting tax from five per cent to four per cent. Thus, bookmakers would still pay five per cent on turnover, but one per cent would be returned to racing. The bookmakers would therefore be better off than before (though the report did not make the point) because they would now be liable for a total of five per cent, instead of five per cent plus levy. The levy and tax would both be based on the same calculations of turnover (an admirable suggestion which has never been put into effect) and if constitutionally possible the levy should be collected by HM Customs and Excise, acting as agents of the authority.

The results

The Benson Report got a mention in *The Times* of 30 July 1968, and provoked an extremely hostile article, headed 'Leave it to the Mugs' in *The Economist* of 3 August. The author could see no good reason for subsidising racing, and could not imagine that Roy Jenkins, the Chancellor of the Exchequer would do so either, since 'The contraction of horseracing in this country would have to be on an enormous scale before any government worried about its revenue from the betting tax'. *The Economist* did, however, support the Committee's recommendations that the administration of racing be brought under one authority, and that the crippling restrictions on the Tote be lifted, to allow it to compete with the bookmakers on something like even terms.

In fact, the Jockey Club seems to have made no serious approaches to the Home Office about the establishment of a new Authority until after the grant of a Royal Charter in February 1970 (*The Sporting Life* of 11 February 1970 applauded its intention to implement Benson's main recommendations) but by then Wigg's influence had made itself felt. The Jockey Club had believed that the Charter would enhance, or at least protect, its claim to rule British racing, and increase the chances of a new Authority being set up. Wigg, therefore, was concerned to show that even if the grant of a Charter had been proper, it was only connected with the Benson report in the mind of the Jockey Club and therefore did not support the case for a new Authority. His arguments against the Charter might well have been put more strongly had he not suspected, as he must have done, that the Queen herself would have taken a personal interest in it. Be that as it may, his intervention seems to have been decisive, since the Jockey Club made no progress with the establishment of the proposed new Authority.

Nevertheless, even Wigg could find much that was good in the report, and said so in a speech at Redcar; in particular, he had always thought that prize money should be increased, and later prided himself on having doubled it in his period at the Levy Board (though after his move to BOLA he thought the emphasis on prize money had gone too far). Nevertheless, the principal value of the report was that it led the Jockey Club to examine itself, in part critically, through the eyes of a trusted and knowledgeable enquirer, who was at the same time not quite an 'insider' on the racing scene.

Further enquiries into the Jockey Club

I have dealt in a separate chapter with Wigg's antipathy to the Jockey Club as a whole, and his love-hate relationship with Feilden. However, it is impossible to leave out his involvement in the continuing period of appraisal of its activities, since one of the examinations of it was conducted at his insistence. This was a report by accountants on the cost-effectiveness of the Jockey Club's administration of racing.[17] The enquiry naturally caused consternation in the Club, but was part of the price it had to pay for the new system of subsidy, whereby racecourses could now receive their allocations in the form of grants for capital works, or have them paid directly to Weatherby's in settlement of the Jockey Club's fixture fees and other charges which had previously been met by racecourses. In paying fixture fees the Board would therefore be paying the salaries of Club staff and officials, albeit indirectly. Hence, Wigg was able to argue that, since the Board would be paying a large proportion of the Club's expenditure, it was only reasonable for the Board to satisfy itself that the expenditure was cost-effective. It must be added that the investigation could not have been wholly unwelcome to General Feilden himself, since it included a detailed examination of Weatherby's operations, and of the effect of dependence on the firm for almost all administrative work. This aspect of the study seems to have reflected Feilden's doubts as to whether the Club's total reliance on Weatherby's was in its best interest.

In general the accountants found the Jockey Club and Weatherby's cost-effective, and there is no need to go into their detailed recommendations. However, their remarks about Weatherby's are of some interest.

They pointed out that only twelve of the sixty staff engaged substantially on the Jockey Club's work were directly employed by it (the sixty excluded racecourse officials and printing staff). The twelve included the three senior executives, of whom two were members of the Weatherby family.

Nor did the Club own the premises at Portman Square and Wellingborough, and a charge for their use (approximately £22,500) was included in the Weatherby contract charge. The estimated charge in 1970 was £165,169, to include a profit margin of £15,000. The cost to Weatherby's of the services provided (registry office and secretariat, overnight declarations, *Racing Calendar* office, names and horse records) was £169,555, a loss (on which the accountants did not comment) of nearly £20,000 being expected on the last two departments, which would more than absorb the £15,000 profit margin. (This does not, of course, mean that the firm was bankrupt, since it had other clients and activities.) Departments not covered by the contract were general administration, security, personnel, officials, ring inspectors and the veterinary field force, which together cost the Club £328,666 against a revenue of £327,544. The greater part of the latter, £249,144, came from racecourse fixture fees.

Until 1969 Weatherby's charges had been on a cost-plus basis, the profit element being twenty-five per cent of direct labour costs, but it had been proposed that the fee should be set for five years, subject to variation in the amount and kind of work, and to movements in the retail price index. At the time of the report the Jockey Club had accepted the new form of contract for 1970 only, but the accountants saw no objection to its being entered into for five years. They considered the fixed price form of contract the more advantageous to the Jockey Club, since it would encourage Weatherby's to increase their efficiency, which in turn would be reflected in the cost of their services, when the next contract was negotiated. They also considered the proposed £15,000 profit margin, which compared with £17,979 in 1969, to be reasonable. They added that data processing at Wellingborough would be entirely computerised by the end of the present contract, and that the Club ought to negotiate the basis for computer charges before then. Otherwise it would be in a weak position to negotiate, since the systems and programmes would belong to Weatherby's, their use would be completely dependent on the computer, and none of the Jockey Club's own staff would understand the system.

Although Weatherby's were cost-effective and efficient, the accountants pointed out that if they at any time ceased to be so it would be very difficult for the Jockey Club to take short-term corrective action, as it would take a long time for it to build up an alternative team of its own with the necessary expertise. They suggested that, if the long-term aspects of the relationship were to be examined, such questions should be tackled as whether there was any means of ensuring Weatherby's continued effectiveness, what the Jockey Club's role was likely to be in future, and 'the extent to which the effectiveness of the Jockey Club administration is dependent upon being conducted side by side with the other services currently being provided by Weatherby's'.

The Levy Board baldly noted that the accountants had presented their report to the Joint Racing Board in March 1971 and that 'The Levy Board were gratified with the conclusion which indicated that those parts of the Jockey Club administration to which the Levy Board contributed were administered on a cost effective basis'.[18]

This report had exasperated the Jockey Club , because it had been imposed upon it. But it seems also to have made the Club realise that there was a value in such scrutinies by complete outsiders, and shortly afterwards it commissioned further studies.

McKinsey's studies

In August and September 1972 McKinsey's, a leading firm of management consultants, submitted two reports, one on the Jockey Club's organisation and the other on its public relations and financial viability.[19]

The organisational report observed that the sport, and industry, of racing had become greatly more complicated in recent years. The professional associations had become far more self-assertive, and the Levy Board now shared decision-making in many areas which it financed, which had previously been the Jockey Club's exclusive responsibility. The Club, as its difficulties with the Levy Board had shown, needed to re-examine its relationships with the Board, and Wigg's impending retirement gave a good opportunity for improving them. It was also desirable to look at the Club's internal organisation, in the light of the recent retirement of the Chief Executive, Peter Weatherby (a misleading title, since the most senior official was the Secretary to the Jockey Club, David Weatherby), and the approaching retirement of General Feilden, the Senior Steward.

Difficulties had arisen with the Levy Board because there had been differences of opinion about the Board's and the Club's respective responsibilities. These needed to be clarified and agreed through a series of meetings; thereafter differences should be prevented from

turning into serious issues by fuller collaboration between permanent staff, below the level of the Board and the Stewards. The Levy
Board's subsidiaries should be more fully consulted (McKinsey's
here made the mistake of referring to the Tote as one of these subsidiaries), and thought should be given to the setting up of an independent statistical office to serve the whole racing industry.

The Jockey Club, then as now, had three members on the Levy
Board. McKinsey's were, of course, writing eight years before the
Horseracing Advisory Council (which will be discussed in Chapter
X) started work, when they said that for some years the Club and
the associations had felt that the Jockey Club members of the Board
had not adequately championed their cause. This was partly because
they were outnumbered, but they needed also to brief themselves
more fully on the associations' views and therefore to obtain longer
notice of what items were to be on the Levy Board's agenda.

Internal reorganisation was also needed. General Feilden was, by
all accounts, a man of extraordinary energy, who was prepared to
devote far more of his time to the Club than could possibly be
expected of any future Senior Steward. His corresponding weakness,
which of course the consultants did not mention, seems to have been
that he thought his very wide personal contacts gave him an adequate
knowledge of what the various interest groups felt, whereas the
individuals whom he happened to know may well not have been a
true cross-section, and may, therefore, sometimes have given him
a distorted or incomplete view.

McKinsey's thought that in future the Senior Steward's work
should be primarily representational, that his two deputies should
play a larger part in the Club's affairs, and that the Stewards as a
group should be concerned mainly with major matters of policy.
Two new Sub-Committees, in addition to the existing Administration
and Finance Committee, should process proposals before they were
put to the Stewards, and individual Stewards should be asked to
specialise in certain areas of the Club's work. Since the setting up
of the Joint Racing Board, the Turf Board was redundant and could
be abolished.

The report noted that the Stewards had felt the service given them
by the secretariat to be insufficient, because times had changed and
the work had become more complicated. There was no direct criticism of Weatherby's; indeed, none would have been appropriate,
since the three senior executives were directly employed by the

Jockey Club. However, the Weatherby family may have felt threatened by McKinsey's recommendation that there should be a single chief executive, since, although one of the two who remained after Peter Weatherby's retirement was the Secretary, David Weatherby, the General Manager, Brigadier Kent, was an outsider. The real point of debate was whether the most senior official should be employed by Weatherby's or the Jockey Club. Kent might well have been a candidate for the new post, but shortly after the retirement of Feilden, who had brought him into the organisation, and the death of his friend, David Weatherby, Kent also retired, five years early, and Simon Weatherby became Secretary.

Kent's chief function had been to act as personal assistant to Feilden. When Lord Leverhulme, who initiated the modern practice whereby Senior Stewards serve for three years, succeeded Feilden in 1973, he saw his own role as that of chief policy-maker and representative of the Club, and his principal task as being to mend relations with the Levy Board, in the same way as Wigg's successors, Sir Stanley Raymond and Sir Desmond (later Lord) Plummer saw it as *their* main task to get back on reasonable terms with the Jockey Club. It followed that, though no less dedicated to racing than Feilden, Leverhulme needed to spend much less time at the office, and had no particular need of a personal assistant. It seems, therefore, that the threat to Weatherby's as hereditary administrators of racing fell away at about this time. It is impossible to judge how serious the threat was, though it must have diminished greatly once Wellingborough, with its computerised services, was fully operational. Since then there have been rumblings,[20] but the firm's position seems not to have come under attack; indeed, it was strengthened by the Rothschild Commission's recommendation that a future British Horseracing Authority should retain the firm, of whose relation with the Jockey Club the Commission said: 'It is a curious but perhaps appropriate feature of the Jockey Club that its secretariat should be bred rather than recruited in the usual manner.'[21]

McKinsey's soon presented their report on public relations and the Club's financial viability. The continuance of what the report on public relations rather loosely described as 'public funds', i.e. the levy, depended on maintaining governmental confidence in the Jockey Club.

McKinsey's thought that the Club's image must depend on its fairness and competence, and that in promoting its image it should therefore concentrate more on what it did, and its underlying attitudes, than on how it presented them. Actions, in other words, would speak louder than public relations. The Club should therefore frankly identify its own aims and values, develop a more systematic and professional appróach in achieving its objectives, and project itself to the public as an active, rather than reactive, body. In the short term the Club should continue to use an outside public relations firm, though McKinsey's could not judge whether the existing Racing Information Bureau would be suited to the more active approach now advocated.

The consultants had presented the case against their clients as cogently as any enemy could have done. At the same time, the skilful formulation of their proposals, with its emphasis on deeds rather than words, cannot have failed to appeal to that 'copper bottomed' quality of integrity (as one fairly new member has called it) which is more important than any number of academic qualifications in maintaining the reputation of a body like the Jockey Club. The result has been that in recent years the Club has taken public relations seriously. Its connection with the Racing Information Bureau (which also represented the Levy Board through all the years of bitter in-fighting) came to an end in 1980. Now it employs an in-house public relations officer, as well as a senior consultant outside, and a specialist parliamentary consultant.

On finance, McKinsey's considered that so far as possible the Jockey Club must set fees which would cover the cost of the services provided and allow it to build up reserves. The alternative was partial or total subsidisation, which would be bad for the Club's image, and bad for racing, since its ability to contribute disinterestedly to decisions about spending Levy Board funds would be impaired if it were a major beneficiary from them. Some services were already funded by the Levy Board and jointly controlled, but of those directly controlled by the Club, it should allow only overnight declarations to be paid for by the Board. 'O/Decs', as the system is known at Weatherby's, was largely for the benefit of punters and bookmakers, and it seemed reasonable to pay for it with funds raised from the bookmakers. (McKinsey's seem to have forgotten that the Jockey Club's own employees were indirectly being paid by the Levy Board.)

With regard to Weatherby's the consultants thought the Club should take note of the value to the firm of that part of its banking business which arose from its position as stake-holder, and take this into account when negotiating the next contract.

Thus there came to an end a period of intense appraisal of the Jockey Club. It was soon to be renewed when the Rothschild Commission was appointed, just about the time when the Club's morale reached its nadir. After Rothschild had reported, although the Government rejected its main recommendation, for the establishment of a British Horseracing Authority, the Club seems to have come to life again, recovered its confidence, and entered a new period of modernisation. Meanwhile, however, there occurred a number of important events in the period of self-examination. They included the hiving off of the Jockey Club's properties to Newmarket Estates and Property Company and the establishment of Racecourse Holdings Trust. I have no space to chronicle these events, fascinating as they were, both in themselves and as further illustrations of the extraordinary relationship between the Jockey Club and Lord Wigg. Instead I discuss, by way of conclusion to this chapter, the Jockey Club's acquisition of a Royal Charter, and the amalgamation with the National Hunt Committee that preceded it.

Amalgamation

Amalgamation of the Jockey Club and National Hunt Committee was necessary in order to meet the Privy Council Office's criteria, codified in 1966, for the grant of a Charter, one of which was that a chartered body must be fully representative of the activity to which it relates. The amalgamation, which went through in December 1968, was not universally popular, as Lord Rosebery showed when hunting for his mislaid binoculars at the first meeting where National Hunt Committee members were admitted to the Jockey Club Stand at Newmarket. 'Comes of having all these damned jumpers about' he muttered angrily.

Nor has amalgamation fully 'gelled' yet. Just as a Foreign Office man can still spot a Commonwealth Relations Office man from the moment he opens his mouth or drafts a minute – and that amalgamation also took place in 1968 – so will the devotee of National Hunt distinguish himself from those addicted to the flat. The reverse is less often the case, perhaps because National Hunt meetings attract fewer regulars whose natural home is the flat than *vice versa*.

The National Hunt enthusiast will say that he is not in it for the money. Prize money is too low (it has always been a grievance that so low a percentage of Levy Board money, thirty-five per cent until recently, now forty per cent, goes to National Hunt) for riches to be the spur. The economics of breeding jumpers are quite different, and at the end of their careers many horses will have no stud value because they have been gelded. Your National Hunt man, or woman, may go on to say that the owner or breeder on the flat is *only* in it for the money, though this is unlikely to be true of more than a small minority.

Since amalgamation, members of the two bodies have mingled, and those who take part in administration have no choice but to concern themselves with both branches of the sport. Socially, however, they have not fully merged. Jumping enthusiasts are visually distinguishable by their clothes; some of them do not feel comfortable at Newmarket (at the racecourse, or in the Jockey Club rooms), which is why there are now more meetings of the Club in London than in Newmarket; and there remains a feeling among some members that the Club embraces two separate interests. The sense of distance between the two interests, though diminishing, will, no doubt, persist for a long time, perhaps until there are no members left who are old enough to pass on the oral tradition of the National Hunt Committee. Usually it does not greatly matter, though some members' lack of interest in jumping may have had some adverse effect on the Grand National appeal of 1982/3.

The Royal Charter

Wigg's public attitude, that the Charter was an irrelevance, and his likely private feeling, that it was a slap in the face, have been noted already. But there are still questions to be asked about why the Club, or those members who were in touch with what was going on, wanted a Charter at all.

There was, of course, a general fear of socialism, even of the kind practised by the then Prime Minister, Harold Wilson, and a fear of the extension of State control in the world of sport. The Jockey Club may also have feared losing its autonomy, either to an entirely State-funded and State-controlled Sports Council, to which it would be one of many specialist advisory committees, or by being taken over by the Levy Board, or by some other form of nationalisation. With declining attendances, the smell of nationalisation was in the air,[22] and the Jockey Club knew that it must defend itself, even if it did not know how effective the chosen instrument of defence would be.

The Jockey Club could have got the idea of a Charter from the bookmakers, who in 1957 had been searching for some kind of constitution which would give them the authority themselves to raise a 'financial contribution to racing' (as what later became the levy was generally known), but in fact it came from Lord Porchester, whom Harold Wilson had appointed Chairman of the Sports Council's Planning Committee in 1965, and who was therefore well able to assess the attitudes of his Chairman, Denis Howell, the Minister of Sport. Howell had shown signs of wishing to abolish the National Playing Fields Association (NPFA), which was funded almost entirely by private enterprise, and in which the Duke of Edinburgh took a great interest. Porchester had reminded the Minister that the NPFA had a Charter, and therefore could not be abolished, and thereafter very naturally thought that it would be a wise precaution for the Jockey Club to obtain a Charter for itself. The idea was adopted enthusiastically by Norfolk and Feilden; the members of the Jockey Club and National Hunt Committee accepted amalgamation as a necessary preliminary (and by a miracle kept the negotiations for a Charter secret), and the Charter was finally granted in February 1970.

The Charter may have offered some protection, though the Jockey Club may also have exaggerated the threats to its position posed by socialism in general or Wigg in particular. Wigg was not a threat to the Jockey Club's very existence; he always insisted that it did its traditional job of administering the Rules admirably, but he did not believe it to be the right kind of body, self-elected, autocratic and of the wrong class, to administer public funds or deal with the complexities of the modern world.

So the fears may have been unfounded and the acquisition of the Charter unnecessary. Nevertheless, a Charter once given would be very difficult to remove. Any chartered body can apply to have its Charter amended (as the Jockey Club had done on occasion), or may voluntarily surrender it. In theory it is also possible for the Crown, on the advice of the Privy Council, to revoke or amend a Charter against the body's wishes, but the procedure is complicated and appears not to have been used in recent centuries.

Of course, it would be possible for Parliament to revoke a Charter by legislation, though in the case of the Jockey Club such a Bill would be bound to be controversial. Furthermore, it would be necessary to signify the Queen's consent to the interference with the exercise of her prerogative, and although in giving her consent the Queen would act on Ministerial advice, it would be a brave Prime Minister who would seek to persuade the present Queen to remove the Jockey Club's Charter.

If a hostile Minister had wished gradually to whittle away the Jockey Club's powers, he would have been frustrated, because its powers are specified in the Charter. Indeed, the possession of the Charter has sometimes been a nuisance to the Club, because it was so tightly drawn that the Privy Council's permission had to be sought for quite trivial changes, such as the number of Stewards.

Whatever its value as a protective device, it is certain that the Charter did not help the Jockey Club to promote legislation which would set up a single authority, as had been proposed by Benson. This was not just because Wigg stirred the pot. The Home Office, ever since 1961, had been trying to hold racing at arm's length. It would hardly have advised Ministers to establish a statutory authority, with something very like the present Jockey Club as its disciplinary arm, for fear that the Home Secretary might end up defending disputed decisions in Parliament. Had the political will been there, no doubt such a nightmare could have been avoided, but the political will, at least at civil service level, ran in exactly the opposite direction.

At first sight it is odd that the Jockey Club should obtain a Charter to protect its autonomy, and immediately seek to give up that autonomy by becoming a subordinate body to the new Authority proposed in the Benson Report. The answer must be that Feilden and his friends were either being naive and muddled, or skilful, and the latter seems more likely. They may have calculated that they would have a very fair measure of control over the new Authority; that the Authority would be very unlikely to seek to interfere with the technicalities of racing, of which the Club was, and remains, the undoubted master; and that in return for giving up the shadow they would gain the substantial bonus of an end to George Wigg's schemes and depredations. Relations between two respectable bodies could hardly have been worse than they were between Levy Board and Jockey Club by 1970, and the prospect of any sort of improvement must have been like an oasis in the desert to the staff of both bodies.

Conclusion

Although the social composition of the Jockey Club may not have changed greatly since the war, much has altered beneath the surface. The Club, it is true, retains its absolute control of the conduct of racing, but with dependence on the levy has come the need to share power with the Levy Board, and to consult the professional associations.

Internally, the Club's organisation has become more streamlined. The Senior Steward now serves for three years and is backed up by a network of committees, professionally run by Weatherby's. (The current Secretary to the Jockey Club and Keeper of the Match Book, Christopher Foster, is the first non-Weatherby to hold that office.) In 1972 the firm leapt into the late twentieth century by establishing its computerised headquarters at Wellingborough,and where the firm led the Jockey Club has, perforce, followed.

Notes

1 R.Mortimer, *The Jockey Club*, London, 1958, p. 10.
2 Jockey Club, *Report of the Racing Reorganisation Committee to the Stewards of the Jockey Club*, London, February 1943.
3 R. Mortimer, 'A war on racing's bigotry', *Pacemaker International*, August 1984. pp. 120-4.
4 Joint Racing Board, *The Racing Industry: Report of the Working Party on Racecourse Management*, London, June 1969.
5 P. Willett, *Makers of the Modern Thoroughbred*, London, 1984, p. 37.
6 *Ibid.*, p. 54.
7 Jockey Club, *The Report of the Duke of Norfolk's Committee on the Pattern of Racing*, London, August 1965, para. 51.
8 Alan Skinner, circular letter to members of the West Suffolk County Council, 8 November 1965.
9 721 *H.C. Deb.*, cols. 1386 & 1389, 30 November 1965.
10 *Cambridge News*, 8 November 1965.
11 Jockey Club, *Report of the Howard Committee*, London, 1964.
12 *The Sporting Life*, 1 October and 17 December 1964.
13 Jockey Club, *The Racing Industry: Report by the Committee of Inquiry*, London, June 1968 (Benson Committee).
14 *Ibid.*, para. 174.
15 The Commentary Fund is collected from off-course bookmakers by Exchange Telegraph and paid to the Racecourse Association (RCA) in return for the right to receive Extel's race commentary over the 'blower' in betting shops. The RCA divides the fund among all its member racecourses.

16 Benson Committee, *Report*, para. 328.
17 Touche Ross & Co. and Deloitte & Co., *Cost Effective Study: the Jockey Club's Administration of Racing*. Presented to the Joint Racing Board, 31 March 1971 (unpublished typescript).
18 Horserace Betting Levy Board, *Tenth Report, 1 April 1970–31 March 1971*, London, 1971, para. 143.
19 McKinsey & Co., Inc., *Strengthening the Jockey Club Organization* and *Improving Jockey Club Public Relations and Maintaining the Financial Viability of the Jockey Club*, London, July and September 1972 (unpublished typescripts).
20 H. Wright, 'Minding the business of owners: Howard Wright talks to Nick Robinson, the retiring President of the Racehorse Owners' Association', *Pacemaker International*, August 1984, pp. 58-62.
21 Royal Commission on Gambling, *Final Report*, vol. 1 (Cmnd. 7200), London, July 1978, para. 9.31.
22 See, for example, *The Times*, 4 August 1969.

VIII
Internationalism in racing

After the war both racing and breeding became increasingly international, thanks to the growth of air transport. Peter Willett records
that:

> In the 1960s there was an annual exchange of about four hundred
> mares for mating each way between England and Ireland, and about
> the same number each way between England and Ireland on the one
> hand and France on the other. Some mares were flown across the
> Atlantic to visit stallions. International exchanges of bloodstock pro-
> ceeded at an ever increasing rate; and the rapid expansion of the
> Japanese breeding industry depended heavily on air transport, as the
> fact that J. A. Peden Ltd., the English bloodstock transport agency,
> flew one hundred and four stallions and mares to Japan in five Boeing
> 707 planes in the winter of 1969-70 clearly indicates.[1]

A convenient point from which to date the internationalisation of
racing is the publication in August 1965 of *The Report of the Duke of
Norfolk's Committee on the Pattern of Racing*.[2] The committee members
were Norfolk, Geoffrey Freer and Peter Willett, with 'the amiable
and efficient Brigadier Sidney Kent' (as Willett describes him)[3] as
secretary. Their terms of reference were 'To make recommendations
on the general programme of all races and stakes, with specal attention to the top class horses of all ages, the prestige races and the
improvement of the thoroughbred'.

The Committee's approach nicely encapsulated the transition
between traditional and modern thinking about the purpose of
racing. It recognised that times had changed since two hundred years
ago, but did so reluctantly: 'In those days and up to quite recently
the object of racing was a sport and the betterment of the
thoroughbred. And many of the rules of racing today were framed
to safeguard this animal through its racing career. Today the sport

has turned into an industry, is looked upon almost entirely commercially and few of those who follow it think anything at all about the welfare of the horse.'

The Committee's reasons for thinking the improvement of the racehorse important were also a mixture of ancient and modern. On the one hand, the thoroughbred was a British creation, part of the national heritage, which was worth preserving, and, like the Mother of Parliaments, was respected by foreigners as typically British. But the bloodstock industry was also a substantial exporter, and both reasons entitled racing to sympathetic consideration from the Government 'no only in times of war and national crisis, but at all times'.

The Committee perhaps went rather too far when it added that if the Turf Authorities failed in their duty to try to preserve the supremacy of the British thoroughbred 'racing is liable to be debased to the level of roulette, and does not deserve to survive'. The sentiment behind the statement is easy enough to understand, and to sympathise with, but twenty years on the statement seems plainly false. In the first place, racing might become so international that the distinction between the British and, say, the French thoroughbred would become unimportant; alternatively, even if the French thoroughbred were supreme, there would be no need for British racing to descend to the level of roulette. Nobody makes any such assertion within a single country (for example, a day at Folkestone races is not likened to a visit to a casino), and there is no reason why it should be made internationally.

But there can be no quarrel with the Committee's main purpose, which was to urge the Turf Authorities to 'ensure that a series of races over the right distances and at the right time of the year, are available to test the best horses of all ages, and they must attempt to ensure that the horses remain in training long enough and race often enough to be tested properly for constitution and soundness. The pattern of racing must combat the temptation to syndicate horses for stud too early in their careers.' Of course, the Committee could not foresee the extraordinary explosion in stud values, which has made it so uneconomic to keep colts in training as four-year-olds: for example, if Golden Fleece (the winner of the 1982 Derby) had lived, he could not possibly have earned in prize money at four anything approaching his potential earnings as a stallion. Nevertheless, the Committee's principles are as acceptable now as they were in 1965.

The Committee made detailed recommendations about races for each of the different ages, two, three and four, which it backed up by reference to the French pattern of racing. It was concerned primarily with top-class races and thought that 'on the whole, handicaps must be regarded as a necessary evil because they put a premium on mediocrity'. Again, the French practice of providing 'all types of weight-for-age races with few handicaps' was cited with approval.

The Committee thought the stakes added to some of the Prestige races in the calendar were too high, and should be redistributed by the Levy Board to some of the less valuable races recommended in the report. The Committee believed that the very high prize money for some races was intended to attract French entries, but thought such reasoning mistaken. In its view, 'The French are well able to win the same amount of money in their own country and it is the name of the race which has attracted them in the past and will attract them in the future'. The report made references to the Ilchester Report of 1943, and regretted that more of its recommendations had not been put into effect. In particular it saw the value of courses being run on a non-profit-making basis, though it did not repeat Ilchester's suggestion that they should be bought by the Jockey Club. Finally, the Committee recorded, in a paragraph already quoted, the special importance of Newmarket 'as the home and headquarters of racing in this country'.

Though the report has turned out to be seminal, nothing was done about it at first, and, but for the energy of Lord Porchester, it might have gone the same way as Ilchester. Porchester was so frustrated by the lack of follow-up that he worked out a chart of British 'Pattern' races, and went with it to General Feilden, demanding action. (A few years later the chart was printed, by then including French and Irish races, and is a familiar sight in the offices of racing's professionals.) Feilden was sympathetic and suggested Porchester might need a committee. Porchester asked for Peter Willett, the noted writer on racing who had been a member of the Norfolk Committee, and had the advantage of not yet being a member of the Jockey Club. (He was elected in 1981.) The Stewards agreed, and in 1967 Porchester, Willett and Kent formed the Race Planning Committee. It reported in May 1967, and 131 races (gradually reduced to 103 in 1987) were adopted as Pattern races in Britain, replacing the former unofficial categories of Classic, Prestige and Feature races.

The International flat race Pattern was very soon accepted in principle by the French (the Irish joined in shortly afterwards), but before it could be put into practice the problem was to work out some form of equivalence between races in the different countries. Otherwise, such was the disparity between British and Irish prize money on the one hand, and French on the other, that winners of important British and Irish races could have run without penalty (that is without carrying any additional weight), and therefore with an unfair advantage, in French races. The consequence was that the French naturally threatened to ban British and Irish horses, except in races in which they met on strict weight-for-age terms, without penalties and allowances. This problem led Porchester, with David Weatherby, to invent the group system, whereby races in different countries were to be assigned to groups according to their quality, irrespective of the prize money given. The system, a British initiative, designed to placate the French and to allow British and French horses to go on running in France, was agreed between the English, French and Irish authorities in 1970, and brought into operation in 1971. Not all breeders immediately saw the desirability of opening their races to foreign horses, and in 1974 and 1975 there was strong pressure from some breeders to close all races except those in Group I. However, other breeders and the race clubs devised a system of premiums for the owners of French-bred winners, which was adopted and seems to have caused the discontent to die away.

Since prize money was so much higher in France, the criteria by which a race was assigned to a group had to be a combination of the quality of field it attracted and the kudos attached to winning it. Both these criteria are difficult to measure, so that decisions had at first to be made by educated intuition, which was a reasonable way of proceeding, given that the people involved had the most highly educated intuition in the business. The trail blazers did not only follow intuition but also made some rules: there was no problem about Group I races, which were for the very best horses from any country; Group II races were also international, but made provision for penalties and allowances, as in the Hardwicke at Ascot in June, or the Lockinge Stakes at Newbury in May. Group III races were essentially domestic and regarded as stepping stones to the higher groups, though foreign horses have frequently run in them. The experience gained since the 1960s, plus the new international handicapping classification, have made the grouping of races much easier than in the past. For example, if a race designated as a Group II attracts Group III fields year after year, the race will be reduced to Group III.

So far as the shape of the Pattern was concerned, it was agreed that Group I races must not clash; the authorities should try to ensure that those in Group II did not, but clashes between the primarily domestic Group III races did not matter. The quality of horses attracted to the various groups may be illustrated by reference to the average ratings (handicaps) of winners of Pattern races for three-year-olds and over in 1983. The averages were: Group I, 86; Group II, 83; Group III, 79. In 1985 a sub-committee of the Race Planning Committee worked out minimum standards for British Group races based on the ratings of the first four horses in all such races over the previous five years. These were (three years old and over): Group 1, 80; Group 2, 75; Group 3, 70; (two years old): Group 1, 75; Group 2, 71; Group 3, 68. The average ratings achieved in 1986 were Group 1: 87.5 (127.5), Group 2: 81.5 (121.5), Group 3: 78.8 (118.8). (The figures in brackets were those actually used in 1986, when the scale of ratings was extended from 0–100 to 0–140.)[4]

The point of grouping was not to invent races, but to grade those that already existed. This is not to say that the Pattern has been static: on the contrary, it has been refined over the years, often because the needs of particular horses have shown up its weaknesses. Some changes have also been made for trainers who want to defer the decision as to a horse's ideal distance: examples are the Earl of Sefton Stakes (Newmarket, mid-April), nine furlongs, for horses which may turn out best at either a mile or a mile and a quarter, and the Yorkshire Cup, formerly two miles, but now a mile and three-quarters, allowing trainers to keep open the option of running a horse afterwards in the long-distance Cup races or going down to a mile and a half.

The Pattern also assisted British domestic racing, because it helped the Levy Board to decide which races it should support in order to meet one of its three statutory duties, the improvement of horse racing. Wigg liked the Pattern for this reason: he also took the view that, since the levy came from bets placed all over the country, and from Scotland, there ought also to be Pattern races in Scotland and the north of England. He therefore tried to introduce new Pattern races to redress the balance. This was not a bad aim in itself, but the new races were not successful.

Though Wigg was in favour of the Pattern, he would not give the

Jockey Club *carte blanche* and insisted that the Flat Race Pattern Committee should have a press representative and a bookmaker, or bookmaker-orientated member. In fact, Charles Layfield, a well-known bookmaker, was appointed to the Committee, and has remained a member ever since, just as Porchester himself remained Chairman from the Committee's inception until 1984. Willett left the Committee in 1977, after twelve years' association with the Pattern, but now he is back again, this time as a representative of the Jockey Club. Thus, the wheel has come full circle. There must, of course, be advantages in so few personnel being involved over the years, yet those within the circle must sometimes wish that there were more people with whom to share the work. Indeed, in January 1985 Lord Porchester retired from the Committee, and was replaced by Tim Holland-Martin, who was still Chairman in 1987.

Over the years the (British) Pattern Committee's work has changed little: the big change has been financial, because Levy Board money has declined and sponsorship greatly increased, and was even extended to the Classics in 1984. However, the review carried out in 1985 led to considerable movement between Groups and to the Pattern Committee taking over responsibility for Listed Races as a fourth layer of quality races. Formerly, the Committee had reviewed these annually in conjunction with the Thoroughbred Breeders' Association.

Germany and Italy joined the international Pattern, at their own request, in 1971. The request was granted, on condition that no group races were limited to indigenous animals. This could not happen overnight, but there has been a noteworthy difference between the Italian and German responses. Only one Italian group race remains reserved for Italian-bred horses, whereas the Germans only agreed to remove the indigenous qualification from all Group races, except the five Classics, by 1989. In 1990 they will have to decide whether to remove the qualification from the Classics, or run the risk of having those races struck out of the Pattern. One argument for protectionism is that in many parts of Germany the climate causes horses to mature later than their English counterparts. At least one major stud virulently opposed Germany joining the Pattern, and there is still some antipathy to it.

The protectionists' case has been strengthened by the example of Italy, where a great many group races are won by English and French horses. By an odd contradiction the German open group races take more winning than the Italian: one informed opinion is that German-bred group horses are six or seven pounds better than their Italian equivalents. Nor do leading trainers regard group races in Italy and Germany so highly as those in Britain, Ireland and France. As Vincent O'Brien said of his horse Esperanto: 'I'm not keen on going to Italy or Germany because I don't think that winning there does much for a horse's value as a stallion. You must win your Group races in Ireland, Britain or France.'[5]

The International Pattern Committee consists of officials from the five countries, who debate and adjudicate upon applications from the various countries for changes in Pattern races for the following year, and report back to their national stewards. The officials' agreement is binding, but any serious points of difference can be taken up at the annual international stewards' meeting (which includes the USA as well as the European five). This meeting takes place earlier in the year than that of the International Pattern Committee, so that the latter can take its views into account when agreeing the Pattern for the next year. The 'ground rules' for the European Pattern, drawn up and agreed by the five countries in 1979, and revised in 1984, cover the requirements for any introduction of new Pattern races, regrading, changes of dates or conditions, and major prize money changes.

The Pattern is not, of course, free from controversy. For example, in 1984, Robert Sangster (through his Swettenham Stud) and the York Race Committee wanted to include an extremely valuable race for three-year-olds and over in the Timeform annual charity day in June. This was not allowed by the Stewards of the Jockey Club, because it would have detracted from similar races which were already in the Pattern: in the event it would, at least, have reduced the fields of the St James's Palace Stakes and the Queen Anne Stakes at Ascot. However, Sangster's wish to do something for racing was not wasted, as when he was approached to consider the alternative of adding the offered money to the Group I Sussex Stakes at Goodwood, he readily agreed.

Owners of group horses who decide to go for valuable races outside the Pattern may win big prizes but not kudos, and therefore not breeding value. The winner of, say, the Grand Prix Prince Rose (Grade I, Ostend, 2200 metres for thee-year-olds and over), will have won nearly £40,000 in added prize money. Even £12,000 is sufficient to render a horse liable for a Group I penalty (in other words, the penalty normally given to the winner of a Group I race if it races outside its Group) and since such a race as the Grand Prix Prince Rose might well be won by a horse of Group III quality, the winner attracts a higher penalty than it will be able to carry successfully if it subsequently runs in Pattern races. The penalty would, of course, be of no consequence if the race were won by a horse of Group I quality, but in that case it would probably not have strayed outside the Pattern.

All this is considered unfair by people who would like the Pattern to be extended to countries whose racing the International Pattern Committee thinks below the required standard. The purist, however, would reply that this example shows exactly what the Pattern is intended to do, namely to stratify horses by quality, and confer prestige on winners in a way which is accepted and understood internationally. This international agreement on what quality *is* (the ability to win group races) also helps to sustain and regulate the bloodstock market, both nationally and internationally. Thus, there need be no objection to extending the Pattern, provided the calibre of the race, and the horses it attracts, can be reliably measured.

There are also people who want handicaps included in the Pattern. They are answered by both purists' and practical arguments. First, the purist will say that a group race is, by its very nature, not a handicap. The handicapper's dream is to arrange the weights so that all the horses in a race, whatever their quality, are within a whisker of each other at the finish, whereas the very different purpose of a group race is competition to provide an absolute test of quality. Secondly, from the practical point of view, a handicap in the Pattern would be limited to a very narrow range, say a stone. In the USA there is a long tradition of very valuable, and therefore successful, handicaps of limited weight range, in which the best horses, especially those of four years old and upwards, habitually run. In Britain there is no similar tradition and such handicaps have tended to attract few runners, and to be won by one of the leading trainers 'carving it up' with a Group III horse. Furthermore, sponsors, whose wishes are becoming increasingly important, naturally prefer handicaps with a large weight range because they provide more exciting racing with larger fields.

Within the Pattern there are some differences of practice. For example, the proportion of prize money provided by owners differs between Britain and France, as does the way the value of a race is calculated.

There is also a difference in the organisation of classic trials. The more important difference is that the Prix Lupin (Longchamp, mid-May) precedes the Prix du Jockey Club (the French Derby, Chantilly, mid-June) by a month, but as a Group I race is of such prestige that in some years it brings together the best three-year-olds, who will later meet in the French Derby, and therefore cannot be regarded as a true classic trial. Secondly there are fewer classic trials in France than in England; they are held at only three or four courses, all in or near Paris, and there is less likelihood that the condition of the ground will vary greatly, so that false results occur less frequently. In England the variations of climate and ground in different parts of the country make alternatives essential. For example, there is usually good ground at Newmarket in the spring, when conditions at, say, York may be very different. Furthermore, training methods are different, and trainers are conservative: they get used over the years to preparing horses for certain races. Thus, although in French eyes there may be too many classic trials in England, there are sound reasons for the number and variety that exist.

Though there are local differences, and occasional complaints in the press that the French dominate the Pattern, on the whole the International Pattern works well. It also, of course, complicates life. Whereas in the old days everyone in racing knew where everyone else would be on a certain day, with the calendar imposing as firm a shape on racing people's lives as does the Church on Christians', now there is alway a chance that a trainer and his entourage will be in Baden Baden or Evry or Rome.

This mobility looks likely to increase, and with it at least an informal pattern is likely to grow. It would, for example, be foolish to allow the Budweiser Million (late August) to clash with the Eclipse (mid-July), indeed, no one framing a new race would wish to upset the European Pattern countries, particularly Britain, Ireland and France. On the other hand, the attractions of America are limited: no English owner would go for the Preakness instead of the Derby, and American racing is often thought less interesting than English, because most American tracks are dirt and tend to be monotonously similar, rather tight, left-handed oblongs. Nevertheless, the grades into which North American Graded Stakes races are classified are regarded as the equivalent of groups in the Pattern for the purpose of calculating penalties, an equivalence which is often questioned by pundits, who argue that American races do not match their European counterparts in quality.

Even if an informal Pattern were to extend worldwide, so that clashes were eliminated, a number of factors would still prevent invitation races, designed to bring together the best horses from all over the world, from becoming world championships. Peter Willett cited some reasons in 1970, when commenting on the Washington International, which had first been run in 1970:

> the difficulties of bringing all the best horses together in a kind of world championship are insuperable. The difference of the seasons and of the age bases of horses in the northern and southern hemispheres, the contrasts in the patterns of racing, the varying reactions of individual animals to long distance travel and changes of climate and environment – all these and many other factors militate against the most ambitions aims of the Washington International. . .[6]

Willett was right about the difficulties, but there has been considerable evolution in international racing since 1970, and now a series of North American middle-distance races in the autumn provides a magnet for the very best European horses. Furthermore, at least one leading authority suggests that such long-distance travel may grow more among fillies than colts and that the great prizes available will persuade owners to keep fillies in training as four-year-olds. His explanation is that, once a filly has won the Oaks or the Arc, she will not shed her paddock value if she subsequently loses races, whereas a colt may lose his attractiveness as a stallion. A filly's estrous cycle normally stops in the autumn, so that, instead of being depleted once a month, she should be in excellent fettle for such major races as the Japan Cup.

Willett went on to draw attention to the health risks inseparable from the international orientation of racing and breeding, and to 'the growing commercialism which has threatened to submerge horse racing as a sport'. The danger, Willett continued, was: 'that breeding will become a department of big business and that racecourses will become casinos with animated counters. Fortunately, the thoroughbred is indeed a creature of blood and heat and spirit, and is perfectly capable, at frequent and salutory intervals, of throwing the rules of big business and investment analysis out of the window and turning rational profit projections on their heads.'[7] He then cited the Prix de l'Arc de Triomphe of 1969, in which all the first three horses were by cheap and unfashionable stallions.

Similar, though perhaps not such striking, examples could be found in subsequent years, but it must be said that Willett's fears (similar to those he had expressed as a member of the Norfolk Pattern Committee in 1965) have, to a large extent, been realised. However, things may not be as bad as they sound. Although all breeders are in business, in the sense that they breed to make money, either by selling the produce or racing it, by winning prize money and by establishing stud or paddock value, few of them breed *solely* for money. A very few breeders are so rich that they do not need to think about money (there were more of these in the past), but it is a matter of daily observation that some of the very rich in fact seldom think about anything else. Some breeders are unsuccessful businessmen, and some go bankrupt.

According to a pamphlet published by the Thoroughbred Breeders' Association in December 1981, the quality of British-bred horses declined in the 1970s.[8] In the early 1970s they were winning more than fifty per cent of British Pattern races; the rate fell to forty per cent in 1980 and 37 per cent in 1979, but improved to 44.9 per cent in 1981. The TBA did not think the quality of foreign horses had risen; they were just winning more races because the native opposition was less keen.

At the same time there was a sharp reduction in the number of large studs. In 1975, 5085 foals were produced; there were ninety-three studs with more than ten mares each, and 4,344 breeders with one mare each. By 1980, when 4,677 foals were produced, there were only sixty-nine studs with more than ten mares, and the number of breeders with only one mare had risen to 4,704. The TBA did not assert a necessary correlation between size of stud and quality of produce, but added that: 'changes of this magnitude cannot be interpreted otherwise than as an erosion of high investment/high quality breeding and its replacement by low investment and hobby breeding'.

If commercialism has increased, as it surely has, it may therefore be linked less to the size of studs than to the changing attitudes and motives of some of their owners. The small breeders are probably neither more nor less commercially minded than they always were, except that, with the vast rise in the bloodstock market, possible rewards and disappointments are greater than in the past. But the average breeder is running a small, and often struggling operation.

At the top end of the market things have indeed changed. If breeders can be persuaded (as a few were) to pay $1 million for a share in Shareef Dancer or £100,000 for a nomination (i.e. the right to send a mare) to the late Golden Fleece, they can hardly be expected to take a non-commercial view of their investments. Nor can the owner of a 'stallion station' in the United States, or a chain of studs, like Coolmore and its satellites in Ireland, be expected to treat the whole operation as a pastime.

On the other hand, if an owner or breeder, however international his scope, runs his racing or stud for pleasure, fun, amusement, the love of horses, or what you will, *as well as* the hope of profit, then he is not essentially different from the one-horse owner or one-mare breeder. Similarly, if he breeds and races in order to achieve something specific, like safeguarding an estate, but goes on doing it for fun once the immediate object is achieved, he is still in the purist tradition. But if, so far as anyone can tell, he is in it solely for the money, he threatens, in the purist's contention, to undermine the whole activity by taking away its heart. And in doing that he destroys what, for other owners and breeders, is not merely a means of making money but a total way of life.

This is an extreme statement of the purist point of view. Fortunately, most owners and breeders have mixed motives, and as long as that continues, racing will still be enjoyable.

The Arabs

When they first came to England the major Arab owners were presented almost as a twentieth-century replica of the eighteenth-century Jockey Club; that is, as a dedicated group, uninterested in money but passionately involved in the sport of racing, and determined to put it on its feet. That interpretation may still be applicable to some Arab owners and breeders, though the hasty syndication of Shareef Dancer at a then record figure (if one interprets the figures charitably) of $40 million gave it a knock. In any case, the more sober view of Arab involvement in British (and more recently Irish) racing and breeding is that it has been good for the industry, both in Britain and America. The Arabs' wealth makes it seem absurd to suppose that their motives are commerical in any ordinary sense, but they do like to break records and are said to be attracted to racing partly because money alone does *not* guarantee success.

However, John Leat, *homme de confiance* of Sheikh Mohammed of

Dubai, the leading Arab owner and breeder, has said that the Sheikh's racing operation is becoming more businesslike than in the past. He is also reducing the number of horses he has in training, and intends to avoid pitting champions against each other.[9] These remarks lend some credence to the pessimistic view that the Classics may ultimately be devalued, if several animals of Classic quality belong to the same owner and are kept from competing with one another.

The Arabs' competitive instincts may have driven prices mad, and they seem very likely to come down when Arab owners have enough home-bred animals to enable them to buy less lavishly at the sales. But the fact that they are buying stud land and setting up large breeding operations disposes of the fear that they might simply fold their tents and leave, or take to tiddlywinks instead of racing. The impression that some, at least, of the Arab owners and breeders are more than birds of passage is increased by the diversity of their interests; not merely the ownership of the Carlton Tower Hotel but also such relatively minor signs of involvement as the gift of £100,000 for an investigation of why grouse is a declining species in Scotland. (The donor, Sheikh Hamdan Al Maktoum, has a grouse moor, and is worried about the poor bags.)[10]

No doubt some far-sighted Arabs also give thought to the stability of their ruling houses, should they ever lose their importance as cold-war allies, or become too unsettled for the West to continue to support them. The prospect seems remote, but so once did the downfall of the Shah of Iran.

Arab involvement in British racing started amazingly recently and in a small way, when Tim Bulwer-Long, the enterprising partner in Heron Bloodstock Agency, decided in about 1975 to try and develop the Middle Eastern market ahead of anyone else. (The agency has a history of foreign enterprise: after the war Ted Corbett, the father of John Corbett, Bulwer-Long's partner, opened up the Japanese market for the British Bloodstock Agency when wartime memories were too fresh for most agents to have any dealings with the Japanese, and John Corbett carried on the tradition until 1978, when exchange control and over-production at home made the Japanese drop out of the market like a stone.) Bulwer-Long made three trips to the Middle East, twice alone and once with trainers Jeremy Hindley and Ben Hanbury, and found out who counted in the various countries. He obtained an introduction to Sheikh Mohammed, who was not yet interested, but when he did come into racing Sheikh Mohammed recruited Colonel Dick Warden from the Curragh Bloodstock Agency to look after his interests. Warden, in turn, brought in John Dunlop as Sheikh Mohammed's first trainer in England, in about 1977, and the Sheikh became his biggest single owner. However, Bulwer-Long's efforts were not fruitless, since he found a new owner in Oman, Tariq al Said. He died at the end of 1980, but his son, Kais, carried on the family interest; he now owns Muscatite, among others, and has bought a stud in Gloucestershire.

The question in agents' minds now is, where are new Arab owners to come from once the existing ones are mainly racing home-breds and therefore no longer large yearling buyers? Oman is a small oil producer, and has to fund a huge defence budget, because of its long borders and numerous neighbours. Dubai and Saudi Arabia are the richest countries, and Saudi Arabia probably the best potential source of new owners, but it suffers from the disadvantage, from the bloodstock industry's point of view, that its oil income goes into the national coffers, and not into the private purse of the ruling family, as in Dubai, where the Royal and public purses are indistinguishable. Kuwait is already in racing (the Royal Family has a stud in Sussex); there is little prospect of new owners from Abu Dhabi or Qatar, and few possibilities exist in Bahrein. It follows that, though the market will stabilise when the Arabs become largely self-sufficient, it will probably do so at a lower level than at present. The answer (from the business point of view feared by Peter Willett) is to see the market as a worldwide entity, and to seek to raise it in areas, like Australia, where it has not yet reached European and American levels. This, in turn, might involve persuading current Arab owners to extend their interests, and so put off, for the time being, the problem of finding completely new money.

Outside the Arab world there are said to be some signs that the Japanese will return to the market, thanks to the strength of the yen.

The European Breeders' Fund

The European Breeders' Fund (EBF) is a very recent and important addition to the range of international agreements in racing. The Thoroughbred Breeders' Association has argued for many years[11] that Breeders' Prizes should be payable to the *breeders* of winning horses, that it, to the owners of dams of winners, from Levy Board money. It has never succeeded in persuading the Levy Board, but it has since 1982 enthusiastically supported the payment of additional prize money from the EBF to *owners* of British, French, Irish and American qualified winners, from money provided by stallion owners and syndicates. The German Racing Authority (Direktorium für Vollblutzucht und Rennen), representing the fifth member of the Pattern, was from the beginning in favour of the EBF but could not initially take charge of negotiations for German entry, since in the other countries the arrangements were being made by the breeders. The German breeders were at first not enthusiastic, partly because membership would entail opening all their two-year-old races and partly because it happened that their leaders were not fluent in English. They gradually became more interested in joining, and asked the Direktorium to conduct the negotiations on their behalf, with the result that Germany acceded to the EBF in 1986. Italy joined at the same time, relatively painlessly, because it had already almost completed the process of opening its races to foreign competition.[12]

Wider membership may pose practical problems, but will not alter the principles on which the fund is run, nor the benefits which it confers on owners of dams of winners. These are indirect, in that it is hoped that the EBF contributions will encourage owners to continue to invest, and so to maintain the bloodstock market. This belief in the link between prize money and willingness to own is, of course, difficult to prove or disprove, or to generalise about at all, since motives probably vary between individual owners, and owners of different classes of horse. But, clearly, there must be *some* link. There is also a small element of direct assistance to breeders, in that £100,000 was allocated by the British EBF trustees to breeders of winners conceived while the EBF stallion was standing in Great Britain. Most of the breeders' prizes in 1984 went, as it has turned out, to small breeders, precisely the people whom the TBA has for many years seen as most in need of them.

The scheme is run by a Co-ordinating Committee of two representatives from each of the three European participating countries, and by national Trustees in each country, who decide how the national share of the pool is to be allocated. The Committee also conducts negotiations with the Americans on behalf of all three countries. The scheme provides that, starting in 1984, fifty per cent of maiden two-year-old races in the three European countries would be confined to the progeny of qualified stallions standing in any country. Thus there would be 210 EBF races in Britain (some of which might be split) and forty-three in Ireland. In France the situation was somewhat more complicated, because although France was to reserve fifty per cent of her maiden two-year-old races for EBF horses, only fifteen of the fifty-four races on Paris courses would be open in 1984 to horses trained outside France. However, in four years all fifty-four would be open, and a further twenty-five races on provincial courses.

To ensure that a stallion was qualified, its owner (or syndicate of owners) had to deposit annually with the fund's trustees a sum equivalent to the average cost of a nomination to the stallion in the previous year, or, if no nominations had been sold, a sum accepted as reasonable by the trustees. (The contributions are calculated on the basis of one hundred per cent of straight fees, seventy per cent of October pregnancy fees; for split payment nominations, one hundred per cent of the first payment and seventy per cent of the second, and sixty per cent of live foal fees.) The 1984 pool (renegotiated for 1985) was split as follows: Great Britain 48.75 per cent; Ireland 26.25 per cent; France 25 per cent.

Cross-registration with the American Breeders' Cup Fund has allowed European horses to enter for the extremely valuable Breeders' Cup, Event Day and Premium Awards Programme. In return, American horses are eligible for European EBF races, in exchange for a contribution to the EBF pool of 7.5 per cent of the American stallion pool of about $10 million and a contribution to the Breeders' Cup of 7.5 per cent of the EBF pool. The principles upon which the two funds are raised differ, since in the Breeders Cup not only is the stallion made eligible by the annual payment of a sum equivalent to the published nomination fee (or 'farm price'), but individual foals by eligible stallions also pay a nomination fee.

The EBF scheme was first announced by Peter Willett, President of the Thoroughbred Breeders' Association, at the Association's Annual General Meeting on 10 January 1983. On this occasion the TBA achieved something of a coup in getting the then Home Secretary, William (now Viscount) Whitelaw, to their post-AGM luncheon, where he described the scheme as 'a wholly admirable example of self-help'. The scheme had been approved in principle by the Jockey Club and Levy Board, the latter having been forced by the recession to make an 11.3 per cent cut in its contribution to prize money.

A few days later, John Hislop and his wife, the owners of Brigadier Gerard, issued their first broadsides against the fund, which Hislop called 'illogical, unethical and dangerous in principle'. Hislop, a member of the Jockey Club since 1971, objected to the element of compulsion in the scheme, to the fact that it had never been discussed at a Jockey Club meeting, so that most members learned of it in the press, and to the large-scale disruption of the racing programme that it entailed. He, and some other stallion owners, refused to join the EBF scheme , partly because they considered that it amounted to blackmail. At least some of the scheme's leading supporters do not try to refute the charge; indeed, one of them agrees that it does contain 'an acceptable amount of *quasi*-blackmail'. Others, however, would see this as too harsh. The scheme was, after all, devised by stallion owners for stallion owners, and naturally included inducements to take part. The Hislops' refusal need, in any case, not have mattered, since the scheme provides for any owner or owners of a stallion's produce to pay the contribution themselves.

So strongly did Hislop feel that he promptly resigned from the TBA, though not from the Jockey Club. He thought few Americans would be interested in joining the scheme, partly because the memory still rankled of the Jersey Act at the turn of the century, under which all horses which did not trace back a hundred years were excluded from the stud book. Mrs Hislop added that the TBA had been ill-mannered in announcing the scheme without writing to stallion owners in advance; it would impose hardships on owners of stallions whose books did not fill, and she disliked the idea of subsidising owners.

The formidable Hislop team might have attracted enough allies in the Jockey Club to destroy the scheme, but the disadvantages of staying out were too obvious and substantial. It had been expected that the 118 British-based stallions which had sired at least one two-year-old winner in 1982 would be entered; in fact a larger number, led by the National Stud, was entered (not necessarily including all the original 118 'targets'), so that a success rate of over a hundred per cent was achieved. Nor were the Americans slow to see that they could hardly afford to stay out. As Tony Morris put it: 'America sold Europe 100,000,000 million dollars worth of yearlings in 1982. Does he [Hislop] really suppose that they will lose that ship for the ha'p'orth of tar that will preserve it?'[13] Hislop would, I suspect, reply that Morris has got his priorities wrong. Many of his arguments are detailed and esoteric, but he rests his case on a major point of principle: 'Fundamentally, racing is about horses, not money; and even if some political holocaust overcame the country, demolishing the whole fabric of racing as we know it, the sport would go on privately in the manner in which it originated.'[14] That statement of faith touches a theme which runs all through this book – the tension in racing between money and love of horses, between sport and industry.

Genesis of the EBF

The proponents of the EBF had moved fast and effectively. The idea had first been mooted at the Highflyer yearling sale at Newmarket in October 1982, when six of its progenitors found themselves sheltering together from the rain. A formal meeting followed at the December sales, where the record was taken by the TBA, and representatives of the owners, the Levy Board, Weatherby's, the Horseracing Advisory Council and the French and Irish Turf Authorities were present. Lord Porchester chaired the meeting and played a large part in persuading those present that the idea was viable. It was eventualy agreed that the TBA was the body best qualified to develop it.

The Stewards of the Jockey Club were consulted very shortly afterwards and, thanks to Simon Weatherby, consented to the scheme, provided ninety per cent of the British stallions engaged in producing horses for the flat were entered. However, in February the Jockey Club was warned by its lawyers that it would be *ultra vires* for it to close certain races, though gentle encouragement would be perfectly in order. It was for this reason that the EBF's formal dealings had to be with the Racecourse Association, leaving the Jockey Club to deal with the EBF as if it were a run-of-the-mill sponsor. The RCA therefore sent out to all racecourses a circular seeking support for the scheme, and received consent from all of them, once minor objections from Warwick and Wolverhampton had been overcome. Nevertheless, it was still considered essential to have the Stewards' blessing, since without the co-operation of the Jockey Club's Race Planning Committee the EBF could not make progress in deciding which races would be EBF races, whether or not the Jockey Club had the power to restrict them. In July, the month after the EBF Co-ordinating Agreement had been signed by British, French and Irish representatives, an *impasse* in negotiations in the Jockey Club/EBF working party was reached over the distribution of prize money for the maiden two-year-old races sponsored by the EBF, but the difficulties were resolved, thanks to months of hard work and diplomacy by Weatherby's.

Meanwhile, negotiations had proceeded internationally. In Ireland the scheme's initial impetus had come from Jonathan Irwin, managing director of Goff's, the auctioneers, but his failure to consult the Irish stallion owners had caused suspicion, particularly in connection with his negotiations with the Americans. However, the stallion owners came round to the scheme, though they insisted on Major Victor McCalmont becoming chairman of the Irish Trust. He, in turn, insisted that Irwin should become Vice-Chairman, partly because McCalmont was reluctant to undertake the considerable amount of travelling that the scheme might entail.

The percentages of the pool which should go to each country were the subject of energetic bargaining. It was reasonably easy for Britain and Ireland to agree that Britain should have the lion's share, because British races provide the major testing-ground for Irish-bred horses and Irish breeders are heavily dependent on the English market, and if the French had refused to join the scheme, as at first seemed likely, sixty-five per cent would have gone to Britain and thirty-five per cent to Ireland.

The French had at first hoped to remain outside the scheme for the time being: a further complication was introduced by Monsieur Jean-Pierre Launay, the new Chef de Service des Haras Nationaux (roughly, Head of the National Studs, the Government Department, within the Ministry of Agriculture, which oversees all aspects of the horse industry in France, including racing), who was initially reluctant to be a party to an agreement which would prevent some French-bred horses (i.e. those by non-EBF stallions) from running in some French races. However, he came round when nearly all the stallion owners agreed to join the scheme. Even then the British representatives at first bid for sixty per cent of the pool, but were well satisfied with the 48.75 per cent finally agreed. Ireland retained 26.25 per cent and France took only 25 per cent, on the ground that it had fewer stallions than the other countries. Many of its best had been exported to the USA, in response to the much higher stallion values prevailing there, and the trend may possibly have been strengthened by the prospect of the socialist President Mitterrand's accession to power. The French, however, gave notice that they intended to renegotiate their percentage for 1985 and successfully did so. (The new percentages, which were not changed in 1986 or 1987, were Britain forty-five per cent, Ireland twenty-eight per cent, France twenty-seven per cent.) Thus, the French percentage remains the smallest; however, thanks to Monsieur Launay's decision that the subscriptions of stallions standing at F5,000 or less should be paid by the Fonds Commun, the French have the highest number of stallions in the scheme. (The Fonds Commun is a fund established by the Fédération Nationale des Sociétés de Courses en France and controlled by a committee of representatives of the racecourse associations, and of the Ministries of Agriculture and the Budget.) The possibility remained open of Germany and Italy joining the scheme later, and meanwhile individual stallion owners or syndicates might join from anywhere.

In Britain the EBF has improved the image of racing, and especially of the breeders, in the eyes of the Government, because it is so much in tune with the self-help philosophy of Thatcherism. Within racing itself it may already have done something to break the industry's psychological addiction to subsidy to which Rothschild referred[15] – and referred unfairly, since no country has found it possible to have properly organised, administered and policed horse racing without drawing revenue from betting. More tangibly, it should in time establish a more honest market for nominations for stallions. In the past, stallions have often been advertised at, say, £10,000, when their real fee was nearer £7,000. No owner or syndicate is going to be so foolish as to exaggerate thus in future, for if he insists that his nominations are fetching £10,000 when they are really fetching £7,000, he will have to subscribe £10,000 to the EBF. There does, however, remain the problem of stallions whose books do not fill easily (i.e. do not attract as many mares as the stallion's owners would wish), so that a fee which started as an honest assessment by the owner has to be dropped as the season progresses. Such owners are, at present, being protected by the EBF's refusal to publish the sums, representing *average* fees, which the Fund actually receives.

Despite the Trustees' forbearance, it is true, as Mrs Hislop said, that the EBF subscription falls hardest on the least successful stallions, whereas the owners of one whose book is full can pay the subscription at no extra cost to themselves, simply by having the stallion cover an extra mare. Some of John Hislop's points of detail also had some validity: the scheme was indeed introduced in a hurry, and ⌐ome loose ends were not tied up in advance. But, given the political will that was present, it was reasonable to push ahead and leave some details to be sorted out on a pragmatic basis, which is what has happened.

The most substantial of Hislop's points is that the EBF takes racing another step down the slippery slope from being about horses to being about money. This argument strikes a chord with anyone who values the traditions of racing, particularly when it is made by someone as widely respected as Hislop. But its importance can be exaggerated. Racing has, after all, always been partly about money: the EBF simply recognises that fact, and tries to improve the financial situation of owners, and indirectly of breeders. The scheme should be seen as a sensible recycling of resources for the good of all, rather than a move towards unbridled commercialism.

The International Conference of Racing Authorities

The international exchange of information about racing, though not direct control of the industry, extends far beyond Europe and America, thanks to the International Conference of Racing Authorities which meets annually (the seventeenth meeting was in 1983) in Paris on the first Monday in October. Nearly sixty countries are represented, over thirty directly, and the remainder through representatives of the four regional organisations (Asia, South America, the Caribbean and the Socialist countries). The preparatory work is done by the American, British, Irish and French Authorities in the course of their regular meetings, and in liaison with the regional conferences, and the secretariat is run jointly by Charles Weatherby and Louis Romanet. (The latter is Director-General of the French Société d'Encouragement, and son of Jean Romanet, who served as Director-General for many years.) This short study is based on the minutes of the meetings held in 1980, 1981 and 1982.

The Conference starts with reports from the regional conferences, some of which attract an extraordinary number of delegates: for example, four hundred attended the fifteenth Asian Conference, held at Seoul in 1980. Some subjects discussed by the regional conferences, and by the international conference itself, have been matters such as the better exchange of information within regions, doping, blood-typing, identification of racehorses, artificial insemination, vaccination, protected names, insurance, the desirable length of the whip, temporary licences for foreign trainers, and so on.

The conference also receives a report of the annual meeting of the

International Stud Book Committee, which first met in 1979, and holds its meeting a few days before that of the main International Committee. The Stud Book Committee appears to have real powers, which it exercises in pursuit of uniform standards of registration, documentation and identification of race horses. For example, in 1980 it turned down a German request that three fillies, conceived in 1973 and 1978 by artificial insemination, under special circumstances and with the Direktorium's agreement, should be accepted as thoroughbreds by member countries. To take another example, in 1982 the Stud Book Committee recorded its view that the 'Israeli Stud Book still bore too many uncertainties and shortcomings to accept Israeli bred horses to be registered in the General Stud Book and in all probability, to allow Israeli horses to take part in races after 1982'.

An example of politics in the Stud Book occurred at the 1981 meeting, when the Polish delegate admitted that Poland departed from the accepted international practice of following an animal's name in the stud book with a suffix to indicate the country of foaling. In a splendid display of national pride combined with socialist dogma, he said that all foals were entered in the Polish Stud Book with the suffix POL, whatever their country of birth:

> Mr Gagorowski justified this by pointing out that all the stallions and broodmares involved belonged to the national stud and that it was inconceivable that their products should be given the suffix of another country and not be entered in the Polish Stud Book. He added that the important factor was not the place where the dam had foaled but the Stud Book in which the product has been entered. This situation occurred in all East European countries, where private property did not exist.

Even vaccination can give rise to *quasi*-political disputes, and recently, with the appointment of M. Jean-Pierre Launay as Chef de Service of the French Haras Nationaux, artificial insemination has become politicised too. Launay attended his first meeting of the International Committee in 1982 and fluttered the dovecotes by expressing doubts, in the name of the French Stud Book Committee, about the necessity of a complete ban on artificial insemination. He thought, evidently approvingly, that artificial insemination would lower stallion fees and bring down the market in their progeny, and he may well have been right. Certainly, these are among the consequences most feared by breeding interests, though they could be guarded against if artificial insemination were practised under very strict safeguards. Launay realised that control methods might not be strict enough in such countries as the United States to avoid confusion over a horse's parentage if artificial insemination were allowed, but in France, he said, control methods were so strict that it could benefit from some sort of waiver of the general rule.

In the short term, Launay was unlikely to make much headway, particularly as the case of Gazolit was fresh in the minds of delegates. This case had been brought up by Louis Romanet the previous year, when Gazolit was the best three-year-old colt in the Soviet Union; his participation in the Preis von Europa had even been contemplated, but he was a product of Anilin, who had been dead for six years! Romanet thought that Gazolit's case showed that a rule was needed debarring products of artificial insemination from running in any race, and to say that a horse must be registered in a Stud Book was not enough.

As a result, at the 1982 meeting, when A. Martinenkov reported on the thirty-third Socialist Countries' racing and breeding conference, he referred to Gazolit and stressed that: 'artificial insemination in the Soviet Union was only a scientific experiment launched by the Ministry of Agriculture, whose objective was to study the consequences of artificial insemination on the racing performances of two and three year old horses, he stressed that no one of these horses had been registered in the Soviet Stud Book and that it had been decided to put an end to the experiment'. In the longer term, it seems unlikely that this dramatic example will prove to be the end of the story of attempts to introduce artificial insemination, and perhaps even embryo transplantation. In that case, since the veterinary procedures are well established, the remaining problem is the political one of gaining international acceptance for foals produced by either technique. Such international acceptance is unlikely to be forthcoming from the International Stud Book Committee, but in refusing it the Committee will hardly be able to avoid playing an increasingly political role.

The International Conference's other principal preoccupations in the years 1980-2 were statistics, cases in various countries where decisions by racing authorities had been challenged at civil law, the revision of the international agreement on breeding and racing, and matters connected with the Pattern, the grading and classification of races.

The statistics are valuable because, although incomplete, they give international data on, for example, prize money, betting turnover and taxation, which show that Britain is consistently the fourth in the world in the amount paid to the Government. Trends in the bloodstock population and in the number of races available for it are also shown.

The International Agreement on Breeding and Racing

The agreement had been first presented to the eighth conference, in October 1974. Many countries did their best to have its articles adopted in their own countries, but by 1980, 'it had become obvious that for a variety of reasons (new officials, modification of internal rules, etc. . .) some countries were no longer able to meet sometimes imprecise prior requirements'.

At the 1980 meeting the secretariat therefore asked the participants to reconsider the Agreement and state which articles they could accept. The Agreement was extensively discussed in 1980, 1981 and 1982, since when it has been reprinted, with a list of countries which have ratified the various articles. The Agreement is intended to provide a model for national rules, and it is hoped that national rules will in future contain a reference to it. There has, however, been no move to set up anything resembling an international court of appeal from the rules of individual countries. For one thing, countries would probably not allow it, and, for another (as the Irish delegate pointed out), a very difficult situation would arise if a civil court set aside the judgement of an international racing 'court of appeal'.

Graded races

Over the years a growing number of countries have produced graded classifications of their races; in 1980 Louis Romanet said lists of graded races from fourteen countries (Scandinavia being counted as one country) had been included as appendices in the Pattern book, and the figure had risen to twenty-four in 1984. Some, like Australia and Chile, had improved their lists by making them more selective than in the past. It was regretted that Mexico had not submitted a list, and it had proved impossible to accept Panama's since, although it had reduced its list from fifty-six to twenty-eight, it remained distinctly unbalanced, with seventeen races in Group I, six in Group II and five in Group III. (In 1981 Romanet was able to report that Panama had produced a revised list, which had been accepted.) Romanet also reminded delegates of the importance of producing supplementary lists of races selected to appear in black type in sales catalogues.

In 1981 Romanet reported that Belgium had requested that one of its grade II races and two in grade III be included in the Pattern. The request would be examined at the December meeting of the European Pattern Races Committee, but it was unlikely that it would be accepted. In the following year Switzerland's request for the Swiss Derby to be included in the Pattern as a Group III race had been turned down.

Romanet also reported in 1982 that West Germany regularly organised races which attracted runners from eastern Europe, and had asked that their major races should be classified, in order to assist handicappers to assign weights. The Soviet Union, Czechoslovakia, Hungary and Poland had published such lists, but not yet East Germany, Bulgaria or Romania.

International classifications

International classifications had first been introduced in 1977 by Britain, Ireland and France, since there was sufficient exchange of horses between these countries for handicappers to draw up a common classification. Italy and Germany were anxious, Louis Romanet informed the 1980 conference, for the scheme to be extended to them, but there was not yet a sufficient number of exchanges between them and the other three countries. However, Romanet was able to announce the first international classification prepared outside Europe; this covered the best horses, of all ages, to have raced in Australia and New Zealand in the 1979-80 season.

Romanet returned to the subject in 1982, when he said that the possibility existed of extending international classification to the USA but, again, there had been so few exchanges that the project seemed premature. However, Romanet added that Britain, Ireland and France informed the organisers of the Budweiser Million and Japan Cup of the official values, as expressed by their handicappers, of the best European horses entered in those events, in order to facilitate the selection of those which would be invited to compete.

Invitation races

At the 1981 annual meeting there had been rather worried references to the growth of invitation races. They consisted of the Washington D.C. (first run in 1952); the Turf Classic, the Canadian Championship, the Clasico Internacionale del Caribe (1966), the Clasico Jockey Clubs Latinos-Americanos (1981: which, however, is not closed to non-invited horses), the Arlington Million, first run on 30 August 1981, and now the Japan Cup, to take place on 22 November 1981 in Tokyo. The worries were expressed both by Charles Weatherby and Louis Romanet.

Weatherby 'thought that international competition was a necessary thing but he deeply regretted that its present development should proceed in such anarchic fashion. He thought that such races should be part of an international schedule and he urged each country to set up its own framework of major races and to integrate it within a continental framework.'

Romanet pointed to three difficulties raised by invitation races: the lack of any worldwide co-ordination; the use of drugs or medication in some of these events (a problem notably in the United States) and the possible participation of horses produced by artificial insemination. Romanet proposed that the conference should set up a sub-committee to co-ordinate invitation races world-wide, though Robert Melican, of the New York Jockey Club, thought 'it would be difficult to enforce any kind of rules in view of the severe competition between various racecourses in the United States and of the necessity of giving owners free choice of entry'. Similarly, even if all forms of medication could be prohibited, the problem would be to find laboratories with the knowledge and equipment to detect the great number of drugs used the world over.

Jean Romanet then asked the delegates to approve five rules for international races. These were: they must be run at weight for age; they must be closed to all products of artificial insemination; the conditions of the races must stipulate that any kind of medication or drug is forbidden; geldings must be excluded; and the rules must allow owners of horses with suitable track records to enter them at their own expense. The first three conditions were unanimously approved, but Japan expressed reservations about the fourth and fifth.

In 1982 Charles Weatherby returned to the subject of invitation races. It seemed impossible to enforce decisions by an international Authority, but there was a great danger of national Patterns being disrupted, if the trend towards more international invitation races continued. He thought that, before launching such races, a country's racing as a whole should be of a high standard. It should have prestigious weight-for-age races, and its Pattern, graded or listed races (including handicaps) should not exceed a certain percentage of its total races. Any body organising an invitation race could avoid clashes by consulting the European pattern races book. Jean Romanet added that, although his idea of a conference sub-committee to co-ordinate such events had turned out not to be the answer, because these races were generally not organised by the racing Authorities, nevertheless any country planning an invitation race should consult the International Conference, so that the Secretariat could assess its significance for the international programme.

Kiyotaka Shioda, of the Japanese Racing Association, who may have been put somewhat on the defensive by some of the discussion, said the purpose of the Japanese Cup was to pit Japanese against foreign horses in order to assess the quality of Japanese breeding and training. The Japanese racing Authorities paid most of the owners' costs, because of Japan's geographical situation. Shioda offered to bring the project back to the conference later, should it so wish. In reply, Weatherby reassured Shioda that 'he totally approved the principle of the Japan Cup; races needed publicity and promotion, and such "shows" provided by the confrontation between horses from various continents should be developed'.

Conclusion

We may conclude from this survey of recent developments in the racing world that it has not only become international but has become increasingly professional and commercial. In former times, at least in the reminiscences of those who remember them, racing and breeding were the activities of a small circle of people who knew each other well, saw each other constantly, and lived as if they were spending most of their time in an exceedingly exclusive club. For some of the circle this was literally true, because the Jockey Club was the centre of their lives.

Economic necessity has forced all that to change. For some breeders, what was formerly a hobby has become big business, and for them racing is a mere adjunct to breeding, designed to establish stud or paddock value. What was primarily a series of small national markets has become a vast international market. which already embraces Europe and North America, and is spreading world-wide.

Stud fees have increased at a rate which no one could have foreseen forty, or even ten, years ago. In 1937 Bahram and Solario, at 500 guineas, were the most expensive stallions in England, and Hyperion stood at 400 guineas. Lower down the scale, a leading sprint stallion like Gold Bridge stood at £49 1s (£48 and a guinea for the groom). In 1986 an equivalent stallion might have been Mummy's Pet (he died that year after the end of the stud season), whose nominations were sold at about £14,000, while at the top end of the scale, nominations to Kris, the leading stallion of the previous year, were sold at about £85,000. In North America the figures are even more striking: the most expensive stallions at Gainesway Farm, Lyphard and Blushing Groom, were advertised at $250,000 and $200,000 respectively in 1985. However, in 1986 unmistakable signs appeared that the long bull market in stallion values was at an end, and in 1987 the response to the weakness at the top end of the international yearling market in the previous years was a widespread fall in the prices of stallion shares and nominations in most of the principal breeding countries.

For some breeders, therefore, breeding has become an activity akin to running a multinational corporation. That does not necessarily mean that its sporting aspect has been destroyed, but it cannot be easy for a man or woman who habitually thinks in tens of millions to retain (except as an occasional luxury) the sporting instincts whose passing has been lamented by the purists of the Turf.

But it may still be argued that they have lamented too soon. Many a breeder is too attached to his animals to treat them merely as units of production. Most members of the TBA are small breeders, many of them existing precariously. The strength of breeding as a hobby, as well as a business, and the continuance of racing as a sport, as well as an industry, depend on the survival of these small breeders, and so far, thanks in large measure to the effectiveness of their 'trade unions', in this country and elsewhere, there is no real sign of their dying out.

Notes

1 P. Willett, *The Thoroughbred*, London, 1970, p. 273.
2 Jockey Club, *The Report of the Duke of Norfolk's Committee on the Pattern of Racing*, London, August 1965.
3 P. Willett, *Makers of the Modern Thoroughbred*, London, 1984, p. 37.
4 I am indebted for this information to Peter Willett. The Jockey Club handicappers produce the handicaps (stated in lb) throughout the season for each horse. 100 lb indicates a truly excellent horse.
5 *The Sporting Life*, 15 August 1984.
6 P. Willett, *The Thoroughbred*, pp. 273-5.
7 *Ibid.*, p. 278.
8 Thoroughbred Breeders' Association, *Methods of Assistance to the Breeding Industry*, Newmarket, December 1981.
9 C. R. Hill, Interview with John Leat, *Pacemaker International*, December 1986.
10 *The Times*, 11 August 1984.
11 Thoroughbred Breeders' Association, *Methods of Assistance to the Breeding Industry*, Newmarket, December 1981.
12 See Peter Willett, 'Now Germany and Italy Join EBF', *Horse and Hound*, 10 January 1986.
13 *The Sporting Life*, 25 January 1983.
14 *The Sporting Life*, 14 June 1983. Hislop set out his own and Mrs Hislop's objections to the European Breeders' Fund.
15. Royal Commission on Gambling, *Final Report*, vol. 1, (Cmnd. 7200), London, 1978, para, 9.42.

IX

The Plummer decade

Lord Wigg departed reluctantly from the Levy Board (though perhaps also with some relief, as he was sick to death of the Jockey Club) on 15 November 1972. He was succeeded for a short time by Sir Stanley Raymond (who resigned on 21 January 1974), but the ten years after Wigg deserve to be known as the Plummer decade. Sir Desmond Plummer – he received a life peerage in April 1981 – served from 22 January 1974 to 30 September 1982, and since Senior Stewards of the Jockey Club serve for only three years, he overlapped with no fewer than four of them (Viscount Leverhulme, 1973-6, Lord Howard de Walden, 1976-9, Captain John MacDonald-Buchanan, 1979-82 and Lord Manton, 1982-5). At the Tote he overlapped with his old friend Lord Mancroft, who was Chairman until 30 April 1976, when he was replaced with the present incumbent, Sir Woodrow (now Lord) Wyatt.

Raymond's appointment by the Home Secretary, Reginald Maudling (acting on the advice of his Parliamentary Under-Secretary, Mark Carlisle) was not totally unsuccessful, but it was surprising, since his post-war career had been on the railways. He had no knowledge of racing, and, indeed, appears to have made no friends or close contacts among racing people other than those required by daily business; he also upset some members of the Jockey Club by not wearing a hat on the racecourse. However, from the point of view of officials in the Home Office, his appointment made sense; indeed, they probably played a considerable part in choosing him, and Wigg probably played a part also, as he was on close terms with some of the officials. Raymond was already part-time chairman of the Gaming Board, and it was thought that he could usefully combine that task with the part-time chairmanship (Wigg, of course, had been full-time) of the Levy Board. Apparently, officials believed that, because both jobs were connected with gambling, they could suitably be controlled by the same person.

This seemed an odd view to anyone closely connected with racing, since gambling in casinos had been an abuse which needed cleaning up, whereas the Levy Board was a very different kind of operation. Nevertheless, it was a view which Raymond himself seems to have shared, if one may judge by his evidence to Lord Rothschild's Royal Commission. He tried unsuccessfully to persuade the Commission that gambling needed an overall supervisory body to bring together the whole mix of gambling and related legislation to protect the punter and control the powerful vested interests which were involved in all sections of gambling. As it was, he believed such bodies as the Jockey Club and the Levy Board were minnows in a sea of sharks.

Raymond did have some achievements at the Levy Board. He streamlined its administration, began to establish a businesslike relationship with the Jockey Club (an objective also devoutly desired by the Senior Steward), set in motion a major new study of the needs of the racing industry, with which he later asked the Joint Racing Board to associate itself,[1] and bought eight shares in Mill Reef, the winner of the 1971 Derby, for the National Stud at what turned out to be the bargain price of £422,178.

Raymond also supervised the formal start of some of Wigg's projects. For example, Racecourse Security Services became responsible for Jockey Club security personnel and became fully operational on 1 January 1973. At that time, extensive use was still being made of guards provided by Securicor (it will be remembered that Wigg had felt this firm had been foisted on him by the Jockey Club), but they were phased out by the end of June 1974. However, it is interesting to note that the Board's twentieth report, for 1980-1, refers to the increased use of casual guards by RSS.

The new grandstand at Sandown, described as a new concept in stand construction, was opened on 22 September 1973. Tattersalls and the Silver Ring were combined and the admission charge was only £1. The cost was met by a loan of £2,500,000 from the Board's subsidiary which owned the course, Metropolitan and Country Racecourse Management and Holdings Ltd (a much greater sum in real terms than the £3,025,000 lent to Goodwood some years later, which excited so much adverse commment in press and Parliament, as well as in racing circles). From the beginning, the importance of

[215]

non-racing activities was emphasised at Sandown, as it was later at another of the Board's acquisitions, Kempton Park.

Another of Wigg's major schemes came to fruition under Raymond, with the agreement on 19 March 1973 of the thirteenth levy scheme, which was the first related wholly to turnover, though turnover had already been the main component of the scheme for several years. Under Raymond the Board remained satisfied with the new structure of the prize money scheme instituted by Wigg, whereby, having completed two major programmes of racecourse improvements, the Board had switched the emphasis of its expenditure to the improvement of prize money. It had also introduced a substantial difference between the basic daily rates paid to racecourses in Groups I and II, and those in Groups III, IV and V, 'in order to achieve a simple means whereby horses of differing standards would become graded automatically'.

Perhaps Raymond's only really unsuccessful inheritance from Wigg was the Admission Charges Option Scheme, which was intended to subsidise courses offering reduced admission to the public. The scheme was never a success, and was dropped in 1974-5 in favour of a new Racegoers' Fund for the improvement of the cheaper enclosures. Empirical work done by Metra Oxford for the Racecourse Association in 1974 had shown that the subsidy on admission, when considered against the total cost of a day at the races, was so small as to be unlikely to bring about a substantial increase in attendance.

Wigg's commitment to the maximisation of the Levy seems not to have been dropped by the Board under Raymond, and there was an ambiguity about its degree of commitment to racing as such, as opposed merely to maximising the levy, just as in Wigg's day. For instance, in Wigg's last Annual Report the Board recorded that 'to meet the needs of trainers special provision was made to encourage racecourses to stage Flat racing in the less profitable months of March, April and October'.[2] In the very same paragraph it went on to reiterate its opposition to evening fixtures because, with the betting shops being closed, they generated little additional levy. So in the evening the trainers seem abruptly to have been fogotten! Nor does the Board ever discuss what the optimum number of horses in training might be, nor whether the provision of additional fixtures was desirable or necessary in order to provide entertainment for the public, or to ensure a large enough pool of horses for animals of real quality to emerge.

The ambiguity was only resolved in the Board's evidence to Rothschild, where it committed itself firmly to the view that, since the extra £5,500,000 prize money which racing needed (in addition to the existing £10 million) was unlikely to be forthcoming, 'it will be necessary in the foreseeable future to trim the size of the industry to a level which can be adequately sustained by the limited amount of money available, rather than to make extravagent demands to increase the amount of money needed to support adequately the industry at its present level'.[3] In fact the number of fixtures and races actually increased at the end of the Plummer decade. In calendar 1974, the first full year of Plummer's stewardship, there were 872 fixtures, 5,511 races and 58,678 runners. In 1981 there were slightly fewer fixtures and races than in 1974, but in 1982 they rose abruptly to 936 fixtures, 5,860 races and 64,253 runners.

Raymond left the Board for personal reasons, though some accounts have it that he was very tired of Wigg's constant telepone calls in his new capacity as President of BOLA. In his handover speech Raymond rebuked those who clamoured for a bigger levy, and said: 'There are some engaged in horseracing who do not seem to appreciate the privileged position the sport is in when compared with other sports of equal or greater public appeal.'[4] It was up to the Board, he went on, to ensure that its subsidy to racing of over £7 million a year was not spent for private gain, and more important than ever, as 'organisations representing the various elements in the industry become more powerful and the lobbying intensifies', to maintain the independence of the Board's chairman and of the other two members appointed by the Home Secretary. This rather sour farewell message ended, *The Sporting Life* noted,[5] without any mention of the pleasure he had derived from working with those with whom his job brought him into contact.

During 1972-3 the Board became aware of growing pressure in the industry for the improvement of staff conditions, and this became one of Plummer's abiding preoccupations, with the result that a high priority was given, when grants were made to racecourses, to the improvement of acccommodation and facilities for stable lads. Perhaps the most famous example of this preoccupation occurred in 1975 after the strike by lads at Newmarket (which, like so many major events, goes unremarked in the Levy Board's reports). Plummer took the opportunity to wield the big stick and said publicly that the additional £1 million prize money provided for in the next prize money scheme was conditional on the establishment by the end of November 1975 of negotiating machinery and on agreement by 1 June 1976 of a minimum wage for stable staff and a minimum training fee.[6] The former was achieved, but there has never been agreement on a minimum training fee because in the view of the Office of Fair Trading it would constitute a restrictive practice.

Industrial relations

A report published by the Joint Racing Board in July 1974 drew attention to the continuing increase in the number of horses in training and the country-wide shortage of staff, especially in the Newmarket area.[7] The difficulty was made worse by the policy of some local authorities not to allocate houses to stable men. Nor could trainers afford to pay increased wages, so that it was now the rule for a lad to do three horses rather than two, as in the past. The Committee had been told that the labour force at Newmarket was down by 5 to 7.5 per cent over the last ten years, partly because of pay and conditions of employment, partly because there was a shortage of apprentices of the right size and weight and partly because of the raising of the school leaving age.

The Committee thought that it was wrong for stable staff to have to rely on presents and their share of the four per cent of winning money which went to the stable. 'In the end it is the regular take home pay which is relevant in considering whether wages are adequate.' Nevertheless, the Committee reaffirmed the conventional wisdom: 'we are convinced that the filter system of deductions from prize money is an effective method of distributing Levy Board and other funds over the industry. We therefore endorse all attempts to increase the prize money.'

The Newmarket trainers (Newmarket Trainers' Federation), the Committee reported, were the only ones to establish wages after formal negotiation with the Transport and General Workers' Union. The basic wage was £23.43 a week from 18 March 1974. The National Trainers' Federation, although in its infancy, could negotiate for all trainers but the Committee noted that the stable staff had no equivalent body. There were only four hundred card-holding trade unionists (almost all of them TGWU members) out of 3,600 stable staff in the country, and about three hundred and fifty of the four hundred were in the Newmarket area. Thus, there was not much enthusiasm for the TGWU elsewhere, and the Committee doubted whether so large a union would have time to organise such a scattered constituency. The Committee thought the racing authorities should encourage the formation of an Association of Stable Employees, for which the recently formed National Head Lads' Association might provide the nucleus. The Jockey Club should also lay down a minimum training fee, which would enable the small trainers to pay their labour properly, and this fee should be deducted from owners' accounts at Weatherby's.

There was trouble at Newmarket in the very month that the Committee reported, because it was alleged that employers were failing to honour a threshold agrement whereby increased wage payments would have been made in accordance with movements in the retail price index. Some trainers, who were already paying wages which exceeded the sum of the standard wage plus the threshold payments, refused to pay the latter. *The Times* of 25 July reported that more than three hundred stable lads were calling for an official strike to give them an extra £2 a week, but the *Daily Telegraph* reported on the following day that the threat of a strike had been averted by the trainers agreeing to the extra £2. Thus the basic wage became £25.43.

Filby shows, in his paper on the Transport and General Workers' Union[8] (from which the following account of union activity up to 1960 is taken), that the union's activity at Newmarket goes back as far as 1937, when stable lads were recruited as an unintended by-product of a recruitment drive among farm workers. Ernest Bevin (General Secretary of the Transport and General Workers' Union, 1921-40) 'undoubtedly had a soft spot for stable lads' and the 1937 agreement over pay and conditions and disputes procedure was essentially made between Bevin and Lord Derby, who used his influence with the Newmarket Trainers' Federation after an earlier approach to it had failed. 'Thus, the agreement formally couched in terms of two collectivities was actually manufactured out of the paternal influence of two individuals.' That agreement provided for a minimum wage of 48s a week, with an undertaking that it would rise to 50s in the spring of 1938. The trainers also made the concession that lads would be allowed one Sunday off in three.

The organisation of stable lads did not really engage the Union leaders' attention again until 1950, by which time there was naturally widespread dissatisfaction with the 1937 Agreement. At Lambourn the trainers continued to resist negotiation with the Union, and at

Malton and Middleham the trainers could not see why a large Union should interfere with their relations with their employees. Nor were the trainers themselves organised, though there were some informal leaders, like Captain Charles Elsey. The result was that in the Malton area in 1958 sixteen individual submissions had to be made to the industrial disputes tribunal, instead of one submission covering all the trainers.

At Newmarket after the war Sir Humphrey de Trafford continued Lord Derby's role by chairing negotiations between the Union and the trainers and, although he was a leading owner and breeder, he was apparently accepted by the Union as an independent chairman. By 1949 the minimum basic wage at Newmarket was 90s a week, and in the same year the appointment of a new national secretary of the Union led to the first explicit attempt to link the lads' wages to those of agricultural workers. In 1955 the first direct negotiations with trainers took place, but the lads themselves seem to have participated little and to have left the negotiations to their national officers. However, an unofficial strike in 1960, which led to a new agreement with the trainers, did evoke some shop-floor participation. It also attracted the interest of Edward Heath, the Minister of Labour, who said that he was trying to bring about a return to work.[9] On that occasion the trainers insisted on negotiating with Union representatives rather than directly with the lads. At first the Union accepted an offer of 10s, but two hundred said they would defy the Union and strike if their claim for £2 were not met.[10] *The Times* reported that the Epsom lads were ready to strike, but the next day it was able to report that an agreement between the Union and the National Trainers' Federation had averted the strike.

The Union was rather inactive for some years, though in April 1967 its General Secretary called for it to be represented on the Levy Board and Tote. Elizabeth Dean shows that the lads' basic wage was above that of agricultural workers from 1967 to 1972, but was overtaken in 1973 and, to an even greater extent, in 1974.[11] From various newspaper reports, she believes that ten per cent of the lads belonged to the Union in 1969 and that this had risen to fifty-four per cent in 1974. In 1970, according to Filby, the Union was reorganised, so that the National Agricultural Trade Group was incongruously subsumed into the Food, Drink and Tobacco Industries Group of 173,000 people. This, of course, led to loss of identity for the stable lads, and was very useful to opponents of the Union.

The year of trouble was 1975. However, the atmosphere between the Union and the Newmarket trainers[12] remained remarkably calm and friendly, partly, no doubt, because Sam Horncastle, the Union's full-time area official, and John Winter, who represented the trainers, are both conciliatory men. They had been in correspondence since August 1974 and were very largely in agreement, though Winter did not believe that it was practicable to introduce shop stewards in stables and had to point out that the blacklisting of Union members by trainers, of which the Union had complained, had stopped many years previously. Horncastle was anxious to ensure that there should be no compulsory redundancies because of the decreased number of horses in training, to which Winter replied that he had told his members to let him know before making anyone redundant.

Some trainers, however, were reluctant to allow the Union to tell them which men should be made redundant, and saw no reason to do any favours to shop stewards. Another thought it a great pity that the stable staff belonged to the TGWU instead of the agricultural workers' union, because the latter understood about horses, whereas the TGWU had to have everything laboriously explained and were 'liable to get their members involved in sympathy strikes over such people as a Pakistani bus driver who might want ten minutes' extra tea break'.

One such trainer was John Oxley. On 11 January *The Times* reported that 120 lads were to go on strike against him after three lads in his yard had been made redundant. The 575 lads who belonged to the Transport and General Workers' Union were threatening to strike (*The Times* said that a further two hundred lads at Newmarket did not belong to the Union). However, on 21 January it was reported that the lads had decided to go to arbitration and that the three who had been made redundant had been reinstated. Filby comments that this decision by ACAS in favour of the lads may have put the trainers off going to arbitration over the strike later in the year.

The trouble this time was about wages. The lads showed their inexperience by giving notice of their intention to strike. *TheTimes* reported on 23 April that they intended to do so from the following Wednesday, 30 April, unless they got a rise of £4.47. On 29 April *The Times* said that the lads planned to picket the racecourse on 1,000 Guineas day (Thursday 1 May 1975) and to picket stables from 30 April. At this point the trainers offered a rise of £3, which was not accepted, and the trainers refused to go to arbitration. On 30 April

The Times reported that Sam Horncastle had expressed the hope that other workers would not cross the picket lines, e.g. horse-box drivers, TV cameramen, and the operators of the photo-finish equipment, and the *Telegraph* said that the lads hoped to stop Newmarket horses taking part in the racing. The threat to picket was taken seriously, by both the police and the trainers, not surprisingly in view of the value of some of their charges. At one point, following a conference between Winter, by then Chairman of the Newmarket Trainers' Federation and Chairman of the Flat Committee of the National Federation, H. Thomson Jones (another leading trainer who was vice-chairman of the Newmarket trainers) and Lord Derby, the police deployed men on the gallops all through the night, and special arrangements were made for the safety of horses going to the 2,000 Guineas on 3 May.

On 1,000 Guineas day the lads sat down across the course. A melée also started between jockeys, who were trying to get to the starting stalls for the second race, and the lads, who were trying to prevent them. Willie Carson was photographed struggling with the lads, who dragged him off his horse, though with police help he remounted. He then rode back to the members' stand and called out to the crowd that if they wanted the racing they would have to clear the track. Carson, Piggott and two other jockeys, assisted by racegoers (subsequent correspondence in *The Times* throws doubt upon whether these were primarily from the members' enclosure, or from the vicinity of the Silver Ring), then forced their way through the line of lads. *The Times* (2 May) reported that:

> As the two groups met, shouting and scuffling began. The lads turned and ran up the course, pursued by the crowd, and then ran off to the side.
> The racegoers, who included owners, trainers and several women, halted, shouting that they wanted to have a go at the militants.
> One of the leaders of their advance was a retired officer, Major-General Sir Randle Feilden, a former senior steward of the Jockey Club.

The second race started twenty-five minutes late. The lads moved back on to the course for the 1,000 Guineas, but eventually retreated, and the race was run without further incident. Michael Seely, a racing correspondent of *The Times*, commented (also on 2 May): 'To say that Admiral Rous would have turned in his grave if he could have seen the happenings on his sacred heath at Newmarket yesterday afternoon would probably be the understatement of all time. Two of the tenets that were held sacred by the supreme dictators of the turf in the mid-nineteenth century were that jockeys should be seen and not heard and that races should be started on time.'

On 3 May *The Times* rebuked the racegoers:

Judging from reports of the fracas which developed at Newmarket Racecourse on Thursday, the sport of kings is in danger of developing into a blood sport. . . Finally, racegoers in the members' stand, determined that their afternoon's enjoyment should not be spoilt, took the law into their own hands and set about clearing the course. The result was a melée involving stable lads, jockeys, highly strung thoroughbreds, normally-sedate ladies, retired military gentlemen, whirling binoculars, stabbing hat pins, thrashing shooting-sticks, flailing whips, boots and fists, and torn jackets. It was a performance which, had it occurred in the Fourth Division football stadium of some fifth-rate town, would have besmirched even the mucky face of professional soccer.

On Saturday 3 May the 2,000 Guineas was started under police protection, from in front of the starting stalls.

The strike continued to attract considerable attention. On 4 May the Newmarket trainers produced figures, showing that of a total 638 lads, 482 were at work. Later figures show that 180 were on strike, 458 at work, and 260 belonged to the Union. The same source lists all the trainers, and indicates that in many yards virtually no staff were on strike. *The Times* (5 May) feared it would spread to other parts of the country, such as the forthcoming Chester Meeting. On 7 May it reported that twelve lads had been fined by the magistrates for causing a breach of the peace, and on 17 May that fifty striking lads from Newmarket had picketed Newbury Races on the previous day. On 27 May it reported that Lord Leverhulme had had talks with the Union about the strike, and by the end of the month the Newmarket Trainers' Federation was able to send out a circular thanking the vast majority of the staff who had remained loyal. 'There is a new atmosphere in the Newmarket yards which is not only refreshing to work in but is reflecting on the horses themselves.'

The lads agreed not to picket the Derby, partly as a result of an appeal by Wigg.[13] Later, Wigg won a libel action against the *Daily Mail*, whose gossip columnist, Nigel Dempster, had suggested that he had intervened at the behest of the big bookmakers. However, it appears that the Newmarket trainers were nervous of a public enquiry being held into labour conditions at Newmarket. They thought any enquiry should be national, and did not encourage an end to the strike at this point, presumably because they thought it would focus too much attention on Newmarket. There was also some feeling that they were being let down by outsiders, and by rich owners, including members of the Jockey Club, who were anxious to settle.

On 16 June, *The Times* reported that the lads were to picket Royal Ascot, and Jack Jones of the Transport and General Workers' Union, appealed to Michael Foot, Secretary of State for Employment, to hold an enquiry into the dispute. On 16 July it was reported that the lads had accepted a formula worked out with the National Trainers' Federation by ACAS, whereby they would receive £4.40 instead of £4.70, but that the Newmarket Trainers did not agree. However, they very soon accepted it.[14] The final settlement of £37 included three and a half hours' overtime during those weekends when a lad was at work, on top of the basic forty-hour week.

Although the return to work had been agreed for 28 July, some trainers were in trouble because they had fewer horses than before the strike began, and therefore did not need to retain their striking labour. Ninety lads were turned off, though the trainers denied victimising them.[15] John Winter wrote to his striking lads on 22 July, saying that he could not keep their jobs open any longer and that they were therefore to be sacked immediately. This resulted in his receiving a notice from the Industrial Tribunal on 23 September; he lost the action, though other trainers in superficially similar circumstances did not. The difference, under the Industrial Tribunals (Labour Relations) Regulations 1974, is that if an employer loses business because his workers are on strike, he is not allowed to dismiss the strikers, whereas if his business is booming and he therefore needs to engage more staff than remain to him, he is entitled to dismiss the strikers and replace them with new staff. Winter fell into the former category in that his yard had only forty-three horses on 29 July against sixty-five on 30 April. Although he said in evidence that this decline was not the result of the strike, the Tribunal found that Winter's ten lads had been unfairly dismissed,[16] but that Wragg's dismissal of eleven lads had not been unlawful.[17]

The growth of representation in the racing industry

These were eventful years. The national scene was overshadowed by the fear of inflation. Within the narrow world of racing the Jockey Club was busy modernising itself; the demand was growing for effective representation of major bodies like the Owners', Trainers' and Breeders' Associations, as well as all the lesser bodies, which are now represented through the Horseracing Advisory Council; the middle years of the decade were dominated by the Royal Commission on Gambling; on-course betting shops became popular (with some benefit to racecourse finances) and the Tote's chequered career continued to attract considerable public notice.

Some of the professional associations in racing are old. The Thoroughbred Breeders' Association dates from 1917 and the Racehorse Owners' Association from 1945, but there was little liaison between the various bodies, and therefore little threat to the over-riding power of the Jockey Club and, latterly, the Levy Board, until relatively recent years. In 1958 a new body was formed, when Sir John Astor was President of the TBA, called the Racing and Breeding Liaison Committee, which consisted of the Racecourse Association, the ROA and the TBA, and was considered rather *avant garde* by the Jockey Club. Ever since then, the piranha fish have been nibbling at the Club's authority, and its members, many of them trained in the Army to take swift independent decisions, must have found the growth of consultation irritating. Nevertheless, they have had the sense not to swim against the tide, and in 1980 the Horseracing Advisory Council was founded. Superficially, there might seem to be a great difference between the HAC and the 1958 body, but the fact remains that the HAC, like all its predecessors, has solely advisory functions. It has influence, to be sure, but no formal power. Thus the Levy Board remains the Jockey Club's only serious competitor, and those two bodies are now living on far easier terms together than was the case under any previous Chairman of the Levy Board before Sir Ian Trethowan was appointed in 1982.

However, the real increase in representation came in 1974, when the Jockey Club took two initiatives. (Plummer also took an initiative, by organising the 'Sandown Conference', a meeting of representatives of the many bodies in racing.)[17] First, the Racing Policy Committee (RPC), which had hitherto consisted of the Stewards and the Jockey Club's members of the Levy Board, was extended to include the president of the Racehorse Owners' Association and its Secretary-General, and the Chairman of the Racecourse Association with its Director-General. In addition, the Joint Associations Liaison Committee (JALC), which had been formed in June 1964, already included some organisations not represented on the enlarged RPC. In 1974, these were informed that they could ask for any item of particular interest for them to be placed on the RPC agenda and be present for the discussion of that item.

Secondly, JALC itself was enlarged in December 1974, partly in anticipation of the newly-formed BRIC – the Bloodstock and Racehorse Industries Confederation (to which we shall come in a moment) finalising its constitution. JALC was enlarged to include the Chairman of the Bookmakers' Committee and representatives of the National Association of Bookmakers, the Tote, the Jockey Club Point to Point Liaison Committee, BRIC (once it was fully established) and the Permit Trainers' Association, and it was to meet four times a year instead of twice; two meetings were to be for matters of policy and the other two for matters of detail (Jockey Club annual report, 1974). Further members were added in 1975, but in its report for 1975 the Club regretted that BOLA had refused to join.

BRIC and RILC

The Bloodstock and Racehorse Industries Confederation, although short-lived, was an important body. It was never popular with Plummer, and is mentioned only once in Levy Board reports.[18] It differed from the other representative bodies in that it took off without any official blessing. It was a spontaneous response to recession by people working in the industry, who feared , for example, that they would have no more horses to train. It was intended to engage in politics on behalf of racing as a whole, because some (at least) of its founders reasoned that if, in a socialist world, privilege was impotent, it was up to the professionals to see if they could do better. But BRIC was soon forced into the role of a political pressure group *within* racing, and became unpopular in consequence.

BRIC started with an open meeting at the Subscription Rooms in Newmarket on 1 October 1974, under the joint chairmanship of John Winter and John Corbett. Winter said that British racing and breeding were dying. The Jockey Club had done its best, but professional assistance was needed. Corbett, speaking as Chairman of the

Bloodstock VAT Committee, thought VAT should be completely removed from the bloodstock industry. He said the Board of Customs and Excise was sympathetic to this view, and would have recommended it to the Chancellor, Denis Healey, had there been no election in the offing. Bob McCreery proposed the formation of a Committee representing the interests of everybody in the bloodstock industry in order to represent to the Government the extremely serious problems that faced it, and this resolution was carried unanimously.

On 15 October Winter was elected Chairman of the Committee and Nick Robinson, publisher of *Pacemaker International* and later president of the ROA, said that a number of owners had offered to help. Corbett reported that an informal meeting had been held at the Jockey Club to discuss its new VAT Committee, chaired by Jocelyn Hambro; however, the BRIC delegates had unanimously decided not to co-operate with the Jockey Club but to proceed with their own already established VAT Committee. This suggests that even from the beginning there was some dissatisfaction with the Jockey Club. BRIC always insisted that it was not intended as a threat to the Jockey Club, but the Club must have been worried both by the challenge to its authority and by the potential diversion of effort, and its relations with BRIC seem gradually to have worsened.

BRIC's first official meeting was held on 7 January 1975, when Winter took the Chair. It was reported that the Jockey Club, as soon as BRIC had become official, had asked it to join its own Liaison Committee (at that time JALC), but the meeting agreed that BRIC must remain separate, although later it joined RILC (Racehorse Industries Liaison Committee), JALC's successor. Representatives of the two bookmakers' organisations and of the Transport and General Workers' Union were not appointed as they had not paid their £1 membership fees.

Very shortly after the official formation of RILC and the enlargement of JALC, the Levy Board's 'Sandown Conference' was held on 5 and 6 February 1975. This was a major exercise in what the Levy Board called 'public participation', with 287 delegates and 91 official delegations. Although it is usually the Jockey Club who are accused of making heavy weather of consultation, on this occasion the exercise seems to have fluttered the Board's dovecotes: indeed, it provoked something approaching panic.

BRIC continued to agitate and to strengthen its organisation. At

the meeting on 9 June 1975, Charles Layfield of the National Sporting
League was present, as was A. W. (Jerry) Wiggin, MP, who later
was retained by BRIC. Its booklet, *The Crisis in Racing – Cause and
Effect*, had been presented to a rather hostile press conference that
morning, and was considered vital for fund raising, particularly as
the Confederation was already over £3,000 overdrawn. It was
reported that the VAT Committee had seen the Chancellor before
the budget. He had been sympathetic but said he could not help, as
he needed every penny he could raise and had sent them to talk to
Customs and Excise.

The General Council of BRIC very soon spawned a number of
committees, of which the most important was probably the General
Purposes Committee (GPC). Wiggin stated at its meeting on 18 July
1975 that Fred Peart, the Minister of Agriculture, was willing to meet
representatives of BRIC, partly as he was interested in getting the
National Stud back into his Ministry, and indeed all other types of
stud farming interests. However, on 4 September it was reported
that he did not, after all, think his Ministry could help as it had no
responsibility for the Levy Board. His earlier statement had been at
an informal meeting at the House of Commons – obviously one of
those meetings which gives so much trouble afterwards to civil
servants.

From the minutes of the same GPC meeting it appears that BRIC
was already on friendly terms with the National Association of Bookmakers. However a meeting between Wiggin and Wigg (who was
by now chairman of BOLA), designed to enlist BOLA's support, had
been disastrous. Wigg had said that he was ready to convey BRIC's
proposals to his Council in September but would not personally
support them. So difficult was he that Wiggin saw no point in ever
negotiating with him again.

On 4 November 1975 Wiggin explained to the GPC how a Royal
Commission works and urged them to start preparing their evidence
very soon; if it was too expensive to do this on their own they should
share it with the Jockey Club. At the January meeting there was
discussion of whether individual member associations or BRIC as a
whole should give evidence to the Royal Commission. As always,
money was a problem, and BRIC was not greatly helped by Brian
Shemmings of ACTT (Association of Cinematograph, Television and
Allied Technicians) saying that his members would only donate up
to £0.25 each per annum. However, in March it was reported that

the TBA had agreed to a levy for BRIC's benefit, but not as a condition of sale. Doncaster Sales had agreed to impose a levy if vendors did not disagree, while Tattersalls would co-operate only if vendors positively agreed. The National Trainers' Federation would give £10,000 and the Jockeys' Association £2 per member. The minutes of the General Purposes Committee for 19 February 1976 showed divided opinions about the Jockey Club's attitude to BRIC, but John Marriage (a QC, who was to join the Levy Board as a Home Office nominee in September 1976) saw no softening. NAB saw no reason to affiliate to BRIC but would co-operate over evidence to the Royal Commission.

On 21 April the Committee was informed that the Jockey Club was to launch RILC on 3 May. The Club had agreed to an amendment to RILC's still not very satisfactory terms of reference, whereby RILC would be consulted over Jockey Club appointees to the Levy Board. BRIC decided to give RILC a chance, though Layfield thought a statutory body was needed. BOLA hoped that the Racing Consultative Council, which was being considered by a Home Office working party, would be set up as a statutory body to counterbalance the enormous increase in the power of the Levy Board since its foundation.

Naturally, the formation of RILC was seen as a Jockey Club counterblast to BRIC. The Club agreed that RILC would be consulted before Jockey Club appointees were chosen to serve on the Levy Board, and BRIC believed that this concession was the result of its own pressure. BRIC itself was one of the constituent bodies of RILC. Other members were the Jockey Club, the Club's members of the Levy Board, the Bookmakers' Committee, the Tote, the Jockey Club Licenced Officials' Association, the Jockey Club Point to Point Liaison Committee, the National Joint Council for Stable Staff, the National Trainers' Federation, the Permit Trainers' Association, the Racehorse Owners' Association, the Jockeys' Association of Great Britain, the Racecourse Association, the Racegoers' Club and the Thoroughbred Breeders' Association. The Bookmakers' Committee dropped out in 1977 and was replaced by the NAB, but BOLA remained aloof.

Lord Leverhulme, the Senior Steward, emphasised to the Press the importance of maintaining contact between the various bodies 'particularly, of course, as during the debate on the Betting, Gaming and Lotteries Act of 1963 it was made clear that the Jockey Club was responsible for representing the whole industry to the Horserace

Betting Levy Board'. Plummer, however, was nervous about the possibility of Levy Board papers being given wider circulation, and Winter was incensed by the way in which the major organisations had been extracted from BRIC and given representation on RILC. This, as one of his protesting letters to Lord Howard de Walden shows, left him still representing an immense number of bodies, but none of them was of much importance. He was also upset that Dr Shirley Summerskill had not included BRIC in the committee estab-lished at the Home Office to consider the setting up of a Racing Consultative Council, for which Wigg had been pressing on BOLA's behalf. He thought BRIC should have been included and quoted a letter from the Private Secretary to Denis Howell, the Minister of Sport, assuring him that BRIC would be consulted.

RILC was a great help to the Club in keeping it informed of the associations' views on subjects which would come before the Levy Board, but there was never any question of the Club relinquishing control. At the first meeting on 14 June 1976 Lord Howard said 'it was the Jockey Club's responsibility to obtain the views of the indus-try on behalf of the stewards and the Levy Board. In all the circum-stances an independent or elected Chairman would not be approp-riate or constructive.'

Many subjects were discussed, including the provision of an all-weather track, overnight declaration of jockeys, breeders' prizes, private testing of samples for trainers by Racecourse Security Services (this provoked considerable opposition from both RSS and the Jockey Club) and later, of course, the response to Lord Rothschild's Royal Commission.

One of the most interesting subjects of discussion was the balance between afternoon and evening meetings, which provides a very neat example of the different attitudes to racing which existed in the Jockey Club and Levy Board. The amount of levy yielded by evening meetings was very small indeed, and the Levy Board would therefore not approve any application for reinstatement of an evening fixture unless the course met the cost of prize money and services.

At RILC's Semptember 1976 meeting, it was agreed to write to the Levy Board expressing dissatisfaction at the way its process of con-sultation with RILC was going, particularly over the Board's new policy on evening racing. The Board was interested above all in the levy, whereas RILC was interested in the long-term future of racing and in attracting the young. Evening racing could be seen as a loss leader. It was *not* the business of the Board to allocate or alter fixtures, and the Racecourse Association would contest any such suggestion with the Home Secretary or in the courts.

To this, Plummer sent a fighting reply to Howard that there could be 'no question of any Jockey Club prerogative when the exercise of that prerogative impinges upon the financial responsibilities of the Levy Board. It is for the Levy Board to decide how many fixtures it can and will finance each year, and if the number of fixtures allocated ever exceeded the number for which the Levy Board considered it could provide finance, the cost of those excess fixtures would have to be met from some other source.'

In the end the Board climbed down by reducing the threatened reductions to the Daily Rate (the sum paid to a racecourse by the Board for each day's racing), and the RCA agreed that a ceiling of seventy-five evening meetings would be satisfactory. This compared with 115 evening meetigs out of 848 fixtures in 1968, and 62 out of 958 in 1977.

Evening racing seems to have been the issue on which RILC made most progress. But even if it had been nothing more than a talking shop, it would have been a valuable means of canalising hostility between the Jockey Club and Levy Board, and so contributing to the growth of harmonious relations between those bodies. As the Club's Annual Report for 1976 recorded, the Committee had 'quickly established a position in the decision making process of the Industry as evidenced by the fact that both the Stewards and the Levy Board have referred major matters to it for consideration before taking decisions'.[19] Captain John McDonald-Buchanan's foreword to the 1979 Annual Report records 'having taken the lead in establishing a working party to consider the question, the Jockey Club subsequently withdrew from the discussions in order that the recommendation should express only the views of those bodies professionally engaged in the industry'. The discussions culminated in the decision to replace RILC with the Horseracing Advisory Council (HAC) early in 1980. The Jockey Club agreed that the Chairman of the HAC should be one of the Club's nominees to the Levy Board, and that he should attend meetings of the Stewards for items affecting horse racing, as opposed to the Club's purely domestic affairs.

Meanwhile BRIC continued in being, but enjoyed rather variable relations with both Jockey Club and Levy Board. BRIC's contribution to the Joint submission to Rothschild caused a minor dispute with the Club, with the result that BRIC participated in a separate submission entitled 'The Organisation of the Control of Racing', in which its partners were the RCA, ROA and TBA. They said that the three Jockey Club nominees on the Levy Board did not adequately represent the views of the rest of the industry. The Board needed strengthening in order better to assess requirements, and to decide on how its income should be distributed. Attempts by the Jockey Club and Levy Board to co-ordinate their activities in the non-executive Joint Racing Board were unsatisfactory because the two bodies were often at loggerheads. Since the Levy Board refused, on Home Office instructions, to allow wider representation on the Joint Racing Board, the submission suggested that a new Racing Board should be set up which would be the Levy Board expanded and given executive powers for the administration of racing. The Stewards would retain responsibility for the rules, discipline, etc. The new Board would have a Home Office chairman, another Home Office nominee, and one nominated by the Minister of Sport. These three would determine a disputed levy.

BRIC's proposed Racing Board incurred Lord Howard's wrath in his 1976 Gimcrack speech on 10 December 1976, in which he discussed the growth of representation. He reaffirmed the Jockey Club's wish that all sections of the industry should make their views known through RILC, but made it clear that it was not the Associations' business to control racing. He therefore rejected the alternative structures which had been proposed to Rothschild, hitting out particularly at the British Racing Board, which had been proposed by BRIC, though he did not mention BRIC by name. He went on, with uncharacteristic sarcasm: 'The Jockey Club, I understand, are not to be disbanded, but as no-one else appears anxious to assume responsibility for the Rules of Racing and discipline they will be given two seats on the Board and tucked away in a corner to get on with this.' Lord Howard may also have been attacking the Levy Board's evidence to Rothschild. Yet later in the speech he paid tribute to the Board, giving a perhaps rather exaggerated impression of the amicability of its relations with the Jockey Club.

In this speech he made his famous remark, 'Power is the name of the game'. This is often taken, especially by 'Jack Logan' in his Friday column in *The Sporting Life*, to mean that Howard was interested solely in maintaining the Jockey Club's power. However, it seems more likely that he also meant to convey that he fully understood that *all* bodies in racing were interested in power.

Another, more substantial, dispute with the Jockey Club concerned proposed amendments to its Charter. The amendments provided for outsiders to serve on 'other committees', but BRIC thought that they should be allowed on all committees and on the so-called Council of Stewards. They intended to put this strongly to the Jockey Club and, if necessary, to the Privy Council, but at the meeting of the Liaison Committee on 9 August 1977 they decided to withdraw their objections. Dame Elizabeth Ackroyd, who in April 1977 had succeeded the much more emollient Winter as Chairman of BRIC, reported that Wigg had asked, via the Privy Council Office, to see the BRIC objections to alterations in the Charter. However, BRIC agreed not to show them to him pending further discussions with the Jockey Club.

BRIC itself suffered internal convulsions. Charles Frank was installed as Director-General at an informal meeting on 24 February 1978, and Winter wrote a firm letter to Dame Elizabeth to inform her of the change. As she had not yet retired, this must have seemed like the operation of a cabal!

BRIC's relationship with the Levy Board was also changeable, as is indicated by the variation between 'Dear John' and 'Dear Mr Winter' in Plummer's letters to Winter. The chief bone of contention was over consultation. Plummer repeatedly emphasised the need for unity in approaches to the Government, and complained about BRIC's lack of consultation, though he rather spoiled his case by jealously guarding papers prepared by the Board. On one occasion he wrote to Winter 'I am sure you will recognise that there are a number of documents, such as our formal submission to the Home Secretary, which, as a statutory body, we are not in a position to release or discuss with any other party.'[20]

BRIC naturally resented the impression conveyed by Plummer that racing matters were the sole responsibility of the Levy Board and Jockey Club, and that BRIC should feel honoured to help. Plummer's firm opinion was that BRIC's proper channel of communication was through the Jockey Club's nominees on the Levy Board, and he seems to have been reluctant to see BRIC do anything independently. For example, he made a great mountain out of the molehill of BRIC wishing to take a census of stable staff, in order to establish which union, if any, they wished to join.

This attitude fuelled BRIC's desire to influence the Club's choice of Board members. In 1976 BRIC supported Astor's appointment, though with some reluctance. There was no personal objection to Astor, but it was thought unfortunate that the first person recommended by BRIC should already be a member of the Club. In 1977 BRIC tried unsuccessfully to get Charles Frank appointed. It experienced the usual difficulty that individual member organisations had approved the appointment of Lt.-Col. P. H. G. Bengough, but BRIC itself had not discussed the matter as a body, nor apparently been consulted. The same difficulty came to light at BRIC's discussion on 31 July 1978 of the new Authority recommended by Rothschild. It became clear that the only member organisations which would like BRIC to represent them on the Jockey Club's working party were ones which thought it unlikely that they would be offered individual seats.

Early in 1978 BRIC's finances began to go downhill. Major Michael Pope, for the trainers, said at an informal meeting at Winter's house that he did not think the trainers would give more than £4,000. McCreery said the TBA would give the same. It was thought that the total budget should be £12,000. McCreery thought that BRIC had outlived its role, but after discussion it was agreed to retain the Parliamentary services of Jerry Wiggin, though BRIC could only budget three months ahead. (In fact, he was retained, intermittently, until March 1980.) However, some present thought that Parliamentary representation should be via RILC and paid for by the Jockey Club. Wiggin seems to have talked good sense about the need for a continuous effort to build up and maintain a lobby in Parliament, even when it was not particularly needed, and an effective lobby meant paying an MP. This was better than relying on the All-Party Committee of MPs, or than employing parliamentary agents, who could upset certain MPs. He did not believe the Jockey Club thought politically, and the Committee was briefed almost exclusively by the Club.

By November 1978 the Newmarket office was closed, and by 1980 BRIC's financial position was very poor. It owed the bank £4,580, and felt that it had no purposeful policies, and that it must either go 'to the Left', that is, make an all-out attack on all the bodies involved in racing, or work with the Jockey Club. Once HAC had been established there was no need for BRIC to remain active on a day-to-day basis, but it was kept alive, as it might be a useful future vehicle for a political lobby. Since then it has, for practical purposes, been moribund, though it holds an annual general meeting. Its most visible legacy had been the reconstitution of its Taxation Committee as the Taxation Committee of the HAC.

The Rothschild Commission

It is often suggested that after the turmoil of the Wigg years and Raymond's calm interregnum, the Board, under Plummer, settled down to a happy period of strain-free co-operation with the Jockey Club. This is an over-simplified picture. The Jockey Club was punch-drunk after five years of Wigg, and anything would have been an improvement. In fact, Plummer was a very great improvement, but he did share Wigg's determination to assert the importance and power of the Levy Board, and his belief that its position as a statutory body gave it a special staus and importance, which put it in some way 'above the battle', sometimes jarred on other organisations within racing. He seems to have seen the Board almost as an outpost of the Civil Service (even in these more relaxed days it still retains something of that atmosphere), and the secrecy with which he surrounded the Board's business was often attacked in the press, notably in Tom Kelly's 'Frankly Speaking' column in the *Sporting Chronicle*.

He did not always please the Jockey Club; for example, he at one time wanted to withdraw Levy Board support from the July course at Newmarket, because he thought it unreasonable to support two courses in one place at a time of serious financial pressure, but changed his mind once he had seen it on a race day. Perhaps even more grave a threat was the inclusion in the Board's evidence to Rothschild of proposals to set up a Horseracing Advisory Council, through which all bodies in racing would make their views known to the Board. The Club would have been just one Council member among many: it would have continued to administer racing 'on a day-to-day basis' but the Levy Board, or some successor organisa-tion, 'must be expected to exert increased control over such areas as fixtures, numbers of racecourses and racecourse contributions to prize money'. Indeed, the Board went so far as to suggest that such a body might end up with total control of the fixture list.

These ideas were, of course, not accepted by the Commission, thanks in part at least to minority recommendations entered by the Jockey Club's and bookmakers' representatives on the Board. But they do show that the drive for power was still at work in the Board.

It is true that the present Horseracing Advisory Council emerged from the Commission, and is fully funded by the Levy Board, but it is not perceived as a threatening body at the Jockey Club's headquarters in Portman Square, and the Board has not gained the wider powers for which it was bidding.

Rothschild said 'The racing world is divided into a large number of interested factions, most of whom hold strong and frequently opposing views about how the sport should be run. We probably received more evidence on this subject than on everything else put together.'[21]

The Commission laboured for two and a half years, and in July 1978 produced a two-volume report of nearly six hundred pages, of which about a hundred concern racing, the Tote and betting shops (the rest is about gambling, fruit machines, etc.). Shortly before he reported, Lord Rothschild showed some optimism that the Commission 'has had some success in producing a practicable and feasible programme for change and action'. He also said that the success of a Royal Commission should not be measured by the legislation which might follow, since that was a matter of political decision by the Government, 'The Report which one aims to produce must be thorough, constructive, hopefully imaginative but above all clear in its reasoning.'[22]

Rothschild's report certainly had all these characteristics, and he must have been correspondingly chagrined when most of his recommendations were rejected or produced no result. Of the 303 recommendations the score by early 1984 was: eleven had been implemented; two partially implemented; five before Parliament (Sir Ian Gilmour's Bill to allow improved conditions in betting shops); thirty-five accepted, but not yet implemented; twenty-three accepted, but no action required; eighty-nine rejected; and on 138 no decision had been reached. Nor does it seem likely that decisions will be taken on many of the last category, since the small legislation unit set up in the Home Office to deal with the Commission's findings has been disbanded as part of an economy drive.

The appointment of a Royal Commission was fairly generally foreseen by the time it was announced on 23 October 1975, though some months went by before it was possible to announce the membership. The impetus came from diverse sources. Lord Wigg, in 1974 and 1975, wrote several letters to the Prime Minister, Harold Wilson, urging that some such enquiry be held. The Duke of Devonshire had written to *The Times* in similar vein on 7 May 1975 and he was disappointed that his letter elicited no support from organisations within racing. His purpose was to get help for racing from the Government, but he did not think it would be forthcoming on the strength of Benson, which had been an internal enquiry. Similarly, pressure by BRIC would be discounted, because it would be seen as self-interested.

Officials in the Home Office were probably the most important group behind the Royal Commission. They tended to be puritanical, and concerned about gambling as a social phenomenon, but not especially interested in racing. They were, however, very worried about the growth of lotteries (as was the Board of Customs and Excise) and about prize competitions. The law relating to gambling looked thoroughly unsatisfactory, particularly since a House of Lords decision had gone against prize competitions. The Home Office felt it must salvage these, since they raised so much money for extremely deserving causes, like the spastics, and a Royal Commission seemed to be the right way towards a general tidying-up of the law. Sir Stanley Raymond took a rather similar view, for he found the regulation of betting far too untidy and lax after the very tight control of gaming houses for which he was responsible, and he would have liked considerable tightening up of, for example, betting advertising.

Unfortunately, however, Rothschild has been a casualty of the factors which contributed to his Commission being set up: lotteries have gone out of fashion, and the need to rationalise the law is correspondingly less urgent.

The Royal Commission gave racing's institutions an opportunity to wash their power games in public. The Jockey Club resisted the temptation (or at least was circumspect) but the Levy Board and the Tote did not, though neither of them gained by it. Plummer, as we have seen, hoped to extend the Board's power. The Commission's final report quoted the 'minatory words' used in the Board's evidence and recommended a much reduced Board. It also savaged the Tote, the burden of whose evidence had been that off-course bookmakers should be abolished through the compulsory purchase of their shops, at a price which would not include goodwill, and that meanwhile clause 3 of the 1972 Act should be brought into force. Rothschild sternly rejected the proposal, because of the faulty arithmetic and reasoning which supported it, as well as the Tote's record of management. He would obviously have gone into the Tote in far more detail had it not, thanks to Wigg, just been investigated by the Select Committee on Nationalised Industries.

By the time of the Royal Commission the bookmakers had become expert both in lobbying and in the presentation of evidence, though it must be added that even the bookmakers did not escape scot-free. Rothschild was particularly scathing about a statement by the William Hill organisation that a 10p bet on the ITV seven could win £100,000. Rothschild commented: 'further inquiry revealed that no bookmaker had ever paid £100,000 on an ITV seven and that the most which William Hill had ever paid on a 10p bet was £27,000.'[23] Nevertheless, he accepted the substance of the bookmakers' arguments: their profits were not excessive; there was no case for a Tote monopoly, though there might have been in 1960; clause 3 should not be activated.

It would be tedious to summarise much of the voluminous evidence submitted to Rothschild, but the Jockey Club's views are of particular importance. It first presented an interim submission, because it knew that the Commission had been instructed to produce an interim report on the possibility of a levy on football pools (or perhaps on other sports) in order to assist sport in general. The Club stated that racing could not do without its levy, and would not wish to share it with any other sport, but it had no objection to other boards being set up to assist other sports. However, the Club was very firmly of the opinion, no doubt with the views of Wigg and Denis Howell in mind, that such boards ought to be independent, not subject to some central sports board.

Thereafter the Jockey Club made a number of submissions. It first made a very substantial contribution to a Joint Submission in July 1976, to which the other signatories were the ROA, the RCA, the Jockeys' Association, the Jockey Club Licensed Officials' Association, and BRIC. An earlier, and much less convincing, version of this document had been prepared by the Racing Policy Committee on behalf of all the associations listed above, except the jockeys. The RPC's draft had been abandoned and the new draft which went to the Royal Commission aroused anger in BRIC because it had been claimed by the Jockey Club that the changes would be only in layout and presentation, whereas in fact they were substantial. Ten years later it appears perfectly true that the changes were more than presentational, but it is difficult to see why BRIC should have complained so vehemently, since the well-researched new document is far more effective than the old, and remains a mine of useful information.

Its burden was that racing was grossly under-financed and needed additional prize money of £13 million per year. A report was rather hurriedly commissioned from the Economist Intelligence Unit, which was expected to support this case but in fact said that racing's resources were adequate. This verdict completely undermined the joint submission, though in retrospect some members of the Jockey Club secretariat thought it had been salutary. The Club, either honouraby or foolishly, or because it had no choice, published the report, with an embarrassed, and rather unconvincing, rebuttal by Lord Howard.[24]

The Joint Submission had made no recommendations as to the administration of racing, on which a number of signatories, including the Jockey Club, presented separate evidence. The Jockey Club's paper, dated September 1976, rejected various schemes which had been put forward, including the Minister of Sport's notion of a Racing Council, Wigg's proposed Racing Consultative Council, and even the British Racing Authority outlined in the Club's own Benson report. At this point the Club believed that racing should continue to be administered much as it was, though it undertook to strengthen RILC. It was perfectly willing to consult RILC before making its appointments to the Levy Board, and if necessary to appoint one or more of its representatives from outside the Club.

There followed a dramatic 'U-turn'. Howard got wind of the Commission's wish to consider other forms of organisation for the industry, and the Club produced a completely different blueprint, whose details Howard made public at a press conference on 20 December 1977, fifteen months after its first submission.

He explained that the Club's purpose in this new proposal had been to design an authority which would keep control of the industry in its own hands, while bringing it under governmental authority by having the Chairman and two members appointed by the Home Office. Howard admitted that the Club had changed its mind since arguing against such an authority in its earlier submssion: 'However, there is a very great difference between the two submissions. The first one dealt with the danger the Jockey Club considered inherent in any Authority imposed upon the racing industry from without. The submission we are discussing today sets out how the Club believes that a Racing Authority could be set up with the full support of the industry.' The new body would leave the Club in control of administration, but would include representatives of the ROA, RCA, TBA, the Tote and the bookmakers. One of the Government nominees would become chairman of RILC. The Jockey Club would accept changes in its Charter if necessary. Financial control would be vested in a committee composed of the Authority's chairman, the chairman of RILC (both Government nominees) and a Jockey Club nominee. At the same time, there was no wish that the Jockey Club should take over the functions of the Levy Board. The intention seems rather to have been that the Levy Board and Jockey Club would both be absorbed in the new Authority.

It seems reasonable to suppose that, just as with the very similar structure proposed by Benson, the Jockey Club expected to be able to count on the support of a majority of the new Authority, while meeting the case for public accountability by asking for a chairman and two members to be appointed by the Home Office.

In the event, Rothschild's chief recommendation in relation to horse racing was not far removed from the Jockey Club's proposal. He recommended that a British Horseracing Authority be set up (which, he hoped, would in due course be given a Royal Charter), and which would take over most of the functions of the Levy Board. If the racing industry, led by the Jockey Club, could not devise the constitution of such a body within six months, then the Government should set up a statutory body. This recommendaton was, of course, diametrically opposed to the evidence offered by the Levy Board, which had hoped that it, or some similar body, would eventualy hold the whip hand in racing.

Once the Commission's report was published, Lord Howard wrote round the various organisations saying he was setting up a working party to devise a constitution for the new authority. At that stage he did not commit himself to saying which bodies would be represented on the working party; that was a decision he would take in the light of their observations on the feasibility of a BHA. He thus gave an opportunity for the frantic democracy of the racing world to show itself in the scramble for places. The working party was duly set up under the chairmanship of Major Michael Wyatt.

After three or four meetings it became clear that Rothschild's BHA was politically a non-starter because it would be insufficiently accountable to Parliament. There were suggestions that Rothschild and his advisers in the Home Office should have seen this objection for themselves, which caused Rothschild to state that the new body *would* have been accountable, in that its accounts would have been attached to those of the Levy Board.[25] Members of Parliament did not like the idea of a truncated Levy Board, with a non-statutory BHA (in effect the Jockey Club writ new) having responsibility for £15 million of 'public money'. The Jockey Club, on the other hand, was very much against the setting up of a statutory body to control racing, so the working party began to turn towards the idea of a consultative body, which the Levy Board was able to support, since it had canvassed such an idea in its own evidence. At this point the Club withdrew from the discussions in order to allow the Associations a free hand in working out the kind of consultative body they would like.

There followed meetings between the Jockey Club and the All Party Racing Committee (then chaired by Sir Timothy Kitson, Conservative MP for Richmond, Yorkshire), which, in turn talked to William Whitelaw, Home Secretary in the Conservative Government which came into office in May 1979. On 19 July Whitelaw announced that the kind of body envisaged by Rothschild was not needed at present, but that he welcomed the steps being taken by the industry to set up a new and independent body. He made the same point in the debate on the Commission's report on 29 October 1979, in which the Horseracing Advisory Council was widely acclaimed, though Walter Johnson saw it as a cosmetic exercise pleasing to the Jockey Club.[26]

Plummer and the bookmakers

Despite his disagreements with the Jockey Club, Plummer delivered the goods, and at bottom the policies pursued under his guidance were in tune with the views of the racing 'establishment'. For this attitude Wigg frequently attacked the Board, in Parliament and elsewhere. He thought it had turned racing from an industry which had been hard up but viable in 1961 into one wholly dependent on subsidy, and seems often to have ignored the fact that he had himself greatly contributed to that dependence by maximising the levy. By October 1981 his relations with Plummer were so bad (because he telephoned individual members of the Board's staff) that Plummer told him that any enquiries he wished to make of the Board should be channelled through its secretary.

Under Plummer, the total prize money rose from £7,053,400 in the calendar year 1974 to £22,998,200 in 1982 (itself sixteen per cent up on the previous year). The increase was not considerable in real terms, but Plummer's major achievements were to handle the bookmakers firmly (several levy schemes had to be determined by the Home Secretary and there was, as we shall see, considerable friction over the twenty-first, for 1982-3), and greatly to increase the proportion of prize money paid by the Levy Board. In the calendar year 1974 it paid only 34 per cent of the total, but in 1982 it rose to 49 per cent. This, in turn, meant that the owners' contribution fell from 31 per cent to 25 per cent, that of the racecourses themselves fell from 20 per cent to 13 per cent, and the sponsors' contribution, having gone as high as 15 per cent during the decade, fell to 13 per cent. Of course, all three of these groups' contributions increased enormously in money terms.

At the same time, Plummer was faced with widespread evasion of the levy, because at the beginning of his period it was paid on the turnover of the previous year. Thus, if a business closed down just before the end of a year, there was no way of establishing in the following year the levy which it ought to have paid. Plummer dealt with this problem by persuading bookmakers voluntarily to pay the levy on the current year, and to maintain the Board's cash flow by paying in instalments rather than at the end of the year. He induced them to do this by making interest payments on amounts paid in excess of the eventual assessment, and in 1980-1 as many as 1,200 bookmakers received interest payments. These payments naturally excited adverse comment in the press but without them it would have been very difficult to persuade bookmakers to pay by instalments. The Board, however, realised that it could not necessarily rely on bookmakers to assist it voluntarily, and tried unsuccessfully to persuade the government to allocate parliamentary time for an amendment to the Act. No time was found, but in 1981 the Hon. Charles Morrison, MP, was fortunate in the ballot for Private Members' Bills and introduced a Bill to regularise the situation, with the support of the Home Office, the bookmakers and all sections of the racing industry. The bookmakers were, however, indignant because just after the Bill received the Royal Assent on 2 July 1981, Plummer wrote to the Bookmaker's Committee stating that the Board expected the Committee to produce proposals for the twenty-first levy scheme (for 1982-3) which would yield £26,500,000, £8 million above the estimated yield from the previous scheme and over £5 million more than had been asked for in April. In September the Board reduced its demand to £24.382 million, but after harsh words between Plummer and the Committee the scheme had to be determined by the Home Secretary; he fixed a rate of levy which might have produced rather over £20.5 million if turnover had remained constant.

The Langdon Report

In connection with the dispute over the twenty-first Scheme, Richard Langdon, the senior partner in the accountants Spicer and Pegler, was invited to advise the Home Secretary as to how a levy of £24.3 million might be raised and the effect on the bookmaking industry of doing so. He reported on 22 February 1982,[27] The Bookmakers' Committee also took advice, and the symbiotic relationship between the Committee and the Board is nicely illustrated by the latter's agreement to pay the £45,000 cost of the Committee's submission to the Home Secretary.[28]

Langdon found (the mathematics are too complicated to go into here) that a bookmaker paying the average levy (at that time 0.768 per cent of turnover) who charged the punter a deduction of 10 per cent was thereby exceeding his Duty and levy liability by only about 0.2 per cent. The largest bookmakers were exceeding their liability by about 0.1 per cent (a figure which differs somewhat from the one produced by the bookmakers themselves, possibly because it was based on slightly different assumptions). Before the increase in Betting Duty of 0.5 per cent and the bookmarkers' increased deductions from 9 per cent to 10 per cent, the bookmakers had therefore been making some contribution towards the Duty and the levy, but this had been eliminated when they increased their deduction.

Langdon thought that the deduction had now reached the point where it could prove a discouragement to the punter to bet: this contention is almost impossible to prove but there has been some theoretical work done by economists in the United States and reported in this country by Bloom[29] which tends to support the view that betting is a good like any other; when its price goes up, consumers buy less of it.

Langdon estimated very tentatively that turnover might grow by one per cent in 1981-2 and a further four per cent in 1982-3, and these estimates were very close to those offered by the bookmakers.

They turned out to be incorrect, since in 1982-3 the turnover actually declined. Given his assumptions, however, Langdon thought that the levy would have to be increased by 40.3 per cent over the Board's latest estimate of the yield of the twentieth scheme if the twenty-first scheme were to produce the required £24.3 million. This, in turn, would cause the bookmakers to raise their deductions to eleven per cent, which might well have the effect of reducing turnover and so invalidating Langdon's forecasts.

He concluded that the bookmakers did not have the capacity to pay a levy at a significantly increased rate over that ruling in the nineteenth and twentieth schemes. If the levy were so increased the bookmakers would take the opportunity to increase their deductions, probably by one per cent, and such an increased deduction would depress turnover. The decline in turnover which actually occurred gave the Board a revised estimated yield, according to its annual report for 1982-3, of £19,117,000.

Plummer and the 'Establishment'

The Board under Plummer continued wedded to the, to my mind, highly dubious view that major increases in prize money can in part be justified on the grounds that they benefit stable staff. The view finds its classic statement in the fourteenth annual report: 'The Board maintains the view that the improvement of the terms and conditions of the industry's workforce is of the greatest importance and that this can best be assisted by an increase in prize money not only from the Board but also from racecourses and owners, so as to ensure that, through deductions from win and place money, adequate sums percolate down to those working in the industry.'[30]

The sentiment is unexceptionable, but the benefits percolate only to the connections of successful horses.

The Board did not forget the interests of owners and breeders. In its 16th Report (1976-7) it refers for the first time to its 'initial basic policy objective which is to ensure that the owner of a horse which wins a race on a Group I or Group II racecourse receives, after deductions, guaranteed winnings which are at least equivalent to half the basic annual cost of keeping a horse in training'.[31] In the following year it made the innovation of allocating £169,050 of its prize money contributions to fillies' premiums and recorded that 'This allocation was widely regarded as having contributed to a buoyant yearling market in 1977'.[32]

The pattern of prize money allocation was also changing. In 1976-7 there took place the first major review of the groups into which racecourses were divided by the Board for prize money purposes. Six were promoted, none was demoted, Group V was conflated with Group IV. The Board also proposed, with the Jockey Club's endorsement, to institute some new northern Pattern races, but this idea was turned down by the International Pattern Committee (it will be recalled from a previous chapter that an unsuccessful attempt had been made to institute northern Pattern races in Wigg's time). In the same year, Basic Daily Rate was increased for Group I and II courses 'as it was considered appropriate to place the emphasis on increasing prize money for the higher quality races.' As so often, the Board does not explain its judgements: no indication was given of the reasons for which the change was considered appropriate. However, in the light of hindsight, they were clearly connected with Plummer's announcement at the April 1979 meeting of the Racehorse Industries Liaison Committee of a proposal for the joint study with the Jockey Club of the future size and shape of the industry. This study resulted in the famous and, in some eyes, notorious 'Blue Report'.

This committee of enquiry, instigated and chaired by Plummer, developed thoughts already expressed in the Board's evidence to the Royal Commission. It believed that the emphasis of prize money allocation should be towards quality and selectivity: the Committee thought that ideally racecourses should be self-sufficient and in any case should be less dependent on Levy Board funds. Unsuccessful courses might not survive, but:

> we consider that racecourses should not be arbitrarily forced to close or people prevented from owning racehorses and keeping them in training, on the grounds of the size of the industry. We do consider, however, that the main aim of those responsible for the financing and administration of racing should be to promote the quality of racing and its attractiveness as a spectacle, as a spectator sport, as a sound betting medium, as a test of racehorses, and as an important and worthwhile feature of the national life.[33]

The Board, not surprisingly, in view of Plummer's role on the Committee, followed the policy recommended, partly on the grounds that it was a necessary response to declining turnover. Racecourses were divided into three categories, which qualified for capital grants for specified types of project and, in the words of the twentieth annual report:

> The Board, supported by the Stewards of the Jockey Club, accepted that the levy had proved insufficient to meet all the legitimate demands upon it and was at present spread too thinly. It therefore agreed that in future its assistance by way of prize money and funds for racecourse improvements should be applied more selectively. It further agreed that self help should be rewarded, that racecourses should be encouraged to be more self-sufficient and should be given greater flexibility as far as prize money was concerned, and that a greater share of the money should be applied to support better quality races.[34]

The emphasis on quality was not, of course, universally popular in the racing world; indeed, it split the Jockey Club, many of whose members were, and remain, deeply attached to the small courses which provide the life-blood of racing. The report was strongly attacked by the HAC and was seen, even by people who favoured a degree of centralisation, as far too much of a businessman's document 'like a remonstrance from Lord Weinstock to a loss-making subsidiary' as one acute observer has put it (the then Sir Arnold Weinstock was a prominent member of the Committee). Furthermore, the report contained no real argument nor consideration of the various options open to racing, but was simply a statement of what might almost be called the prejudices of the Committee's leading members.

By espousing the report, Plummer aligned himself with the more prosperous and 'hard-minded' faction in racing, and, in doing so, may have lost some popularity at the end of his term at the Levy Board. But the line he took does not merely indicate that he wished to favour that faction above others. It is at least as much a demonstration that, by training a politician, he remained attuned to the political atmosphere of the time, which was dominated by the Thatcherite *ethos* of self-help.

When Plummer retired, Tom Kelly wrote that he had been wrong about the three most important issues of his later years at the Board.[35] These were Aintree (for which the Board had been able to do nothing), the twenty-first levy scheme and the Blue Report.

Kelly was, perhaps, rather harsh. The complaint that Plummer failed to save Aintree may have ben unfair, since he undertook long and exasperating negotiations, which brought the price down from some £10 million to £4,500,000. Furthermore, he had had a clear indication from the racing industry as a whole, and particularly from the flat side, that Levy Board funds should not be spent on Aintree but that the jump side should rescue it by its own efforts. Plummer also took over the Levy Board when its morale was very low, steered it successfully for eight years, and left it on an even keel. He deserves to be remembered for that achievement, rather than for his failures.

Notes

1 The study was published in 1974 under the title *The Future Requirements of Racing*.
2 Horserace Betting Levy Board, *Eleventh Report: 1 April 1971 – 31 March 1972*, London, 1972, para. 69.
3 Horserace Betting Levy Board, evidence to Royal Commission on Gambling, 7 October 1976, para. 129.
4 *The Sporting Life*, 22 January 1974.
5 *Ibid.*
6 *The Times*, 5 March 1976.
7 Joint Racing Board, *Report of the Committee of Enquiry into the Manpower of the Racing Industry*, London, July 1974.
8 Michael Filby, *The T & G Industrial Relations and Racing*, unpublished, undated.
9 *The Times*, 9 February 1960.
10 *The Times*, 10 February 1960.
11 E. Dean, *An Analysis of the Labour Market for Stable Lads in Newmarket*, 1976, unpublished BA dissertation, University of East Anglia.
12 The National Trainers' Federation kept out of these negotiations, and left everything to the Newmarket trainers. I am indebted to John Winter for access to his papers relating to this period.
13 *The Times*, 2 June 1975.
14 *The Times*, 25 July 1975.
15 *The Times*, 30 July 1975.
16 *The Times*, 30 January 1976.
17 *The Times*, 28 July 1976.
18 Horserace Betting Levy Board, *Fourteenth Report: 1 April 1974 – 31 March 1975*, London, 1975, para. 5. Again I am much indebted to Mr Winter for access to papers on BRIC.
19 Jockey Club, *Report by the Stewards 1976*, London, p. 6.
20 Plummer to Winter, 23 December 1975.
21 Royal Commission on Gambling, *Final Report*, vol. I, July 1978, p. 8 (Cmnd. 7200), para. 9.1.
22 Rothschild, Lord, 'Royal Commissions', an address to the British Academy, 29 June 1978, reprinted in *Random Variables*, London, 1984, pp. 85-91.
23 Royal Commission, para. 6.28.
24 See *The Times*'s leading article on the EIU report, 6 June 1977.
25 See Lord Rothschild's letter in *The Sporting Life*, 19 April 1979.

26 972 *H.C. Deb.*, col. 886, 29 October 1979.
27 R. Langdon, *Horserace Betting Levy: Enquiry into Certain Matters Relating to the 21st Levy Scheme*, 22 February 1982, unpublished.
28 See Tom Kelly's column in the *Sporting Chronicle*, 2 April 1982.
29 S. Bloom, *The Economics of Gambling*, May 1984, unpublished BA dissertation, Preston Polytechnic.
30 Horserace Betting Levy Board, *Fourteenth Report*, para. 10.
31 *Ibid., Sixteenth Report: 1 April 1976 – 31 March 1977*, London, 1977, para. 10.
32 *Ibid., Seventeenth Report: 1 April 1977 – 31 March 1978*, London, 1978, para. 14.
33 Joint Racing Board, *The Report of a Committee of Enquiry into the Distribution of the Horserace Betting Levy in Support of British Horseracing*, April 1980, para. 3. The report is commonly known as 'The Blue Report'.
34 Horserace Betting Levy Board, *Twentieth Report: 1 April 1980 – 31 March 1981*, London, 1981, para. 8.
35 *Sporting Chronicle*, 1 October 1982. For a rare interview with Plummer see Ivor Herbert, 'He Holds the Reins', *Pacemaker International*, April 1980, pp. 29-31.

X
Racing into the nineties

It must never be forgotten that racing is about pleasure. Its professionals become as passionate, absorbed, indeed obsessed, as do those in any other sport. But most of the issues I have been discussing are political, where politics is about the distribution of resources for which individuals and institutions compete. Those resources are money and power. The two nearly always run in tandem, but they are not, or not always, different names for the same thing.

Of course there are also questions which on the surface appear technical, but whose real significance is generally political. There is no technical problem about letting off a Polaris missile: the real question is where, and when, to fire it. There is no crucial technical problem about artificial insemination or even embryo transplantation. But if they were introduced (the odds shortened with Monsieur Launay's appointment as head of the French National Studs in 1982) and inadequately controlled, the bloodstock market might collapse. The question, therefore, is of keen financial concern to a mass of interested parties all over the world, and their battle is political. Similarly, the difficulties of the Racecourse Association or the Racehorse Owners' Association (but much less of the Thoroughbred Breeders' Association) are the political ones of representing constituencies whose members have very diverse, and sometimes irreconcilable, interests.

In this final chapter I sum up the current state of racing's major institutions and the increasingly harmonious relationships between them, and speculate about the institutions' possible future development. I discuss the challenges and opportunities presented by the introduction of television in betting shops and the recent removal of on-course Betting Duty, and go on to argue that continuing governmental approval will depend upon racing's ability to display a capacity for self-help. There has recently been a shift away from the traditional effort to persuade the government to give back to racing some of the tax raised on gambling, towards a new preoccupation with persuading the public, and ultimately Parliament, that Sunday racing and betting should be legalised. I conclude that strength comes from unity and that great progress has already been made towards it.

Conflict between racing's institutions has revolved, at least since Lord Wigg's day, around the competitive, and sometimes vitriolic, relationship between the Jockey Club and the Levy Board. Even under Lord Plummer the Board not only consolidated the gains made by Wigg but sought to extend them still further, taking the line that 'he who pays the piper calls the tune'. However, it was under Sir Ian Trethowan (whose acceptance in 1985 of a second three-year term of office was generally welcomed) that old rivalries were at last laid to rest. He used the oppportunity of his speech at the 214th Gimcrack Dinner at York in December 1984 to emphasise the great respect felt by all in racing for the Jockey Club's integrity and for its effectiveness as the administrator and regulator of racing. At the same time, while making it clear that the Levy Board had no further territorial ambitions, he made it equally clear by omission that he did not consider the Club to be the leader of the industry in all respects.

In a statesmanlike and witty reply, Lord Manton, who retired as Senior Steward on 30 June 1985, said that at one time inviting a Levy Board Chairman to air his views on the Jockey Club in public, let alone at the Gimcrack Dinner, would have been as inadvisable as inviting Count Dracula to manage a blood bank. But those days, he added, were over.

By international standards the Board's income is small; in its first twenty-five years (1961-86) it raised £231 million, less than the Royal Hong Kong Jockey Club takes in commission in two years. The Board's small resources have made it bear cost-effectiveness and value for money very much in mind. In May 1984 the accountants Peak Marwick Mitchell were appointed to investigate these aspects of its activities, partly because of the dispute with the Bookmakers' Committee which was hampering its operations, and partly as a matter of routine, in accordance with the recommendations of a recent governmental report.[1] The Peak Marwick report was, broadly speaking, favourable, though it did suggest that the Board should tighten up its procedures in some respects, for example, the examination of requests from racecourses for loans, and that it should re-examine the complicated system whereby numerous kinds of grants were paid to racecourses.

Although the Board and the Jockey Club now pull in the same direction, they may not always agree. There will be little disagreement about the Board's aims, which are laid down in the Act, but the main bone of contention has always been the rate of levy which it is reasonable to expect the bookmakers to pay on their turnover. The Levy Board sees its duty as the balancing of demands from the Jockey Club and professional associations for an ever-increasing levy, against its own estimation of what a reasonable rate will be and of what the bookmakers will consent to pay without forcing a reference to the Home Secretary. The Board's task was complicated in 1984 and 1985 by the dispute between the two Bookmakers' Associations, BOLA and the NAB, over the Chairmanship of the Bookmakers' Committee. It is true that the Committee's only essential function is to agree the rate of levy with the Board, but its failure to hold any formal meetings, and to provide a Chairman who could represent the bookmaking industry directly at Levy Board meetings, made relations between bookmakers and the Board uneasy, to say the least.

Thanks, however, largely to Trethowan's diplomatic skills, all sections of the racing industry were brought to agree in 1986 that for three years no higher rate of levy would be demanded, so that the amount raised would depend solely on the bookmakers' turnover. This agreement freed the industry from an exhausting annual ritual, and gave it a breathing space in which to deal with more substantial problems. The most important of these are: what case should be made to the Government on racing's behalf; how should the industry best take advantage of the removal in 1986 of the prohibition of television sets in betting shops; and how is the question of Sunday racing to be tackled?

The overriding importance of these questions contributed to a period of profound reassessment at the Levy Board, which perhaps was only made possible by the stability achieved in its relations with the Jocket Club and the bookmakers. Its financial contribution to racing had been of considerable significance for all racecourses, and the smaller ones had depended on it almost totally. Its relative weight has now decreased, so that it has begun to appear almost peripheral in the light of the huge growth in commercial sponsorship of races and the Racecourse Association's negotiation in 1986 of a valuable agreement over television rights with a consortium led by the 'big four' bookmakers. (Both these developments will be discussed below.)

It has, therefore, become possible for the Board to pare down its activities and alter their emphasis. For example, there has been a movement in the distribution of prize money away from the top towards the middle tier of racing (leaving the owners of the worst horses to race for little more than their own money). The Board had always been required by the Home Office to distance itself from the day-to-day running of United Racecourses Ltd. Now, as the result of a report received in 1986, it has adopted a similarly indirect relationship with the National Stud, whose Director formerly reported directly to the Board.[2]

Diminishing though the Board's importance may be, it would be foolish, as Sir Ian Trethowan has pointed out, for racing to provoke the government into doing away with its private levy and letting it take its place in the queue for Treasury subsidies along with swimming and the Arts Council.[3] But even if the levy continues the Levy Board will not necessarily retain its present importance: the Rothschild Commission accepted the Jockey Club's proposal that the Club should be replaced by a new British Horse Authority, and thought such an authority should take over many of the Levy Board's duties, though the Board would retain its status as a statutory body. Such ideas are not dead, and will become more plausible as the percentage of racing's total costs paid by the Board diminishes and that raised from other sources increases. On the other hand, Parliament would insist on a statutory body controlling the Levy, and the Jockey Club could not be sure of retaining the influence it has. Racing would probably be best advised not to get involved in fresh legislation, which could lay it open to all sorts of Parliamentary caprice.

Meanwhile the Board remains committed to the Horseracing Advisory Council, and pays all its expenses. The HAC was set up on the recommendation of a working party chaired by Air Commodore Brookes (chairman until 30 June 1985 of the Racecourse Association) and brings together the organisations which proliferate in racing. It provides an outlet for the frantic democracy which has characterised the industry ever since the birth of the Bloodstock and Racing Industries Confederation (BRIC) in 1974 and a base from which its secretary, Stanley Jackson, conducts solid research which otherwise might not be done at all. It was set up with a two-tier constitution, consisting of a non-Executive General Council containing representatives of many organisations, and a more compact Executive Committee. The first chairman, Phil Bull, expected the General Council to be a forum for the pursuit of sectional interests, but hoped that the Executive Committee would consider the welfare of racing as a whole.

The HAC suffers from the strengths and weaknesses of many bodies which have to represent very disparate constituents. Bull resigned in July 1980, after only a few months in office, and his successor, Major-General Bernard Penfold, found morale very low. Although his diplomatic gifts quickly improved matters, difficulties remain. The HAC's members are representatives of specialised interests, and in the last resort are liable to use their own organisations as the vehicles for direct pressure on the Levy Board or Jockey Club, instead of using the HAC as their intermediary. Furthermore, individual bodies may take the credit for successes which have really been achieved by the HAC.

On the other hand, the HAC is useful. The Jockey Club can call it in aid to support an initiative of which it approves, or remit to it one about which it has doubts. It also enjoys the approval of Lord Whitelaw and of the All Party Parliamentary Committee on Racing which contributed to its setting up, and it is undeniably true that the HAC has persuaded previously isolated bodies to communicate with each other. Even if it were no more than a talking shop, it would be of value, but it has also on occasion persuaded member organisations to abandon sectional interest in favour of the greater good.

Even a short account of the problems besetting racing requires a few words about the Tote. Its history has been chequered, ever since it was set up in 1928 with the twin objects of providing the public with an alternative means of betting and earning money for the benefit of racing (though only the second object was mentioned in its first annual report).[4] It conducts its operations in its own kiosks and buildings on course, by telephone (for credit customers), and in betting shops both on and off course. It has always believed, though it is difficult to see why, that it has a duty to provide pool betting facilities on *every* course, even on days when it is bound to make a loss, so that it is not surprising that its profits have been low and sometimes non-existent. Its turnover has also been low: the record was £136,785 million in 1980-81, a little under the equivalent of twelve days in Hong Kong in the same year. In the betting shops only a very small percentage (5.8 per cent) of the business is done at Tote odds, which seems to invalidate the claim repeatedly made in its annual reports during the 1970s that by opening betting shops it was offering the off-course punter a widely-desired additional service. It seems also to vindicate the judgement of the bookmakers who refused to pay large sums for the authority to strike bets at Tote odds. However, there are signs that in recent years Tote betting (particularly the Placepot) has become more popular, and there are now over 3,500 betting shops, including those owned by Coral's , Hill's and Mecca, which offer bets at Tote odds.

In 1984 the Tote made a new agreement whereby it continued to pay the racecourse on which it was operating a site rent and a daily payment to cover free entry by Tote personnel, and added an additional sum to bring the total to 3% of turnover. In 1985 the 3% was extended to cover credit betting relating to that course, and in 1987/88 the agreement was refined, so that the Tote paid 3% of turnover in its buildings, 4% of kiosk turnover and 5% of any increase in turnover over that attained in 1986/87. The new money was not great at first, only £150,000 in 1984, but it gave the racecourses immediate new confidence, and the amounts given were soon greatly increased. These measures seem, at least for the present, to have killed the idea, which is canvassed from time to time, that each racecourse should run its own Tote.[5]

The Tote has been bedevilled by uncertain management, badly sited buildings, and endless difficulties, both financial and managerial, over modernisation. However, under the energetic leadership of Lord Wyatt (who also had his ups and downs in his first years at the Tote), the organisation has become altogether more effective. Kiosks have sprung up at strategic points on most racecourses and are a boon to the lazy or slow-moving punter who does not want to walk as far as the bookmakers, and in return the Tote has made substantial contributions to the capital cost of some racecourse improvements. The computerised information on the Tote screens has improved beyond recognition, and its target of regaining the twenty-five per cent of on-course business which it had in 1970 seems realistic. Furthermore, the Tote hopes to instal equipment in 1988 whereby bets made in betting shops can immediately be transmitted to the pool, and those made at one course tranferred to the pool at another, if racing is taking place at both on the same day. The considerable progress the Tote has made may be bringing it to the point where privatisation is an option, a course which would, no doubt, be popular on ideological grounds with some Conservatives. Naturally, it would have to be done without prejudicing the benefit racecourses now gain from the Tote's operations, though a privatised Tote might reasonably be allowed to make its whole contribution directly to the racecourses, and in the form of sponsorship, and to cease its annual contribution to the levy.

The possibilities I have discussed so far, such as slimming down the Levy Board, making more use of the HAC, privatising the Tote, are internal to racing, but the greatest problem is how to present its collective case to the Government of the day, bearing in mind that Labour has on the whole been kinder to racing, as to farming, than have the Conservatives. The difficulty is that the racing world is so divided that it can hardly be said to have a collective mind to make up. All sections would agree that more money is needed, but how it is to be raised and spent is another matter.

Douglas Hurd, as Home Secretary, expressed views on racing in 1986 strikingly similar to those of R. A. Butler and the Home Office itself in 1960. Then, as now, the Government hoped to keep racing at arm's length. Hurd had no wish to be called in again to decide the rate of levy, and pointed out how much racing was envied by other sports for its possession of this private source of revenue. Unfortunately, he also believed that the levy was a substantial asset, despite the readily available figures which show that it is derisory, by comparison with other major racing countries.[6]

The case generally made to the Government is that racing needs more money from outside the present levy system, which must entail (as Phil Bull said in his evidence to the Royal Commission) a diversion to the industry of part of the betting tax. If the Government fails to do this, it is claimed that employment will suffer; good stallions will move abroad; small racecourses will be obliged to close; part of the national heritage will be lost, and so will votes. On top of all this, the goose which lays the golden egg of tax revenue will be lost.

In reply, it has to be said that the tax raised from betting is unimpressive beside the vast sums raised from tobacco, £4,140 million compared with £293 million from racing in 1984-5.[7] It is interesting, too, that a single company, GEC (whose Managing Director is Lord Weinstock, a keen member of the Jockey Club), paid almost exactly the same amount in tax in 1984-5 as was raised from betting duty,

£298,500,000.[8] Furthermore, yet another rise in the rate of betting duty seems unlikely. As Sir Geoffrey Howe said in 1981, when justifying the big increase which he had just imposed on petrol and derv, while raising betting duty by only 0.5 per cent to the eight per cent at which it still stands: 'Any further significant increase [in betting duty] would fail to raise anything like the amount of extra revenue needed. And it would risk driving gambling underground into the hands of the criminal world.'[9]

It is hardly surprising, therefore, if the various arguments put forward by racing interests for the diversion to the sport of some of the Betting Duty cut little ice with civil servants or their masters. However, a famous victory was gained in 1987, when the Chancellor of the Exchequer removed the four per cent tax on betting on course. This concession does not in itself put money into racing, but it may encourage people to bet on course instead of in betting shops, and so safeguard a healthy on-course market.

Now that the on-course tax has been removed and (as we shall see) governmental support expressed for Sunday racing, it is unlikely that the government will do more in the immediate future. No doubt it has done so much already because it has been impressed by such examples of self-help as the saving of Aintree and by the Thoroughbred Breeders' Association's part in setting up the European Breeders' Fund. However, the fact that much has been achieved does not mean that the industry should allow the Government to lose sight of racing's eventual aim of recovering some of the tax revenue raised on betting. Meanwhile the racecourses will have to generate more money by their own efforts. Various methods of doing so are available; they have already made arrangements to realise the potential offered by television, both national and on closed circuit in the betting shops; they can establish even closer relations with the Tote (perhaps to the detriment of bookmakers, particularly the smaller ones who form the backbone of the National Association of Bookmakers); they can make a still greater offort to attract sponsors; and they can insist on framing exciting cards which will both please sponsors and attract racegoers from the betting shops back to the course.

Unfortunately, the large racecourses are in a far stronger position to make such moves than are the smaller ones, with the important exception that both large and small courses will benefit from television in betting shops, though there are bound to be difficulties over the division of the spoils. In other respects the existing disparity of interest between the big battalions and the small fry is liable to grow. This would not worry the big owners and the leading trainers and jockeys, for whom racing is about winning top-class races. Some of them would hardly care if half Britain's racecourses were closed, though of course they would miss the opportunity of raiding remote northern courses to win small races with animals which have failed in the south.

If racing were a company set up to make money the obvious answer would be to centralise operations at the major courses, giving each as many fixtures as the turf would bear and abandoning the rest. The horse population would be reduced accordingly, an altogether more efficient organisation would be the result. But that answer ignores the fact that racing is more than a rich man's pursuit. There are a host of small owners and breeders, and minor jockeys and trainers, not to mention the small windswept racecourses whose vociferous local followings protest that racing is about sport and sociability as well as money. There is, too, some feeling in the Jockey Club that to provide a few days' racing at, say, Fakenham, is a kind of social service, which should be rendered as long as it is not a drain on central funds.

The small man's friends are also helped by the fact that if the Government were asked to help an industry organised for the big battalions, it would surely refuse, because there is no way in which racing could present such a case with a unified voice. The small man could not be muzzled, and the Government would quickly realise that to back what looked like a rich man's business might be a vote-loser. It would not believe that the goose needed any fattening, and would probably assume that it could go on laying golden eggs, even if it claimed to be half starving. Common sense dictates, therefore, that the industry should press the case for the *whole* industry, in the varied interests of sport, employment and tax-gathering. If later some racecourses were to fall by the wayside, their failure would be seen as the result of market forces, not the fault of the industry's leaders.

It remains to consider what racing has done for itself, and may yet do. There are still those who say that the bookmakers have a moral duty to contribute more than they do at present by way of levy. Lord Rothschild rejected that claim, in my view rightly.[10] The question is not one of morality but of the market place. The book-makers naturally complain about both tax and levy, but in fact contribute virtually nothing to them, as they pass both on to the punter.

The argument has in a sense become out of date, since the agreement made in 1986 over the provision of television programmes in betting shops. This was an agreement based on commercial prudence on all sides, not on morality. It was made possible by a Private Member's Bill, sponsored by Sir Ian Gilmour with the encouragement of the Home Office, making it possible for the Home Secretary to make regulations to improve the facilities offered by betting shops.[11] This he duly did (though he still insisted that his purpose was to make betting shops tolerable, rather than enticing[12]) and the most important improvement now permitted was the provision of television programmes.

It was common ground that the racecourses owned the copyright in pictures transmitted, and all of them sensibly allowed the Racecourse Association to negotiate on their behalf with the various consortia that presented themselves as candidates to transmit the pictures via Direct Broadcasting by Satellite (DBS) to the betting shops. Meanwhile, those courses which had contracts with the national television companies for public programmes, as opposed to ones shown only on closed circuit (DBS) continue to negotiate independently with the companies.

During protracted negotiations two consortia emerged. At first the front runner was a group consisting of Exchange Telegraph (Extel, the company which delivers the race commentary to the betting shops), Mercury Communications (a branch of Cable and Wireless) and GEC. Their rival, at first named Satellite Racing Development (SRD), was dominated by the big four bookmakers – Ladbroke's, William Hill, Mecca and Coral. Initially its bid was rejected, partly because there were worries over control being exercised by the big four which already owned over a third of Britain's 10,300 betting shops, and whose continued expansion was considered unstoppable. However in the end SRD, renamed Satellite Information Services (SIS), won the day with a revised bid and a new constitution. Fifteen per cent of its shares were to be held by Ladbroke's, ten per cent each by Hill's, Mecca and Coral, five per cent by the Tote, ten per cent by the Racecourse Association itself, with forty per cent remaining to be allocated.

Bookmakers would be able to subscribe to the service on a tariff ranging from £3,500 to £6,800 per year. It would of course be some time before it became known how many bookmakers would be able to afford the service and how many would prefer to remain with Extel, which naturally intended to offer improved services in order to retain as many as possible of its existing customers. Nevertheless, General Sir Peter Leng, Chairman of the Racecourse Association, was able to forecast that the RCA would benefit to the tune of at least £10 million over the next three years, and that '£25 million over five years was not wide of the mark'.[13]

What is not known is the extent to which the more comfortable betting shops will discourage people from going to the races, despite the removal of the on-course tax. It may be that, instead, they will draw new people into gambling who before would have patronised neither the betting shop nor the racecourse. Such a development would no doubt upset the Home Office, though not the Levy Board, since higher turnover brings increased levy. On the other hand, the programmes shown in betting shops might diversify away from horseracing to greyhounds, and other events on which bets are not liable to levy. The proportion of turnover attributable to such events was showing worrying signs of going up, even before the introduction of television, and, if it were to continue, even significantly higher turnover might not benefit the Board. The empirical evidence on the relation between betting shop attendance and racegoing is rather meagre. Some research conducted for the Racecourse Association by Metra Oxford in 1974 found that two-thirds of their sample of betting-shop punters also went racing, most of them only occasionally. The main reasons for not going more often were time and money, though others mentioned included the wife, traffic, and distance from the racecourse. Those who claimed to watch racing on television often were more likely than others to go racing as well, as were the most frequent visitors to betting shops, and those who placed the most and the highest value bets.

A Gallup poll in 1983 found that 17 per cent of men and 2 per cent of women (making 10 per cent of the sample) used betting shops. This compared with 41 per cent of the sample who filled in football coupons, 55 per cent of men and 29 per cent of women, and only 4 per cent (7 per cent of men, 2 per cent of women) who bet at the racecourse or dog track. A high proportion, 68 per cent of the betting-shop users, also bet on course, and 31 per cent of the on-course punters also used betting shops.

These figures tell us nothing definite about what effect television in betting shops will have on racecourse attendances, though the

Metra results suggest that there is no incompatibility between enthusiasm for the betting shop and enjoyment of the racecourse. Both this Metra report, and another done for Goodwood racecourse in 1973, emphasised the importance of marketing racing, both to attract the betting-shop public and to bring in completely new racegoers.[14]

The other areas in which the Government might expect the racecourses to help themselves are those of commercial sponsorship, and racing on Sundays.

The former presents in a sharp, almost ugly, form the tension between racing as a sport and racing as an industry. Sponsors do not merely influence the type of races to be run and then put up the prize money but have recently shown increased willingness to pay for improvements to the course itself. The most striking example is the commitment Ever Ready, the sponsor of the Derby, has made to the development of Epsom racecourse and its associated facilities. But for the sporting racegoer such developments lead far from the sport he has known and loved, into a world where elaborate buildings are put up in order that businessmen may spend vast sums (by most people's standards) entertaining their customers. Then, once racing is over, the buildings can be used as hotels and conference centres, so that a course may earn more from non-racing than from racing itself.

It all makes good commercial sense, but it turns some stomachs. Company entertaining has become so widespread that racing almost gets in the way. For example, at Cheltenham companies wine and dine five thousand or more people on each day of the Festival meeting in March, at a cost of £100 to £150 per day each, providing a 'take' of, at the very least, £1.5 million. By contrast, American companies seem to dislike mixing business and pleasure in this way, with the result that their British subsidiaries take relatively little part in sponsorship.

The feeling that sponsorship, and the commercial atmosphere that goes with it, have gone too far is not confined to racegoers. There are, it is true, plenty of articles about Ascot in colour supplements, which manage to deride what they think of as the 'genuine upper-crust' while snobbishly poking genteel fun at the less genuine, but similar articles are to be found about numerous other traditional British enjoyments, like Henley or Wimbledon. Such articles may be light in weight, but they do reflect a serious dilemma for the administrator of any sport, who wants at the same time to make a commercial success of the activity and to retain the best of its accustomed character. Unfortunately, the dice are not evenly loaded. Commercial influence is here to stay; some aspects of it may diminish, or be abolished, like sponsorship by tobacco companies, but the trend is unlikely to be reversed.

Unlike television and sponsorship, Sunday racing remains in the future. It can, of course, be argued that if racecourses wish to race on Sunday, they should simply go ahead and do so, and in the process disregard the Sunday Observance Act of 1780. This Act provides that those who admit the public to places of entertainment on Sundays shall be treated as if they were the keepers of disorderly houses (brothels). This is not a fate to which any Senior Steward of the Jockey Club is likely to lay himself open, although many sports already disregard the Act with complete impunity.

Merely to race on Sundays would, in any case, not solve the problem of Sunday betting for cash, which could be introduced only after legislation. There are three schools of thought about Sunday cash betting (credit betting by telephone is already legal): first, that the racecourses could manage very well without it, relying on their entrance money and other sources of income instead and leaving betting to those with credit accounts; secondly, that there should be betting on course but not in the betting shops; thirdly, that there should be betting both on and off course.

Those who favour Sunday racing with no betting appear to be in a minority, and unlikely to win the day. The second school was initially favoured by the National Association of Bookmakers (NAB), but not the Betting Office Licensees' Association (BOLA). It has the further disadvantage that the levy would be greatly reduced; nevertheless, the Levy Board's chairman, Sir Ian Trethowan, did not reject it out of hand. As he has pointed out, the Board's purpose is to benefit racing as a whole, and if racecourses could make more additional income from non-levy sources on Sunday than they might have made from the levy on another day, it would not be for the Board to stand in their way.[15]

Tom Kelly, Director-General of BOLA, has, however, made it clear that, if there is to be Sunday racing, there must be betting both on and off course. He argues that, without off-course betting, illegal betting, and therefore evasion of betting duty, would expand dramatically. BOLA is also doubtful about Sunday betting on other grounds.

If it is allowed off course, there may be difficulties with trade unions, whose members would no doubt demand high recompense for disturbance to their Sundays. On the other hand, if Sunday betting is to be allowed at all, BOLA's members naturally do not wish to cut themselves off from the benefits it will bring. Kelly made no bones about saying that BOLA would opposed any legislation to introduce cash betting on course only, and would thereby frustrate it, since the Government would be bound to demand unity before proceeding.[16]

These commentators, though taking care not to reveal confidential information, were speaking with the benefit of inside knowledge, since they were members of the Jockey Club Working Party on Sunday racing, which had been set up in January 1985, and released its report in January 1987. The Committee recommended that a campaign for changes in the law should be started, to allow Sunday racing to take place with betting both on and off course, despite the NAB's earlier reservations. The report recognised that there was weighty opposition from the Churches and their supporters in the fight against Sunday trading, and that it would be necessary to win over the workforce to the proposals. The Committee was aware 'that a good deal of explanation, consultation and lobbying will be needed before we can expect Parliamentary support for legislation to allow betting on Sunday. We are mindful of the Home Secretary's view that all the preparations need to be soundly carried out if Sunday racing is to become a reality.'[17]

Douglas Hurd, as Home Secretary, was in favour of it, as he made clear at the Gimcrack dinner at York racecourse on 9 December 1986, but his fingers had been badly burned earlier in the year over the Shops Bill, which he had introduced to legalise shopping on Sundays and which had failed in the face of widespread unpopularity in the country and the House of Commons. His major recommendation (echoed shortly afterwards by the Jockey Club Working Party, with which he had been in close touch and whose report was published a few weeks after his speech), was that a campaign, which might take some years, should be undertaken to gather public support. He also came down against Sunday racing with no betting, on the ground that it would lead to an unacceptable increase in illegal betting – again foreshadowing the Working Party's report.[18] Hurd did not exclude a Private Member's Bill and, as it turned out, matters moved forward earlier than had been expected. On 11 May 1987, the Earl of Caithness, in a short late-night debate in the House of Lords, said that the Government might find that it would be able to support a Private Member's Bill, were one to be introduced, and that it could see no reason for Sunday betting or racing not being allowed.[19]

Many difficulties lie ahead. Nevertheless, it seems probable that in the fullness of time Britain will follow the example of Continental Europe, where Sunday racing has been long established, and of Ireland, where it was introduced in 1985. Having already achieved a very fair degree of internal unity, the industry's task is now to cultivate a favourable image with the public and with Members of Parliament. To carry weight it will need to broaden the base of its lobby, by establishing, even more than it is doing already, common ground with all those whose business or pleasure lies with horses. The objective will no longer be the traditional one of getting back into racing some of the money taken out in the form of tax, but to move public opinion towards Sunday racing.

Perhaps the single most important task of a more powerful 'horse lobby' will be to build on the strengthened co-operation with the bookmakers that may result from the Racecourse Association's deal with Satellite Information Services.

The bookmakers have much to offer. Successive Governments have been wryly aware of the strength of their lobby, at least since 1972, when the bookmakers emasculated the Tote Bill. Since then BOLA has built on the foundations laid by the NAB in making bookmaking a 'respectable' profession, and provides research and security services which are becoming indispensable. Bookmakers have for years taken part in annual deputations to the Chancellor of the Exchequer, urging the reduction of betting tax, and there is no reason why the trend towards closer links between the racing and betting industries should not be strengthened, particularly now that the difficulties over the Bookmakers' Committee are settled. As the Duke of Devonshire said in the House of Lords as long ago as 17 December 1975: 'To pretend that bookmakers are not vital to racing is like pretending that the lions are not in Trafalgar Square.'[20]

Racing, to conclude, is an extraordinary mixture of greed, good-fellowship, love of horses, snobbery, and a hundred other qualities. From this small self-contained, complex world radiate the great moral and political issues of class, money and power. The Jockey Club is also an extraordinary body, self-elected, with many members who are rich and influential in other fields than racing. It has retained its power because it has had the wit to share it, and because its members' publicly expressed attitudes have so changed that it is widely seen as genuinely less autocratic than in the past. According to where one stands politically, it is either a happy example of tradition at work, or a disastrous comment on the corrupt state of English society, that this is the body which is leading racing into the 1990s and towards the twenty-first century.

Notes

1. *Report on Non-Departmental Public Bodies* (Chairman Sir Leo Pliatsky), HMSO, January 1980, Cmnd. 7797.
2. A distinguished committee chaired by Sir John Sparrow, was appointed in February 1985 to look into the future of the National Stud, and reported in November.
3. C. Hill, 'Racing's Money in Good Hands' (an interview with Sir Ian Trethowan), *Pacemaker International*, April 1986, pp. 38-40.
4. For a fascinating and detailed account of the Tote's origins, see Racecourse Betting Control Board, *First Annual Report and Accounts 1929*, HMSO, 29 April 1930 (H.C. 116).
5. I am indebted to Lord Wyatt, Chairman of the Tote, for the figures in the foregoing paragraphs.
6. C. Hill, 'A View from the Home Secretary' (an interview with the Rt. Hon. Douglas Hurd), *Pacemaker International*, September 1986, pp. 94-7.
7. 76th *Report of the Commissioners of Her Majesty's Customs and Excise, for the year ended 31 March 1985*, HMSO, December 1985, Cmnd. 9655.
8. General Electric Company, plc, *Annual Report*, London, 1986.
9. Sir Geoffrey Howe, Chancellor of the Exchequer, speaking at St Mary Hall, Oxford, 10 April 1981.
10. *Royal Commission on Gambling, Final Report* (Cmnd. 7200), HMSO, July 1978, especially paras. 9.95–9.108.
11. Betting, Gaming and Lotteries (Amendment) Act, 1984. The Act received the Royal Assent on 26 June 1984.
12. Hill, 'A View from the Home Secretary'.
13. See *The Sporting Life*, 30 September 1986, from which this account is taken.
14. I am indebted to the Racecourse Association, the Earl of March and Social Surveys (Gallup Poll) Ltd. for permission to refer to this material.
15. Sir Ian Trethowan, 'Steer a straight course on Sunday', *The Times*, 3 October 1986.
16. Tom Kelly, 'Complexities rumble beneath the surface', *Ibid.*
17. *The Report of the Jockey Club Working Party on Sunday Racing*, London, 1986, para. 6.6.
18. *The Times*, 10 December 1986.
19. 487, *H.L.*, Deb., cols. 523-532, 11 May 1987.
20. 366, *H.L.* Deb., col. 1466, 17 December 1975.

Abbreviations

BAC	Bookmakers' Action Committee
BBDO	Batten, Barton, Durstine and Osborne, Ltd.
BHA	British Horseracing Authority
BOLA	Betting Office Licensees' Association
BRIC	Bloodstock and Racehorse Industries' Confederation
DBS	Direct Broadcasting by Satellite
EBF	European Breeders' Fund
EIU	Economist Intelligence Unit
GPC	General Purposes Committee of BRIC
HAC	Horseracing Advisory Council
JALC	Joint Associations Liaison Committee
NAB	National Association of Bookmakers
NBPA	National Bookmakers' [and Associated Bodies' Joint] Protection Association
NEWE	Newmarket Expansion Without Entanglement
NPFA	National Playing Fields Association
NTF	Newmarket Trainers' Federation
NUDC	Newmarket Urban District Council
RBCB	Racecourse Betting Control Board
RCA	Racecourse Association
RILC	Racehorse Industries Liaison Committee
ROA	Racehorse Owners' Association
RPC	Racing Policy Committee
RSS	Racecourse Security Services, Ltd.
RTS	Racecourse Technical Services
SFA	Newmarket and District Stud Farmers' Association
SIS	Satellite Information Services
SP	Starting Price
SRD	Satellite Racing Development
TBA	Thoroughbred Breeders' Association
TGWU	Transport and General Workers' Union
WSCC	West Suffolk County Council

Bibliography

Adams, C. E. (ed.), 1982, *Mammalian Egg Transfer*, CRC Press, Inc., Florida.

Allen, W. R. and Paster, R. L., 1984, 'Production of Monozygotic Horse Twins by Micromanipulation', *Journal of Reproduction and Fertility*, 71.

Bloodstock and Racehorse Industries Confederation Ltd., n.d. but 1975, *The Crisis in Racing – Cause and Effect*, London.

—, 1980, *V.A.T.: A Revised Guide to Value Added Tax and the Bloodstock Industry*, Newmarket, September.

Bloom, S., 1984, *The Economics of Gambling*, unpublished BA dissertation, Preston Polytechnic.

Bookmakers and Backers Racecourse Protection Association, 1921, Speeches made at their first banquet, 6 December 1921 (unpublished).

Butler, R. A. 1971, *The Art of the Possible*, Hamish Hamilton, London.

Churches Council on Gambling, 1964, 'Gambling – Why?', *Annual Review of the Churches Council on Gambling for the Year ending 31 December 1963*.

—, 1965, *Annual Review of the Churches Council on Gambling for the Year Ending 31 December 1964*.

Crossman, R., 1976 and 1977, *The Diaries of a Cabinet Minister*, vols. 2 and 3, Hamish Hamilton and Jonathan Cape, London.

Dean, E., 1975, *An Analysis of the Labour Market for Stable Lads in Newmarket*, unpublished BA dissertation, University of East Anglia.

Dixon, D., 1980, '"Class Law": the Street Betting Act of 1906', *International Journal of the Sociology of Law*, 8.

Economist Intelligence Unit Ltd., 1969, *Report on the Administrative Structure, Methods and Procedures of the Horserace Betting Levy Board*, London.

—, 1977, *Finance for British Horseracing*, London.

Filby, M., n.d., *The T. & G. Industrial Relations and Racing*, unpublished paper.

[266]

Fowler, N., 1967, *A Policy for Gambling*, Bow Group Memorandum, Bow Publications Ltd., London.

Fuller, P., 1974, 'Introduction', J. Halliday and P. Fuller (eds.), *The Psychology of Gambling*, Allen Lane, London, pp. 1-114.

General Electric Company, plc, 1986, *Annual Report*, London.

Hamilton of Dalzell, Lord, n.d. but 1940, 'The Tote', in Lord Harewood and Many Authorities, *Flat Racing*, Seeley Service, London, pp. 378-94.

Hargreaves, J., 1986, *Sport, Power and Culture*, London.

Herbert, I., 1980, 'He holds the reins' (interview with Lord Plummer), *Pacemaker International*, April, pp. 29-31.

Hill, C., 1986a, 'Racing's Money in Good Hands' (interview with Sir Ian Trethowan), *Pacemaker International*, April, pp. 38-40.

—, 1986b, 'A View from the Home Secretary', (interview with the Rt. Hon. Douglas Hurd), *Pacemaker International*, September, pp. 94-7.

—, 1986c, 'The Sheikh and I' (interview with John Leat), *Pacemaker International*, December, pp. 90-2.

HMSO, 1930, Racecourse Betting Control Board, *First Annual Report and Accounts 1929* (H.C. 116).

—, 1951, *Report of the Royal Commission on Betting, Lotteries and Gaming*, chaired by Henry Willink, QC, Cmd. 8190.

—, 1960, *Report of the Departmental Committee on a Levy on Betting on Horse Races*, Chairman Sir Leslie Peppiatt, Cmnd. 1003.

—, 1978, Royal Commission on Gambling, *Final Report*, 2 vols., Chairman Lord Rothschild, Cmnd. 7200.

—, 1980, *Report on Non-Departmental Public Bodies*, Chairman Sir Leo Pliatzky, Cmnd. 7797.

—, 1985, *76th Report of the Commissioners of Her Majesty's Customs and Excise, for the Year Ended 31 March 1985*, Cmnd. 9655.

Hood, C., 1972, 'The Development of Betting Taxes in Britain', *Public Administration*, 50 (summer), pp. 183-202.

—' 1976, *The Limits of Administration*, John Wiley & Sons, London.

Horserace Betting Levy Board, 1962 and annually, *Annual Reports and Statements of Account of the Horserace Betting Levy Board and the Horserace Totalisator Board*, London.

International Conference of Racing Authorities, 1980, 1981, 1982, *Minutes of Meetings*, unpublished typescript, Paris.

Jockey Club, 1943, *Report of the Racing Reorganisation Committee to the Stewards of the Jockey Club*, Chairman Lord Ilchester, London.

Bibliography

Jockey Club, 1961, *The Doping of Racehorses: Report of the Committee set up by the Jockey Club*, Chairman the Duke of Norfolk, London.

—, 1965, *Report of the Duke of Norfolk's Committee on the Pattern of Racing*, London.

—, 1966, *The Report of the Working Party on the Introduction of Starting Stalls*. London.

—, 1968, *The Racing Industry: Report by the Committee of Inquiry*, Chairman Sir Henry Benson, London.

—, 1974 and annually, *Report by the Stewards*, London.

—, 1986, *Report of the Jockey Club Working Party on Sunday Racing*.

Joint Racing Board, 1969, *The Racing Industry: Report of the Working Party on Racecourse Management*, Chairman Sir Rex Cohen, London.

—, 1971, *Report of the Committee on the Scheme for the Suppression of Doping*, Chairman Professor W. D. M. Paton, CBE, London.

—, 1974, *Report of the Committee of Inquiry into the Manpower of the Racing Industry*, July, London.

—, 1974, *The Future Requirements of Racing*, December, London.

—, 1977, *Report of the Working Party on Assistance to the Breeding Industry*, Chairman Major M. G. Wyatt, London.

—, 1980, *The Report of a Committee of Enquiry into the Distribution of the Horserace Betting Levy in Support of British Horseracing*, London.

Kaye, R. and Peskett, R., 1969, *The Ladbrokes Story*, Pelham Books, London.

Khan, P., 1980, *The Sport of Kings: a study of traditional social structure under change*, unpublished Ph.D. thesis, University of Swansea.

Lambton, G., 1963 (first published 1924), *Men and Horses I Have Known*, J. A. Allen, London.

Langdon, R. N. D., 1982, *Horserace Betting Levy: Enquiry into Certain Matters relating to the 21st Levy Scheme*, Spicer and Pegler, London.

Livingstone-Learmonth, J., n.d. but 1972, *The Horserace Betting Levy Board: Its Political and Economic Implications*, unpublished paper, University of York.

Loder, E. P., 1982, *Bibliography of the History and Organization of Horseracing and Thoroughbred Breeding in Great Britain and Ireland*, J. A. Allen, London.

McKinsey & Co., Inc., 1972a, *Strengthening the Jockey Club Organisation*, July, London.

—, 1972b, *Improving Jockey Club Public Relations and Maintaining the Financial Viability of the Jockey Club*, September, London.

Bibliography

Moody, G. E., 1972, *The Facts about the 'Money Factories': an independent view of betting and gaming in Britain now*, The Churches Council on Gambling, London.

Mortimer, R., 1958, *The Jockey Club*, Cassell, London.

—, n.d. but 1966, 'Viewpoint', *The Tote Racing Annual 1966*, Tote Investors Ltd, London, pp. 10-15.

—, 1979, *The Flat*, George Allen & Unwin, London.

Newmarket Society, May and June 1967, *Newmarket Society News*, Newmarket.

Peat Marwick Mitchell & Co., 1984, *The Horserace Betting Levy Board: Review of Activities*, London.

Persse, H. S., n.d. but 1940, 'Training', in Lord Harewood and Many Authorities, *Flat Racing*, Seeley Service, London, pp. 309-48.

Racing Information Bureau, n.d. but *c.* 1975, *The Racing Information Bureau: a report on the development of the organisation, its role and its future, with particular reference to the Racecourse Association*, Newmarket.

Rothschild, Lord, 1984, *Random Variables*, Collins, London.

Submissions to the Royal Commission on Gambling, Betting Office Licensees' Association Ltd., 1976, London.

—, Bloodstock and Racehorse Industries Confederation Ltd., n.d. but 1976, London.

—, The Horseracing Industry Joint Submission, 1976, London.

—, The Jockey Club, 1976, *The Control of Horseracing*, London.

—, National Association of Bookmakers Ltd., May and June 1976, June 1977, Three Memoranda, London.

—, Racing Policy Committee, n.d. but 1976, London.

—, Thoroughbred Breeders' Association, 1976, Newmarket.

Thoroughbred Breeders' Association, 1981, *Methods of Assistance to the Breeding Industry – a review*, Newmarket.

Touche Ross & Co. and Deloitte & Co., 1971, *The Jockey Club Administration of Racing*, London.

Towers-Clark, P. and Ross, M. (eds.), 1980 and 1984, *Directory of the Turf*, Pacemaker Publications Ltd., Newbury.

Vamplew, W., 1976, *The Turf: a Social and Economic History of Horseracing*, Allen Lane, London.

Wigg, Lord, 1972. *George Wigg*, Michael Joseph, London.

Willett, P., 1970, *The Thoroughbred*, Weidenfeld & Nicolson, London.

—, 1984, *Makers of the Modern Thoroughbred*, Stanley Paul, London.

Wright, H., 1984, 'Minding the business of owners: Howard Wright

Bibliography

talks to Nick Robinson, the retiring President of the Racehorse Owners' Association', *Pacemaker International*, August, pp. 58-62.

Wyatt, W., 1985, *Confessions of an Optimist*, Collins, London.

Index

Horses' names appear in italic type

Index

Grand Prix Prince Rose, 191
Greater London Council, 157, 158
Green, Brigadier Henry, 112-15
Griffiths, Eldon, MP, 156
Group races, 188-192

Hall-Walker, Colonel (later Lord Wavertree), 84
Hambro, Jocelyn, 227
Hamilton of Dalzell, Lord, 7
Hamilton Stud, 154, 155, 156
Hamilton, Willie, MP, 60
Hamling, William, MP, 105
Hanbury, Ben, 197
Hancock, Mr., 31, 36
Harding of Petherton, Field-Marshal Lord, 73, 76, 78, 79, 81, 83-90, 92, 94, 146, 168
Hardwicke Stakes, 188
Harris, 'Tom', 13
Head, Viscount, 96
Healey, Denis, MP, 227
Heath, Edward, MP, 96, 226
Heron Bloodstock Agency, 197
Hickey, William, 112
Hicks, Sir Denys, 78, 92, 96
Highflyer yearling sale, 202
Hill, Warren, 44-5
Hill, William, 9, 29, 33, 34, 44 *see also* William Hill Organisation
Hindley, Jeremy, 197
Hislop, Mr and Mrs John, 200-2, 204-5
Hodgson, Harold, 129
Hoggart, Simon, 129
Holland-Martin, Tim, 196
Holt, Arthur, MP, 53
Home Office
    Betting, Gaming and Lotteries (Amendment) Act, 1984, 258
    bookmakers, 3, 11, 17, 24-6, 27, 30, 34, 35, 37
    Horserace Betting Levy Act, 1981, 242
    Horserace Betting Levy Board, 70-2, 77, 84-5, 243, 251, 252

Horserace Totalisator and Betting Levy Boards Act, 1972, 131
Horserace Totalisator Board, 122-6, 131
Jockey Club, 3, 11, 27-8, 34, 35, 37
    levy and legalisation of off-course betting, 16, 18, 19, 36, 38
    Peppiatt Report, 65
    Rothschild Commission, 240-1
    statutory horseracing authority, 182
Home Secretary – *see* Home Office
Hong Kong,
    Jockey Club, 250
    tote turnover, 253-4
Hood, Christopher, 80
Horncastle, Sam, 221-2
Horserace Betting Levy, 3, 7, 8-9, 17, 38, 44, 62-3 – *see also* Peppiatt Committee
    Benson Report, 171
    introduction, 11, 18, 31, 32
    levy schemes, 77, 78
        determined by Home Secretary, 242-3
        evasion, 242
        seventh and eighth, 100-6
        twelfth, 128
        thirteenth, 216
        twenty-first, 242-4
    Langdon Report, 243-4
    maximisation, 76, 116, 216, 217
    paid on profits, 68
    on turnover, 77, 83-4
Horserace Betting Levy Act, 1961, 3, 11, 38, 41, 63, 65, 68, 70-6, 102, 152
    1981 amendment, 242
Horserace Betting Levy Act, 1969, 106, 162-6
Horserace Betting Levy Act, 1981, 242-3
Horserace Betting Levy Board, 2, 52, 61, 65-140 – *see also* Wigg, Lord
    announced by Butler, 70
    Bloodstock and Racehorse Industries' Confederation, 226-35

Index